The Brixham Branch

by

C.R. Potts

THE OAKWOOD PRESS

© Oakwood Press & C.R. Potts 2000

British Library Cataloguing in Publication Data
A Record for this book is available from the British Library
ISBN 0 85361 556 X

Second (enlarged) Edition 2000, first published 1987.

Typeset by Oakwood Graphics.
Repro by Ford Graphics, Ringwood, Hants.
Printed by Oakdale Printers, Poole, Dorset.

A PW train at Brixham hauled by '55XX' 2-6-2T No. 5573 on 7th August, 1960. The engine shed siding used to be to the right of the telegraph pole. The signal box still carries its nameboard, although this was closed at the same time as the shed siding, in September 1958.
R.E. Toop

Title page: Brixham inner harbour at high tide with several sailing trawlers in evidence.
D.K. & M. James Collection
Front cover: '14XX' class 0-4-2T No. 1466 waits to depart Brixham with the 3.15 pm to Churston on 28th December, 1959.
J.R. Besley/Colour-Rail
Rear cover, top: A busy scene at Churston with 2-6-2T No. 5158 departing for Newton Abbot, while 0-4-2T No. 1470 is seen in the bay platform with the Brixham branch train, March 1960.
Peter W. Gray/Colour-Rail
Rear cover, bottom: Diesel railcar No. W55015 at Brixham in February 1962.
J.R. Besley/Colour-Rail

Published by The Oakwood Press (Usk), P.O. Box 13, Usk, Mon., NP15 1YS.
E-mail: oakwood-press@dial.pipex.com
Website: www.oakwood-press.dial.pipex.com

Contents

'14XX' class No. 1439 propels trailer No. W222W, forming the (apparently empty) 3.15 pm ex-Brixham service, slowly to a stand at Churston on 18th May, 1957. This was still the winter timetable and there remained but three return journeys to do, the last leaving Brixham at 5.10 pm. W222W looks fairly tatty, and the paintwork has suffered, particularly from much kicking of the inward-opening driver's and passengers' doors.

Peter W. Gray

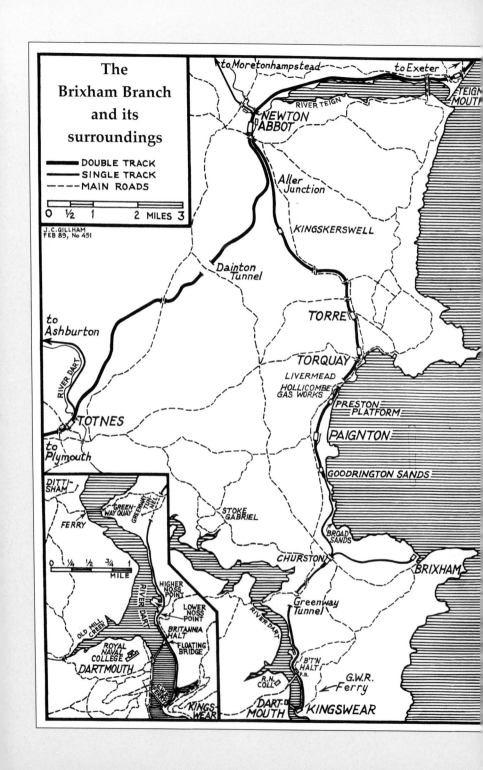

Introduction and Acknowledgements
(Second Edition)

In the Introduction to the First Edition I explained why the book had come to be written. I knew the station for the period 1955-1963 and had been allowed, as a schoolboy, to act as an unofficial worker during my holidays, tolerated by most of the good-natured staff. Since writing the First Edition a little (very little) more has been found about Richard Wolston, but he still remains a 'mystery man'. Quite a lot more has been discovered about the general history, including much more about individual staff members in the early days, as the reader will have noticed by the increased size of the book (the First Edition was 96 pages plus photographs). A new chapter details the tremendous problems encountered at Brixham because of shortage of water for the locomotives. Also I have attempted to put in as many new pictures as possible; those included from the First Edition are only retained because of their historical content.

I ended my first Introduction by saying 'Gone but not forgotten!' As I write these lines I am looking at the front page from the Torquay *Herald Express* for 7th January, 2000 headlined '£4m Railway bid for Port'. It says that a consortium is hoping to 'resurrect a derelict stretch of rail line between Churston and Brixham' to run electric trains along a 1½ mile track, from which passengers would be transferred to Edwardian-style buses to the Town centre. (The building of the houses on Brixham station site precludes the whole of the former branch being used.) The proposal would cost about £4m, which the proposer is quoted as saying would be 'got back in seven to eight years without any problem'. What will happen remains to be seen, but some 132 years after it opened, the Brixham branch is still being talked about!

BRIXHAM FROM BAY VIEW.

Lower Brixham, gathered round its harbour. The difference in height between the fishmarket and the station is emphasised by this picture. On the skyline from right to left are the goods shed, the station building, partly obscured by a line of coal trucks (*centre*), and the bulk of Furzeham School (*left*). This card was posted in 1919.   *D.K. & M. James Collection*

5

A fascinating scene at Brixham town centre (Bolton Cross) in the pre-motor age.

D.K. & M. James Collection

Almost as soon as the First Edition was published, retired signalman Jack Eveleigh contacted me and filled in some gaps in the story, which I am pleased to include this time. Similarly the late Fred Park, MBE, wrote, and was able to correct and amplify the material on Northfield oil depot for which I am very grateful. Alan Babbage, whom I met rather sadly at the funeral of former Torquay signalman (and onetime Brixham porter) Clifford Pearce, kindly supplied some S&T memories of the branch.

David James of Brixham has most kindly allowed the author free access to his magnificent collection of photographs of Brixham and many embellish this new edition. For his generosity I am most grateful.

Dr Philip Armitage, curator of Brixham Museum, kindly arranged for a number of photos in the Museum's collection to be copied and these are credited to the Museum; the question of ownership of some of these is unclear and if a photographer recognises his work, no slight is intended and contact should be made via the publisher. A model of Brixham station, with operating auto-train, is opening in the Museum this year (indeed should be open by the time this book is published) and I encourage all readers to visit it. For those interested in Brixham's history, a Museum visit is a must.

Jim Cook once again lent me his historic staff photos and gave his usual encouragement; it is thanks to people like Jim that this book came to be written. To all photographers credited, many thanks.

Finally, the following all helped in some way, for which thanks are due: Dave Braun, Tony Cooke, Ian Coulson, Bridget Howard, Peter Kay, Ian Kennedy, Chris Turner, staff at PRO Kew and the BR Records Office, and finally my mother in Brixham for keeping me up to date with cuttings from the *Herald Express*. To anyone I have forgotten, my apologies.

Christopher Potts
January 2000

Chapter One

Brixham before the railway

As Brixham is bounded on three sides by sea it is natural that livelihoods connected with the sea should be of great importance to the town. As early as 1535 Brixham was the largest fishery in the south-west, the annual tithes at £17 being almost as much as the rest of Devon outside Torbay. In 1785 there were 76 decked trawlers employing 400 men. In 1801 Brixham was home to 3,671 souls whilst Torquay only housed 838 (this did not include 294 in Cockington). Paignton with 1,575 inhabitants was bigger but still half the size of Brixham.

Brixham fish market was opened in 1799 and in 1803/04 the New Pier was built. By 1811 the population was 4,371 (Paignton 1,639, Torquay 1,350). The trawlers that operated out of Brixham were built in Brixham which gave further employment to the townspeople and the place continued to expand. The 1821 census showed a population of 4,503 (Paignton with 1,796 was now smaller than Torquay with 1,925). In 1822 there were 89 decked and 60 open fishing boats employing 540 men and boys and the weekly catch was 120 tons. By 1830 no less than a thousand men and boys were associated with the fishing industry and fish sales amounted to £1,000 per week. About 1840 Brixham was described as the wealthiest place for its size on the south coast of England.

In 1842 the soil around Brixham was found to contain rich iron oxide deposits, which, when used as a base in paint, was ideal for the protection of iron. Mr Richard W. Wolston, a wealthy local solicitor, leased the land and mined the iron oxide, processing it in a factory he built on the cliffs at Furzeham, overlooking the harbour. The boats could berth right under the factory, some 30 feet above and the products were loaded into them by hoist. Richard Wolston is a key character in this book, for he was later to be responsible for Brixham's railway.

Some additional information on Brixham in 1847 comes from the hand of Richard Wolston in the form of a proof of evidence he gave on behalf of the proposed Brixham branch of the South Devon Railway (in the event not built). Brixham had a population of about 7,000 of which 600 to 700 were permanently engaged in the fishing trade, employing 146 vessels of 4,416 tons. On average (he says) about 60 tons of fish a week were caught, all of it being sent to Ireland, between 3-4,000 tons in a year. [This figure is almost certainly too low because, c. 1825, a writer said annual landings were 6,240 tons.] The average value of a ton of fish was £14. In addition there were some 130 brigs or schooners in the shipping or coasting trade, totalling between 14-15,000 tons, employing a further 800 people. These were employed in the fruit trade of the Mediterranean and Azores, but outside the season some would convey the iron ore mined in Brixham to South Wales and Tyneside. They did not all necessarily work out of Brixham but were owned by Brixham men and their earnings came back to the town. 'Vast quantities of timber' were used for shipbuilding and repairing, brought from Exeter and sail cloth was brought from east of that city.

So far as his lime quarries were concerned, that from Brixham being 'the best for agricultural purposes', he had been forced to abandon a trade he had with Exeter in 1845 because of the unreliability of sea-carriage. He had previously had 450 accounts in Exeter. A railway would enable him to resume that trade. A considerable lode of iron ore had been discovered recently, of which he had already exported 5,000 tons, and he anticipated increasing the rate at which he excavated the ore to 6,000 tons per year. He also mentions that at this time Paignton, 'frequented by visitors as a watering place', had a population of 2,500.

A different document, a brief to the SDR counsel, stated that the annual catch of fish at Brixham was 7,000 tons. Fish was sent 'even so far as Reading and Maidenhead' and such was the urgency of its journey, that as well as public coaches, light caravans and post horses were used to transport the perishable product. This document states that the population of Churston Ferrers was between 2-3,000 at this time, i.e. as big as Paignton. Hence one can see the desire to reach Brixham by railway, although this document gives Brixham's population as 5,700, somewhat less than Wolston's figure.

Appendix Eight gives some brief details of Brixham as a fishing port and shipbuilder in the late 18th century onwards.

In 1843 the present breakwater was commenced but by the end of 1846 only 250 ft had been built. The Torbay & Brixham Deep Sea Harbour of Refuge & Dock Company was floated in 1846 to raise the sum of £170,000 to enable the breakwater to be completed, the original intended length of 1,750 ft extended by this proposal to no less than 3,200 feet. The Engineer was John Ellis and the Solicitor was our friend Richard Wolston again. (He may have adopted the 'Torbay & Brixham' from the harbour company's title for his later railway line.) It does not appear that this scheme got off the ground but the original (1843) scheme continued to be added to bit by bit, financed by the surplus income from the Harbour. In *Brixham in Devonia* published in 1896 the author states that there was: ' . . an annual charge of one shilling per ton harbour dues on all vessels entering the port with which the Breakwater and Harbour are now kept going'.

(In July 1883 the breakwater had reached nearly 1,100 ft. By 1896 1,400 ft had been built at a cost of £22,447. No further work took place until 1909 when a further 600 ft was authorised at a cost of £23,000 (towards which the Government contributed £17,000). A further 1,000 ft (and £40,000, some of which came from public sources) was authorised in 1912. The breakwater was completed in 1916, at 3,000 ft in length and approximately £100,000 in cost. In 1920 the Anglo-American oil company constructed a jetty on the sheltered side, about 120 ft long, so that ships could berth to load or unload oil.)

Although Brixham was prospering, it was recognised that there was a need for better transport facilities so that its products could leave Brixham in greater quantity and more speedily; fish in particular is very perishable. Wolston was a man of vision and even before the railway reached Torquay (in 1848) he was striving to bring the benefits of the new form of transport to Brixham. His principal motive was to move the iron ore to Dartmouth where he formed a company to crush and mill the ore; but he could also see that far larger markets for fish could be reached if a faster means of transport could be found.

Chapter Two

The Struggle to open the Line

As early as 1845 a Prospectus was issued for a 'Dartmouth, Torbay & Exeter Railway' built to standard gauge which would have run from Dartmouth through Brixham, thence via Paignton and Torquay and the Teign Valley to Exeter.

Richard Wolston had been involved in the drawing up of the plans for this line, and had nearly been killed when the special train in which he was travelling to Exeter to deposit the plans was run into by another special train containing opponents of the proposal (the collision was an accident, it should be stressed!). However the 'narrow gauge' interest were not successful in obtaining their Act of Parliament.

In 1846 the South Devon Railway (SDR) was empowered to make a branch to Torquay (the present 'Torre'); then in 1847 additional powers authorised extension of the Torquay branch into Torquay proper together with a branch to Brixham (*referred to in Chapter One*). There are references in the SDR Minutes in 1849 and 1852 to a branch to Brixham but the expense of replacing the atmospheric system on the main line prevented this expansion taking place. Not until 1859 was the Torquay branch extended at all, and then not by the SDR although they gave great assistance to the company involved.

After the opening of the SDR to Torquay (Torre) on 18th December, 1848 the Brixham fish merchants were able to bring their catch, in carts drawn by four horses, to that place - a journey of about 10 miles. However, it frequently happened that the catch was delayed and the urgent traffic arrived after the train had left. Knowing that the train paused for quite some time at Newton, the drivers then pushed on and it was quite a regular sight to see the perspiring horses galloping up past Torre and through St Marychurch to deposit their perishable traffic at Teignmouth, before the train arrived there. The Torquay to Teignmouth road contains some considerable hills and would have required great effort of the poor horses.

A separate and independent company, the Dartmouth & Torbay Railway (D&T) (although worked by the SDR) opened from the latter's Torquay station (then renamed 'Torre') with an intermediate station at Torquay (actually in Cockington parish) to Paignton on 2nd August, 1859. This roughly halved the road journey that faced the fish merchants of Brixham, and prospective passengers for that matter. On 14th March, 1861, the D&T was extended to Brixham Road, bringing the benefits of railway communication slightly more than two miles distant from Brixham, a considerable improvement compared with 1848.

A special dinner was held in Brixham, price 13s. 6d. a head, to celebrate the arrival of the railway close by. Naturally the principal item on the menu was fish but there was very nearly no fish to eat! Because there had been heavy easterly gales for several days beforehand, no fish had been caught. Then someone remembered a lovely turbot caught about a week earlier, and sent to Bristol. That place was telegraphed and the reply came - the fish was unsold (and had been left in ice). So the fish was returned in ice by the mail train and arrived just in time to be cooked, thus saving Brixham's reputation.

TORBAY AND BRIXHAM RAILWAY.

Incorporation of Company—Construction of New Lines—
Arrangements with South Devon and Dartmouth and Torbay
Railway Companies—Use of Railway—Amendment of Acts.

NOTICE IS HEREBY GIVEN, that application is intended to be made to Parliament in the ensuing Session for an Act to Incorporate a Company (herein called the Company), and to confer upon the Company the following or some of the following among other powers (that is to say)—To make and maintain a Railway, with all necessary works, stations, approaches, sidings, and other conveniences connected therewith, commencing in the Parish of Churston Ferrers, in the County of Devon, by a Junction with the Siding of the Dartmouth and Torbay Railway, at or near the eastern end of the Platform of the Brixham Road Station of that railway, and terminating in the Parish of Brixham, in the said county, at a point at the southern end of Furzeham Common, about three-quarters of a furlong from the boundary wall there, and which intended railway will pass from, through, or into the Parishes or places following, or some or one of them, viz., Churston Ferrers, Brixham, Brixham Quay, or Lower Brixham, in the County of Devon aforesaid.

A tramway which will be wholly situate in the Parish of Brixham, Brixham Quay, or Lower Brixham, commencing by a junction made with the last mentioned intended railway at or near the termination thereof, and terminating in the north-east corner of Furzham Common, aforesaid. To purchase and take by compulsion or otherwise, for the purposes aforesaid, or any of them, lands, houses, and other property, hereditaments, and premises ; and to vary and extinguish all existing rights and privileges connected with the lands, houses, and other property, hereditaments, and premises so to be purchased and taken, or which would in any manner impede or interfere with the construction, maintenance, or use of the said railway, tramway, and the works connected therewith, or any of them ; and to confer, vary, and extinguish other rights and privileges ; and also to cross, stop up, alter, or divert—whether temporarily or permanently—any highways, turnpikes, or other roads, railways, tramways, streets, paths, passages, aqueducts, rivers, canals, brooks, streams, sewers, waters, watercourses, drains, and pipes, so far as it may be necessary or is expedient for the purposes of making and maintaining the said railway and tramway, or of any of the works, approaches, sidings, stations, or conveniences connected therewith respectively.

To levy tolls, rates, and duties in respect of the said Railway, Tramway, and Works, and for the conveyance of traffic thereon, and to alter existing tolls, rates, and duties, and to confer, vary, and extinguish exemptions from payment of tolls, rates, and duties.

To enable the Company on the one hand, the Dartmouth and Torbay and South Devon Railway Companies hereinafter referred to as the two companies, or either of them, on the other hand, from time to time to enter into arrangements and agreements with respect to the working, use, management, and maintenance by the two companies, or either of them, of the said intended railway, tramway, and works, or any part thereof ; and the supply of rolling stock and machinery, and of officers and servants, for the conduct of traffic on the said intended railway and tramway, or either of them ; the payments to be made, the conditions to be performed with respect to such working, use, management, and maintenance, and the collection, appropriation, and apportionment and distribution of the revenues arising therefrom, and all incidental matters connected therewith.

To make provision for facilitating the interchange and transmission of all traffic whatsoever to, from, and over the said intended railway, tramway, and the said Dartmouth and Torbay and South Devon Railways respectively ; and to secure through-booking to, from, through, and over the said railways respectively ; and for fixing, ascertaining, limiting, reducing, and settling the tolls, rates, and charges to be levied or charged, and other terms and conditions to be imposed for, or in respect of, any of the purposes aforesaid, as may be necessary ; and to authorise the company and the two companies, or either of them, from time to time to enter into agreements with respect to all or any of the matters aforesaid, and to confirm such agreements as may be entered into, and in default of agreements to confer all necessary powers for effecting the objects aforesaid, or any of them.

To enable the company and any company by whom the said intended railway and tramway may at any time hereafter be lawfully worked or used, to run over, work, and use with their engines, carriages and waggons of every description, and with their officers, clerks, and servants, the Dartmouth and Torbay Railway, together with all stations, sidings, watering-places, water, platforms, approaches, turntables, and other works and conveniences connected with the said Dartmouth and Torbay Railway as aforesaid, with the said stations, upon such terms and conditions, and on payment of such tolls and charges, as may be agreed upon, or as in case of difference shall be settled by arbitration.

And it is intended, so far as may be requisite or desirable for any of the purposes of the said Bill, to amend or repeal the provisions or some of them, of the several Acts of Parliament following (that is to say)—Local and personal, 20 and 21 Vict. c. 103 ; 24 and 25 Vict., cap. 46 ; and 25 and 26 Vict., cap. 192, and all other the Acts relating to the Dartmouth and Torbay Railway Company ; and local and personal, 7 and 8 Vict., cap. 68; 9 and 10 Vict., cap. 402 ; 10 and 11 Vict., cap. 242 ; 14 and 15 Vic., c. 53; 17 and 18 Vict., cap. 122 ; 20 Vict., cap. 1 ; 20 and 21 Vict., cap. 8 ; 21 and 22 Vict., cap. 102 ; 23 and 24 Vict., caps. 10 and 102 ; and all other the Acts relating to the South Devon Railway Company.

Duplicate plans and sections, shewing the line, situation, and levels of the said intended railway, tramway, and works, and the land in or through which the same are intended to be made, together with a book of reference to such plans, and a copy of this notice, as published in the *London Gazette*, will, on or before the 30th day of November instant, be deposited for public inspection with the Clerk of the Peace for the county of Devon, at his office at Exeter, in the said county ; and that, on or before the said 30th day of November instant, a copy of so much of the said plans, sections, and book of reference, as relates to each parish, division of parish, or extra-parochial place, in or through which the said intended railway, tramway, and works will be made, together with a copy of the said *Gazette* notice, will be deposited for public inspection with the Parish Clerk of such parish or division of parish, or in case of any extra-parochial place with the Parish Clerk of some parish immediately adjoining thereto.

Printed copies of the said intended Bill will, on or before the 23rd day of December next, be deposited in the Private Bill Office of the House of Commons.

Dated this 10th day of November, 1863.

R. W. WOLSTON, Brixham,
Solicitor for the Bill.
HENRY MOON,
6, Manchester Buildings, Westminster,
Parliamentary Agent.

Notice of intent to apply for
Torbay & Brixham Act 1864.
*Courtesy Devon Record Office
Ref QI/RUm 288*

Goods traffic commenced to be dealt with between Torre, Paignton and Brixham Road on 1st April, 1861. The people of Brixham had pressed the D&T to reach Dartmouth via Brixham; the company's response was that it would be pleased to do so providing Brixham found the money. This they could not do.

Later in August 1861 a public meeting in Brixham considered a proposition by R.W. Wolston for a railway from Brixham Road, through the centre of Churston village (without encroaching on land owned by Lord Churston) to a station on Furzeham Common about 120 ft above sea level, some 40 ft lower than the station at Brixham Road. The estimated cost of the line was £12,809* and as the value of the fishing vessels alone in Brixham approached £200,000 it was felt this was a trifling sum for the community to find. Since the extension to Brixham Road 'shoals of passengers (had been) brought there' and hotel keepers reported business up by five or six times. There was no doubt in Mr Wolston's mind that shares in a Brixham railway would provide a 'handsome income' paying, he estimated, between 6 and 13 per cent. (That, as we shall see later, was hopelessly optimistic.) The meeting agreed a company be formed to construct a railway from Brixham Road to Brixham and a share list was at once agreed.

Richard Walter Wolston was a solicitor who was also a 'mine owner' because since 1841 he had owned and worked the ore on Furzeham Common. He was also proprietor of the Torbay Iron Paint Works which produced Wolston's Torbay iron paint; he was involved in manufacture of sewerage pipes and iron-stone pottery, doubtless all by-products of his mine. To fill in any spare time that arose, he was also a notary public, Clerk to the Harbour Commissioners and Portuguese Vice-Consul! The last post was no doubt necessary because of a large traffic in port wine between Oporto and Dartmouth.

Things now moved slowly. In 1863 there is a reference in the South Devon Railway Directors' minutes that they would 'consider the propriety of working the Torbay & Brixham Railway' when the capital for making it had been subscribed.

In February 1864 a Torbay & Brixham Railway Bill was presented during the 1864 session of the House of Lords. A capital of £18,000 in £10 shares together with a £6,000 loan was proposed to finance the line, which would be 1 mile 66 chains long from its junction with the D&T Railway to a point at the southern end of Furzeham Common. From there a tramway 21 chains in length was proposed to the north-east corner of the common (doubtless to Wolston's iron ore workings). The cost was split £16,000 railway, £2,000 tramway. The line was to be of broad or mixed gauge and be completed within four years. The Bill also legislated for Brixham trains to run over the D& T and use its stations and to contract with the latter to work the new railway and for interchange of traffic. (*See 'Notice of Intent', illustrated*). It was objected to by the D&T for this reason and because the D&T did not consider it was necessary and it 'is not well selected in an engineering point of view' (legal speak for they did not think much of its planned route and gradients).

R.W. Wolston had purchased no less than 1,770 of the £10 shares himself, the remaining 30 having been obtained by his brother and son and Mr W.P. Spark, his clerk in the legal business. He had been responsible for the preparation of the Bill,

---

* Made up: fencing £525, earthwork £3,000; ballast £450; masonry £975; metalling roads £90; permanent way £2,100; rails £1,575; occupation gates £30, stations & sidings £1,000, junction at Churston £500; land £1,400; total £11,645; contingencies £1,164 = £12,809 [*Western Morning News*, 24th August, 1861].

In Parliament- Session. 1864

Deposited 31st Dec. 1863

Torbay and Brixham Railway

Estimate of Expence.

I estimate the expence of the Undertaking under the proposed Bill in Parliament bearing the above name or title (including the purchase of land) at the following sums. —

Cost of Railway including Land and all incidental expence . . . . } £ 16,000

Cost of Tramway including Land and all incidental expence } 2,000

Total. £ 18,000

Dated this twenty first day of December One thousand eight hundred and sixty three

William Bell
Engineer

The Torbay & Brixham Railway seal. *British Rail*

which duly received the Royal Assent, becoming an Act on 25th July, 1864. The Act required the *agreement* of the D&T before use of its railway or stations, etc.

Meanwhile on 16th August, 1864 the Dartmouth & Torbay Railway reached Kingswear. The D&T had been frustrated in its attempts to reach Dartmouth by the objection of the landowner concerned and had to be content with Kingswear on the east side of the River Dart. Dartmouth became famous as a station without trains, being served by the railway-owned ferry from Kingswear, the journey taking only a few minutes. From 1st January, 1866 the D&T was leased to the South Devon Railway in perpetuity.

The contractor assigned to build the Torbay & Brixham Railway, a Mr Jackson, defaulted before any construction had started and Wolston undertook the work himself. Some delay ensued as doubtless Wolston had to arrange the necessary supervision and dip into his pocket for more funds. The first sod was cut by Richard Wolston on 23rd October, 1865 and building commenced that November; Mr S.G. Stewart was appointed Resident Engineer. At its meeting on 23rd November, 1865 the SDR agreed in principle to work the Torbay & Brixham. In February 1866 Wolston wrote to the SDR asking them to spell out their terms for working the line.

Attached to his letter was an appendix setting out Wolston's estimates for the money the line would earn. At that time the population of Brixham was roundly 7,000 (perhaps confirming that his population figure in the 1847 document (*see Chapter One*) was too high). He anticipated the following goods traffic passing by rail:

40 tons of fish per week, over 2,000 tons per annum
Coal   20,000 tons per annum
Lime   50,000 hogs per annum

Earnings were estimated at £20 per mile per week or £2,080 per annum. After deduction of working expenses (£596), a profit of £1,484 was anticipated, enabling a return of nearly 7 per cent on the share capital. If earnings of only £15 per mile per week were achieved, then the return on share capital dropped to nearly 4 per cent.

Mr Wolston wrote that he hoped to open the line in 'June next' (1866) but was having difficulty in raising funds (a loan of £6,000 had been authorised by the Act) and requested the SDR to assist, suggesting the latter rent the branch with a view to ultimately purchasing it.

The SDR minutes the next day indicate that the Brixham line would be worked 'at cost'.

Wolston tried again in May 1866. He pointed out that he had already expended nearly £9,000 on the line's construction. If the SDR would guarantee the interest being paid he should then have no trouble in raising the £6,000 loan and the line could be finished in four or five months. Unfortunately the SDR minutes do not indicate the company's attitude to his further approach but we know from other records that the loan was raised on 15th October, 1866.

In April 1867 a correspondent to the *Western Morning News* comments that the coming of the railway was bringing increased prosperity to the town. Property had enhanced in value and rents also were rapidly rising. There was a scarcity of houses as every available building was occupied and, with a lack of speculative building taking place, the writer urged the inhabitants to form a Building Investment Society to develop the many vacant sites available and bring about much needed improvements.

The 6th April, 1867 issue of the *Totnes Times* gives a most comprehensive account of the progress of the railway works and is worth quoting in full:

Recurring to the progress of the railway, we are able to quote the report of the resident engineer, Mr Stewart, to the chairman and directors. Mr Stewart says the contractor has been put in possession of all the land required. All the cuttings and embankments will be completed (excepting what is reserved for ballast) in the course of three weeks. The greater part of the bottom ballast has been saved and deposited along the line ready to be broken and spread. Only about twelve hundred yards of single fencing remain to be done. Two under- and one over-arched bridges are completed, and the masonry of three bridges is ready for receiving the timber work. One 16 feet arch remains to be turned, and another to alter. The culverts are all completed. The raised and lowered road approaches may be said to be completed excepting the metalling in one or two cases. All the permanent rails, with the exception of about 45 tons, are on the ground, and that portion, as well as the necessary fastenings, are ordered. Half the timber required is hourly expected in Brixham harbour, and arrangements are being made for the remainder. A new goods shed has to be built at Brixham-road station to replace the present one, and the excavation for the foundation is now being made. In a few days the new access to the goods shed will be completed, and then the present road can be closed and formed for effecting a junction with the Dartmouth and Torbay railway. The plan of junction has been arranged with that company. The ground at Brixham station will be ready for the bottom ballast in about three weeks. The retaining walls are mostly completed. The passenger platform wall is ready for the coping. A new road to give access to Brixham harbour is completed, excepting for about 150 yards. The difficulty in supplying water for the locomotives and general purposes at Brixham station has been successfully overcome by the overshot wheel and pumps placed in the leat at Parkham Wood, the quantity raised 135 feet, through 1,700 feet of pipes, being 17,000 gallons per day, far in excess of what is required. Although the late severe weather has seriously impeded the works, they have not suffered the slightest damage. Should nothing unforeseen occur the line may be completed by Midsummer.

A letter from Wolston to the SDR in September 1867 requests permission to obtain some rails from them for Brixham station, payment to be deferred for four to six months. 'As the platelayers will be waiting for them in the course of two or three days will you kindly instruct Mr Margary (SDR Engineer) at your earliest convenience'. On 31st October, 1867 the SDR ordered that Brixham Road be renamed 'Churston for Brixham' on the opening of the branch to Brixham.

In August 1867 the Secretary of the T&B, John Howard, based at 2 Bridge Street, Westminster, had written to the Board of Trade giving advice of intent to open within one month. On 6th December the Resident Engineer, S. Stewart, wrote to the BoT asking for the necessary paperwork which the company needed to submit requesting a BoT inspection. This was followed a week later by another letter, from Brixham, the Second Notice of Intent to open:

> ... (the line) will be sufficiently completed for the safe conveyance of passengers on the 13th 21st [*sic*] day of December and will be ready for inspection ... in the following 10 days.
> *Signed R.W. Wolston Secretary pro-tem.*

This obviously got back to John Howard in London and on 15th December this worthy wrote to the BoT:

> I beg to inform you that I have not given the Second Notice referred to ... and the T&B Railway Co. have not requested me to do so. May I ask whose signature the notice bears?

Having been supplied with Wolston's name, this appears to satisfy Mr Howard as there is no further correspondence on the matter!

On Christmas Eve 1867 a test of the strength of the permanent way and structures was carried out. The line, at slightly more than two miles in length, traversed fairly flat countryside; the heaviest cuttings, through limestone, were about 18 ft deep with the embankments about the same height; there were eight bridges. The approach to Brixham entailed the only gradient of any significance, 1 in 82½ falling towards the station. Bearing in mind that this was a terminus, all trains were required to stop dead just before reaching Brixham, afterwards drawing slowly to the platform.

The station was sited at Furzeham Common close to a plot of eight acres reserved as a recreation ground for the inhabitants and soon afterwards to be laid out and planted by the Local Board. There was an excellent view from the common over Torbay and up the English Channel, it being possible to see Portland on a clear day. Mr Wolston had constructed a cart road from the harbour to the station, this 'had been cut out of the face of the hill' and rose from sea level to about 120 ft in its course.

Interestingly the water supply for the engines had also to be raised some 135 ft from the mill leat by means of a water wheel in Glenmore Road near Mr Wolston's residence, Parkham House.

The South Devon Railway locomotive *Ajax*, an 0-6-0ST built in 1860 and weighing approximately 40 tons, accompanied by the SDR's Engineer, Mr P.J. Margary, was used for the test. The *Torquay Directory* said:

The novelty of the first locomotive traversing the line and entering the town attracted a large crowd of inhabitants, particularly the sturdy fishermen of the port, who cheered as sailors only can cheer, and drank to Mr Wolston's good health with their usual blunt but hearty good will, accompanied with the usual three times three and three times over; after which several were treated to a ride as far as the Brixham Road Station.

The test was entirely satisfactory.

As an example of how quickly the Board of Trade could react and bearing in mind the incidence of Christmas and the fact that this was a very small line, it is creditable that the BoT inspection was carried out on 28th December, 1867. However, the report was not good news for the little Brixham company and is worth reprinting in full.

Devonport 28th December, 1867

Sir,

I have the honour to state for the information of the Board of Trade in obedience to your Minute of the 14th instant, that I have this day inspected the Torbay & Brixham Railway, which commences at the Brixham Road station of the Dartmouth & Torbay branch of the South Devon Railway and ends at Brixham a length of 2 miles and 6 chains.

This line is single throughout with sidings at Brixham Road and Brixham stations and no provision has been made either as regards the land or works for a double line hereafter. The width of the line at formation level is 18 feet, the gauge is 7ft 0¼ inches and the width between the main line and the sidings is 6 feet.

The permanent way consists of bridge rail that weighs 60 lbs per linear yard for a greater portion of the length and 50 lbs per yard in the Brixham Station in lengths that vary from 18 to 24 feet laid on longitudinal timber of Danlzic Timber averaging about 24 feet in length and 12 in. x 6 in. scantling. The rails are fastened to the longitudinal timbers by ⅞ in. fang bolts at the joints and by fang bolts and wood screws for the remaining fastenings in the proportion of one fang bolt to two wood screws. Transoms of 6 in. x 4 in. scantling are placed at from 10 to 12 feet apart and secured to the longitudinal timbers by iron shop bolts. The ballast is entirely of broken stone and is said to be 1 foot thick under the longitudinal sleepers. The steepest gradient on the line is 1 in 82½ and the sharpest curve at the Brixham Road Station has a radius of about 9 chains. There are 3 over bridges and 5 underbridges or viaducts - the largest span has an opening of 24¾ ft - they are either constructed entirely of rubble masonry or with masonry abutments and wooden platforms. All are well constructed and sufficiently strong. There are no unauthorised level crossings of Public Roads on the line - and the only stations are at Brixham Road and Brixham.

A short piece of railing is required at the end of the Dock at the Brixham Road Station to prevent passengers from falling into it in the dark and some shelter should be put up on the platform. The switches of the facing points are to be locked by the distant signals when taken off - so as to have them open for the proper lines - the same thing is to be done at Brixham Station where a portion of fencing is required at the back of the platform and a portion of a wall at the side of the steps leading up from the road is to be removed - and the platform ramped off for some little distance further back. The line is in fair order but the drainage in the cuttings requires to be attended to.

The line is I understand to be worked by the Torbay & Brixham Railway Co. and by one Engine in steam not weighing more than 10 tons in weight; but at the present time the Co. has neither engine nor other rolling stock and no arrangement has yet been concluded with the South Devon Rly Co. by which these requirements are to be provided.

I have therefore to report that by reason of the incompleteness of the works, and the insufficiency of the Establishment the opening of the Torbay & Brixham Railway for traffic cannot be sanctioned, without danger to the Public using the same. I have the honour to be, Sir,
Your most obedient servant,
W. Yolland, Colonel

Accordingly on 30th December the Board of Trade wrote to the company directing that opening must be postponed for one month.

Note that there is now no mention of a tramway from the end of the passenger line but that the length of the line, as completed, is about the same as the previous railway and tramway combined. Possibly declining output from Wolston's mine now made the tramway unnecessary and a terminus site for the railway was selected nearer the town than previously intended. *Bradshaw's Railway Manual 1869* says that 'the tramway has merged into the railway with the sanction of the Board of Trade'. The whole of the £24,000 authorised by the Torbay & Brixham Act 1864 had been expended on the construction of the line. Probably the cost of the new road and the water arrangements at Brixham should be added to this figure.

Richard Wolston must have been upset by this set-back but decided to go-ahead with formal opening of the railway on 1st January, 1868. The day was a general holiday in Brixham, with shops and businesses closed and flags and triumphal arches erected to celebrate the coming of the train. A special train hauled by a gaily decorated *Lance*, a large 4-4-0ST of Gooch's 'Corsair' design built in 1851 left Newton about noon arriving at Brixham Road at 12.40. Here the train was joined by Mr Wolston and guests and Mr Seale Hayne, the Chairman of the Dartmouth & Torbay Railway; the officials of the South Devon Railway and a band from Torquay were already on board.

After *Lance* had run-round the special, departure for Brixham took place shortly after 1 pm. Probably this first trip was run at a sedate pace to allow the invited guests to see the engineering works that had been undertaken; after passing through the village of Churston Ferrers where flags were in evidence, Brixham was approached at about half-past one, according to the local paper.

As the train ran in the band on board played 'See the conquering hero comes'; everyone who could walk was at the station on this momentous day. As soon as a path could be cleared Mr Wolston stepped off the train to tumultuous cheering and was led outside the station where an 'exceedingly handsome and massive tea and coffee service' (costing £100, subscribed by the public) was presented to him by Lord Churston. The latter congratulated him on his perseverance 'in spite of the greatest difficulties and notwithstanding every conceivable discouragement' and hoped 'that when, with this service upon your table, you are enjoying the quiet exhilarating but not intoxicating cup', (applause and laughter), 'You will have the satisfaction of knowing that it was given with the sincere approbation of your fellow-townsmen'.

After a suitable reply Richard Wolston joined a procession, led by the band of the Brixham Artillery Volunteers, to the town where a 'Wolston Testimonial Dinner' was held in the Assembly Rooms shortly after 3 pm. Lord Churston was in the chair and in his speech referred to the opposition that Richard Wolston had first suffered when promoting his railway, but that now the people of Brixham were almost unanimously in his favour. In addition to the beneficial results for the fish trade, Lord Churston looked forward to the line producing a great advance in the shipping and shipbuilding trades.

Richard Wolston in reply said that he had been endeavouring to bring the railway to Brixham since 1845 (when the incident mentioned at the beginning of the chapter occurred). That project had failed because of the opposition of the broad gauge faction. Four years ago he had decided that a town of 7,000 inhabitants with a large fish trade must have a railway and determined to provide it. The line had been brought to the town 'at a high level' to avoid heavy works and demolition of house property so as to keep its construction cheap. (His first intention had been to bring the line to Parkham Wood much nearer the town, but strong opposition prevented that. Unfortunately the line's situation was eventually to be its undoing - Brixham station was too inconveniently sited in the motor age.)

In the evening Mr Wolston, supported by the Resident Engineer, Mr Stewart, gave a supper for his building superintendents, Messrs W. George (cutting of the line), Lyte (bridges and masonry) and H. Maddick (erection of the station and carpentry) and the navvies, carpenters and platelayers. Also invited were the employees of Wolston's lime quarries, paint works and iron mine. Mr Stewart complimented the men on their good conduct and said that he had never fallen in with a better behaved set of men. No accidents had happened during the construction nor had any man been brought before the magistrates for any offence.

During the day the train ran to and fro between Brixham and the junction enabling a large number of people to have a first ride on the new line. It must have been an anti-climax to close down afterwards, pending Board of Trade approval.

There was a rather unfortunate sequel for *Lance*. Several years later, on 3rd December, 1873, *Lance* was piloting an up goods train which was standing at Menheniot, as was a down goods train waiting to proceed westwards. Menheniot was a crossing place, the line in each direction being single. Having obtained 'Line Clear' for the down train, the signal porter shouted 'Right Away, Dick' but coincidentally the guard of the up train was also called Dick and that train started. Halfway to St Germans, in a cutting, there was a collision with another down goods. One driver was killed and, although all three engines were badly damaged, only one, *Lance*, was completely wrecked and had to be scrapped.

On 9th January, 1868 the SDR Minutes record:

A proposed agreement with the Torbay & Brixham Co. was submitted and as that Company proposes to perform the locomotive working of the line it was RESOLVED that should the Brixham Co. desire to Through Book, security be required to the amount of £5,000 to meet any claims which may arise for compensation in respect of accidents.

A further inspection took place on 24th January, 1868 but Col Yolland was again unable to sanction opening. The company had not yet erected the required shelter on the platform at Brixham Road, nor 'obtained possession of the engines with which they proposed to work the traffic'. Another notice of postponement to open for one month was sent. (A postscript on Col Yolland's report said this should be sent to the Secretary, Brixham, Devon, i.e. not John Howard in London.)

On 17th February, 1868 R.W. Wolston wrote to Colonel Yolland direct (which probably did not go down very well in Whitehall) to say that

1. The T&B now possessed the engines with which it intended to work the traffic.
2. The shelter had been put up at Brixham Road.
3. The SDR had provided the necessary rolling stock (passenger and goods).
4. Under the terms of the Working Agreement, the SDR undertook to provide a replacement engine with driver, etc., if the Brixham-owned engine was disabled.

Mr Wolston asked Colonel Yolland to make representations to the BoT that as all necessary stipulations had been met, the line might be opened immediately.

Protocol required Col Yolland to pass the letter over to the BoT and that august body duly replied on 21st February that there was no longer any objection to the line being opened for traffic.

The South Devon Railway minutes show 27th February, 1868 as the opening date but MacDermot and other recognised authorities record 28th February, 1868 (a Friday) as the day when at last Brixham was able to enjoy the long awaited benefit of 'railway communication'. Goods traffic was also dealt with from 1st May, 1868 and Brixham Road was renamed Churston on the latter date.

DIAGRAM OF AN OLD BROAD GAUGE TANK LOCOMOTIVE.

RAILWAY FOUNDRY, LEEDS, Dec., 1853.

ORDER 1630.

length of barrel 105 tubes

6' 3"

120 lb.

30"

Cylinders: 10¼ Water Tank

8' 0"

4' 0" dia.

Drawing of the Queen.

Chapter Three

Worked by the SDR: 1868-1875

The engine with which Richard Wolston ('General Manager and Secretary' according to *Bradshaw's Railway Manual*) commenced operations on what was, in effect, *his* railway (although worked and staffed by the South Devon Railway), was the *Queen*. This little 0-4-0 well tank was built by E.B. Wilson in 1852 and used during the construction of Portland breakwater. Bought second-hand by Wolston in 1868, her known statistics were as follows:

Inside sandwich frames
Wheelbase: 8 ft, wheel diameter: 4 ft
Cylinders: 10½ in. x 17 in.
Well tank capacity: 150 galls
Boiler: 6ft 4½in. x 3ft in.
   containing 94 2 in. tubes

Heating surface: 280 sq.ft
Firebox heating surface: 49 sq.ft
Grate area: 7 sq. ft
Working pressure, 120 lb.

These details come from Part Two of *The Locomotives of the GWR* (published by the RCTS); the accompanying plan taken from *The Locomotive* (1908) has one or two differences. The latter publication tells us that the chimney was hinged 'to allow of passing under low stagings'.

Although Wolston's letter of 17th February, 1868 to Colonel Yolland mentioned possession of engines, plural, he only had *Queen*. He needed a back-up in the event of repairs making the engine unavailable for service. As early as 7th May, 1868 the SDR Minutes state that the Board had authorised 'a charge of £3 per day to be made to Mr Wolston for the engine now working the Torbay & Brixham'. A week later Mr Wolston agreed to the SDR having a lien on the *Queen*, 'in respect of money owed by him to the SDR'. At the end of June the SDR Board were

. . . looking for the transfer of Mr Wolston's engine to the SDR in lieu of advances, coal etc. made to him, with a power of redemption available to Mr Wolston.

On 30th July, 1868 Mr Wolston agreed to mortgage his only locomotive to the South Devon company, for £350; he was presumably unable to find any other way of raising the money.

The first appearance of the Torbay & Brixham Railway in *Bradshaw* was in the June 1868 issue, when the following service was shown (running time 10 minutes):

Brixham to Churston (weekdays): 7.5, 8.45, 9.50, 10.30, 11.12 am, 2.0, 3.20, 4.35, 5.30, 6.30, 7.40 pm.
Churston to Brixham (weekdays): 7.30, 9.10, 10.15, 10.55, 11.37 am, 2.25, 4.0, 5.0, 6.0, 6.53, 8.25 pm.

Brixham to Churston (Sundays): 7.25, 8.50 am, 1.10, 7.10, 8.30 pm.
Churston to Brixham (Sundays): 7.50, 9.16 am, 1.40, 7.35, 8.55 pm.

Because Mr Wolston had decided to charge 3*d*. for the third class fare to Churston, and this was more than the charge of 1*d*. per mile for this class sanctioned by Parliament, it was necessary for these passengers to re-book at Churston. However, first and second class passengers could be issued with through tickets at Brixham.

The November 1868 issue showed some minor retimings and the following services withdrawn:

> From Brixham: 10.30 am (weekdays); 8.50 am, 1.10 and 8.30 pm (Sundays).
> From Churston: 10.55 am, 6.53 pm (weekdays); 7.50 am, 1.40 and 7.35 pm (Sundays).

Bradshaw's Railway Manual 1869 say that the earnings for the last six months (to 31st December, 1868) 'having averaged over £100 per month, fully justify the conviction that the expectations under which the construction of the line was undertaken will be fully realised'.

At the beginning of January 1870 there was a rock fall overnight (probably in the deep cutting at the Bascombe Road overbridge near Churston village) and the first train from Brixham the next morning ran into the debris, causing substantial damage to the engine. Luckily there were no injuries.

Between 1868 and 1870 financial results must have been encouraging enough for Richard Wolston to order another engine, *King*, from the Avonside Engine Co. This was a 2-4-0 side tank with 3 ft diameter coupled wheels and 4 ft 9 in. wheelbase. However, by March 1870 Wolston had to write the following, rather despairing letter to Mr L.J. Seargeant, the SDR's Secretary and General Manager at Plymouth.

> In the now present uncertainty of being able to place my debentures I feel that I have no alternative but to accept your offer of taking the new engine off my hands at the cost price to me. I do it the more willingly as it is to be attached to the Newton station. I can, as you observed, in case of need have the use of it instead of one of your large engines. Would not the more simple mode of putting you in possession be that I should complete the contract with the Avonside Company, you favouring me with the funds, and I will immediately hand it over to you or authorise them to deliver it to you direct? I should be glad if you will kindly let me know the probable cost per day of the new engine.

Unfortunately the SDR side of this correspondence has not been found, the only references being brief entries in the SDR Board Minutes. In May 1870 the SDR Board were prepared to work the Torbay & Brixham for a period of five years on terms of 80 per cent of the receipts and Mr Wolston's providing the new engine (*King*). Wolston asked the SDR to put these terms to independent arbitration but the larger company refused. But in July the SDR put up an amended offer to work the Brixham for 70 per cent of gross receipts for five years. They would pay for *King* (subject to inspection by the locomotive superintendent) and reserved the right to terminate the agreement at any time with 12 months' notice.

Still the matter dragged on, and on 16th August, 1870 Wolston wrote to the SDR:

I fear I shall have a breakdown unless I get the new engine on the line at once - as I have relied on the agreement with the South Devon Company being carried out I have not provided for the first instalment of £440 [for the new engine]. I must therefore ask your immediate good offices for an advance or the loan of one of your engines but as the hiring of which as you are aware is ruinous - I hope on the new engine being placed in your Company's hands either by assignment or otherwise as you may advise. You will oblige me I consider the matter so urgent that I am coming down by next train to see you on the matter.

The request for an advance was declined by the Board who were doubtless holding out for the best terms (to them) that they could force upon poor Richard Wolston.

No intermediate correspondence is available but on 10th November the SDR Board agreed to purchase the Torbay & Brixham new engine 'on the best terms available'. Mr Wolston gave up all claims to the engine.

A letter from Arthur Wolston (Richard's brother living in Exeter, and a Director of the T&B) to the SDR in December 1870 points out that he had never received any interest on his debenture holdings, any surplus of income over working expenses being used to reduce the Torbay & Brixham's debt to the SDR. So the Wolstons were running their railway for nothing better than Directors' fees/Secretary's salary (possibly not even Directors' fees at this time).

Sometime after 1870 Richard Wolston (who had been born in 1799) removed to Weston-super-Mare. As will be seen in Chapter Five, in December 1870 he was declared insolvent. He sold his mining and paint businesses around 1872; the Torbay Hematite Iron Ore Company, which placed a full page advertisement about the purchase of two mining businesses in Brixham in the *Railway News* for 22nd June, 1872, would appear to be the purchaser of the former.

By 1873 the Wolstons had realised that something was seriously wrong with the South Devon Railway's accounting methods - at least as far as the Torbay & Brixham was concerned. By this time Richard Wolston was ruined and some friends employed an experienced railway accountant to look at the South Devon Railway's accounts. He found that the SDR had not credited the Brixham company with the terminal charges for originating traffic but had been invoicing all the traffic as if it had originated at Churston (i.e. its own station) and simply paid for the two miles from Brixham at mileage rates.

At first Richard Wolston attempted to negotiate. He met the superintendent of the SDR on 26th August, 1874 but no agreement could be reached. A new face now came on the scene; Henry Ellis of Exeter was appointed Chairman of the Torbay & Brixham. Ellis bought a half interest in the Torbay & Brixham for £3,250 according to John Batten, a Parliamentary agent and friend of Wolston. The lively correspondence that passed between Batten and J.C. Wall, the goods agent of the Bristol & Exeter (B&E) over an allegation that Wall was behind the purchase of the Torbay & Brixham is reproduced as Appendix Three. Ellis had been a Director of the Bristol & Exeter Railway since 1868 so must have had some experience of the South Devon Railway, the latter being a neighbour of the B&E and both companies, together with the GWR, forming the 'Associated Companies'. In November 1874 the T&B intimated its desire to sell or lease to the Associated Companies or the LSWR (this was after Mr Ellis' arrival one notices!).

A special meeting of the shareholders was held on 30th November, 1874. This was in fact the first meeting of shareholders since the line opened, business in the meantime having been conducted by Richard Wolston. The four surviving Directors appointed by the 1864 Act were re-elected (A.H. Wolston, C. Lempriere, W.T.P. Wolston and W.P. Spark), and new Directors H.S. Ellis and R.T. Campion joined them. H.S. Ellis, who had just bought a half-share in the company, and was an experienced railway director, had no doubt soon agitated to introduce Directors' meetings and half-yearly meetings of shareholders so as to conduct the company's business properly. Bridget Howard who has been researching Richard Wolston for many years, and who supplied some of the additional information about him which appears in this edition, considers that Ellis was in the family, probably a cousin, but has not yet been able to prove it. Two of Wolston's sisters married Ellis's. Why else would he, a Director of the Bristol & Exeter Railway, want to put a substantial amount of money into a concern that had never paid a dividend?

A very minor matter that was revealed at this meeting was that the work involved in carrying mails for the post office four times a day only earned the company £25 a year, or 4¾d. per journey!

On 16th October, 1874, during shunting operations with some empty fish trucks, the engine was 'thrown off the rails and the 12.00 to Churston could not start. Upwards of 20 passengers were left behind'. [*Dartmouth Chronicle*]

As well as becoming embroiled in the SDR negotiations, Henry Ellis entered battle on another cause that cost the Brixham company dear - that of Government Duty. This was duty payable to the Government on ticket sales, but exemption was granted under certain conditions, one being that 'the fare or charge for each 3rd class passenger by such trains shall not exceed 1d. per mile'.

Unfortunately the Brixham line, being just over two miles long, charged 3d. for a 3rd class ticket and was thereby disqualified from exemption. Mr Ellis was unable to convince the Inland Revenue that this duty was unfair on the T&B. Government duty in 1875, for example, was over £48 out of originating passenger revenue of £971.

The half-yearly report to 31st December, 1874 noted that the Directors were unable to submit any statement of accounts as none had been received from the SDR (due to the continuing dispute). However, the Directors were advised by 'the Company's Superintendent at Brixham that the whole traffic on the railway continues to show a steady progressive increase'. The dispute had been referred to friendly arbitration. The following table of traffic trends was included:

Year Ending	No. of Passengers	Receipts (Pass. only)	General Merchandise (tons)	No. of Parcels	Fish (tons)	Minerals (tons)
31/12/1868	60,729	£695 17s. 11d.				1,248 (a)
31/12/1869	68,856	£767 12s. 2d.				2,133
31/12/1870	73,822	£806 3s. 0d.			1,200	3,802
31/12/1871	69,154	£904 3s. 0d.	4,412	6,833	1,144	
31/12/1872	69,190	£916 7s. 3d.	4,952	5,700	1,174	
31/12/1873	73,160	£984 14s. 11d.	5,341	5,658	1,407	

NB The returns for general merchandise and parcels for the years 1868, 1869 and 1870 and for fish for the years 1868 and 1869 being imperfect are omitted in the above statement. Since 1870 the Lime Works have been discontinued but are likely to be soon recommenced.
(a) 1868 is 10 months only.

White's Directory 1878-9 records that 800 tons of fish were moved in 1869, comparing that with over 2,000 tons in 1877 to demonstrate how the railway had brought prosperity to the town. See Appendix One for traffic and revenue details 1868-1882.

So there were steady increases in nearly every department, yet the Directors had to declare in the body of the report that the company had never paid any dividend to its shareholders or any interest to its debenture holders. Obviously something was very wrong somewhere.

At the meeting dealing with this report, Mr Ellis thought it would be a great advantage if the Board of Trade relaxed its regulations to enable them to stop the train at any part of the road to take up passengers as the omnibuses did. On such a short line it mattered little whether five or ten minutes were occupied in the journey.

W.P. Spark, a Director, advocated a station being built at Northfields Lane, little more than half a mile from Brixham (although Spark placed it, wrongly, about midway to Churston). In his view this would encourage many people who at present walked to Churston (because they could be halfway to Churston by the time they had walked to out-of-the-way Brixham station) to use the train. He also wanted a 'little station or stoppage' in Churston village. Richard Wolston supported the latter and said it would be a great convenience to the many shipwrights who lived in Churston and now walked to work.

Mr H. Cecil Newton was elected to be one of the auditors.

In the 1875 session of Parliament the Torbay & Brixham promoted a Bill to obtain powers for raising additional capital (£9,000 in shares and loans) and to abandon the broad gauge when the SDR Co. adopted the narrow or mixed gauge.

The preamble to the Act drew attention to the fact that the earnings of the railway had always been insufficient, after paying working expenses, to discharge the mortgage interest, arrears of which were considerable (over £3,000). The share capital raised by the new Act would, with the consent of the mortgagees, be used to pay off the the interest by an issue of new shares. The money could also be used for provision of new rolling stock or altering the gauge. The Act received the Royal Assent on 28th May, 1875.

Writing only 20 years after the event G.A. Sekon, in his *History of the Great Western Railway*, states that:

. . . the Brixham Company was so exasperated that, in 1875, it obtained Parliamentary sanction to alter the gauge of the line, the idea being that if the gauges of the lines were different, no interchange of traffic could take place, and the South Devon Railway would be effectively prevented from making any charges for such accommodation; but this change of gauge was not carried out until the final conversion of the GWR in 1892.

Sekon may have had access to some information not available to the present writer, who does not reach the same conclusion. The Act says:

. . . it is expedient that [the Company] should have power to convert their railway and tramway [a reference back to the 1864 Act] to the narrow gauge only *as soon as the narrow or mixed gauge is laid down on the adjoining railways* [my italics] or on that part thereof which communicates with the Company's railway.

and later:

When the mixed gauge or the narrow gauge is laid down on the Dartmouth and Torbay Railway, and on the South Devon Railway, or on that portion which communicates with the Company's railway, the Company shall be relieved of the obligation contained in the sixteenth section of the 1864 Act, and may remove the broad gauge from their railway, and lay down and henceforth maintain the narrow gauge exclusively thereon.

On 22nd June, 1875 Mr Ellis met the Chairman of the SDR, Mr A. Hubbard, and presented a compromise settlement proposal to the SDR. He suggested that the SDR pay £1,000 in respect of past differences and in recognition of the Torbay & Brixham's legal costs of £800 (in obtaining the 1875 Act). In addition he submitted that the SDR should work the line in future for 50 per cent of the gross receipts including terminals, or at a fixed rental of not less than £1,000 pa. Mr Ellis assumed that £2,000 would be needed to repair the line.

The SDR mulled this over for a month and then met Mr Ellis on 19th July. They counter-proposed that the SDR retained two-thirds of the gross receipts including terminals up to £1,800 pa. Above that amount the Brixham Co. would retain half of the remainder. The SDR would accept the line in its present condition, i.e. needing repair, and also pay a reasonable sum for the recent Parliamentary expenses.

Two days later the Torbay & Brixham declined these terms and asked the SDR to hand back the entire working arrangements to the owners. By return (22nd July) the SDR determined that they would relinquish the working of the line from 1st August.

This was probably too soon for the Torbay & Brixham for on 29th July Mr Ellis proposed that the SDR should keep the receipts from 1st January, 1875, handing back £600 for the present year, with an increase of £100 annually afterwards up to a maximum of £1,000. He also asked for £800 in settlement of past disputes.

But the South Devon would not give any further; on 12th August the SDR Board confirmed their terms as presented on 19th July and declined Mr Ellis' bid of 29th July. The minutes do not state that the decision to withdraw from the working of the Torbay & Brixham was postponed but all the evidence shows that it was. The half-yearly accounts for the period July-December 1875 include the usual charge for hire of rolling stock from the SDR, and wages are about the same. It would appear that the SDR continued to work the line until the SDR was taken over by the GWR on 1st February, 1876. There is an indication in the report of the shareholders' meeting for the first half of 1876 that independent working only commenced in June 1876, which presumably means that the GWR continued to work until then in place of the SDR.

Mr Ellis reported on 30th August (at the shareholders' meeting for six months to 30th June, 1875) that negotiations with the SDR had fallen through and a Railway Accountant had been employed to examine the accounts with a view to taking steps to settle the matter. It must have been a bad period for *Queen* for no less than £153 had been expended on hire of engines, plus £185 on own locomotive wages and £135 on locomotive stores making a total of £473 out of a total expenditure for the six months of £786. Receipts totalled £753, leaving a deficit on operations for the half year of £33.

The original T&B engine *Queen*; its extremely limited coal and water storage capacity is immediately obvious, even for a short branchline like Brixham.   *Real Photographs*

The general balance sheet showed a net deficit of £3,158, most of which was unpaid interest on debenture loans since their creation on 15th October, 1866 (£3,060), but included £82 'claimed by the SDR on account rendered to 31/12/1874 but disputed'. Train mileage run was 6,724 (passenger) and 84 (goods/minerals) in the six months.

Mr Ellis commented that, although the line was carrying a large quantity of fish and merchandise and between 70,000 and 80,000 passengers a year, it was not earning a penny piece for the proprietors. It was quite clear that the line could become a valuable property but that in the interests of the company and the public a proper working agreement was needed with another, larger, company leading to absorption.

This plea was to go unheeded for several more years until at last its neighbouring and very much larger company did absorb it.

An unlikely character to appear in these pages is Sarah Brown, a fish dealer of Newton Abbot. Although only having a tenuous connection with the Brixham branch, the two occasions where our story and hers crossed make interesting reading and are worthy of inclusion. Sarah, or Sally, Brown appears to be a lady ahead of her time and would be in her element in today's compensation culture.

In the first instance, in September 1875, Sarah Brown had made one of her regular visits to Brixham to buy fish. It was her practice to stay overnight at a public house run by an innkeeper named Hill. The next morning she was arrested at Brixham station and accused of stealing over £20 from Mr Hill. In court Hill's daughter, whose only evidence connecting Sarah with the crime was that she had seen her go upstairs, was proved to have been unable to see that happen from her position in the bar. Mysteriously some of the missing money had been found. She was discharged. In November 1875 Sarah Brown brought an action for false imprisonment and asked for £20 damages. Her attorney (Creed) admitted that she was of previous bad character, having been sentenced to five years' penal servitude for stealing cheese in 1856 (she served 28 months), and one year's imprisonment and five years' police supervision in 1872 for uttering counterfeit coin - 'all the more reason why she should be protected against such a charge'. The attorney for the police tried to show that Sarah had gone upstairs 'to catch a flea which was troubling her' but Brown said that the flea in question was caught on the train going home and she had a witness to prove it! After several defence (police) witnesses were heard his Honour said that as a matter of law the police had no right to give the plaintiff into custody, and the question for the jury was the amount of damages; the jury had a right to take into account the woman's previous character [heavy hint?]. The jury found for the plaintiff; damages one shilling.

Sarah's other incident was much more closely connected with the railway and occurred on Ash Wednesday, 6th March, 1878. Arriving at Churston on the first down train from Newton Abbot, she was in the process of handing in her ticket before proceeding to the Brixham train, when an assistant guard named Foster threw out a hamper or 'maund' of fish weighing 15 cwt against her ankle. She asked him why he did it but he only laughed. Another woman witnessed the incident. Being anxious to continue with her business she did not see a doctor immediately but was forced to give up going to Brixham after 15th March. She finally saw a doctor on 28th March with a very swollen and inflamed ankle; she was confined to bed for a month and did not resume her trips to Brixham until 31st May.

On Monday 17th June, 1878 in Churston County Court Mr Creed again appeared for Sarah in an action against the GWR for £40 damages. His client, aged 66, had never had a day's sickness before this incident. Her ankle was still extremely tender and she could not put her foot on the ground without considerable pain. The defence lawyer pointed out that if she had gone to a doctor straight away, doubtless she would have been back to normal by now. Foster, the GWR guard, supported by Luscombe, a porter, maintained that the maund fell out of the door when he opened it; Mr Creed quickly pointed out that if that was the case the GWR was still responsible for the accident. His Honour said that he agreed with Mr Creed and left the jury to decide the amount of the damages; after retiring the jury decided on £15.

The editor of the *Dartmouth and Brixham Chronicle* wrote quite a long leader praising Sarah Brown for her 'plucky action'. He seems to have had a bit of a bee in his bonnet about the GWR and fish carried on passenger trains, as witness the following extracts:

> The plucky action brought by Sarah Brown against the GWR . . . was a rather amusing episode in an otherwise dry day's work. It shows that an 'intelligent jury' considered a fisherwoman's ankles as valuable as those of the 'grandest lady in all the land', and although they may be a trifle larger, are not to be knocked about and 'laughed at' by every railway porter who cannot appreciate symmetry, or who does not admire natural development of size and muscle.

Perhaps the payment of this £15 and costs will teach the GW Directors a lesson, and cause them to pay a little more attention to the hampers of fish which they allow to be carried by passenger train. It is not an uncommon occurrence, particularly at Kingswear, to see a number of these maunds . . . on the pontoon, or near the platform . . . generally landed at the last moment, and just when passengers are leaving the steamer from Dartmouth, and if all the 'pumps' [stains, damage,etc. through coming into contact with them?] received were paid for at the rate of the injury to Sally's ankle, a pretty heavy bill would result, to say nothing of the sweet-smelling leakages, which in summer time particularly, are anything but agreeable . . . Two or three such actions as the one noted above may . . . be the means of stopping what is now a great nuisance.

The *Dartmouth Chronicle* of 8th October, 1875 reported that Richard Wolston had resigned as Secretary and been elected a Director. (The Great Western Board Minutes of 6th July, 1876 recorded an application from him for renewal of his pass from Weston-super-Mare to Brixham, and it was agreed 'to continue the pass for the present'.)

A letter to the *Dartmouth Chronicle* of 12th November, 1875 complained that the number of connections from Newton trains at Churston for Brixham had been reduced from seven to four, two in the morning and two in the afternoon. The 3.38 and 5.30 pm trains had been discontinued.

The year 1875 ended on a rather unhappy note with a fatal accident. On Friday 19th November, 1875 a man named Earle, aged 72, had been cutting mangolds all day in a field near Northfields Lane, less than ½ mile from Brixham station. He left work just before 5 pm, to walk home in the dark, using the branch line as a short cut to his house. When passing over Northfields Lane he was joined by another man, Millar, a ropemaker, and the two continued, Earle walking inside the rails and Millar outside them. A high wind was blowing and neither man heard the 4.50 pm from Churston approaching until the driver saw them at the last moment when, he said, he was 25 feet away, and shouted. Millar stepped aside but Earle was knocked down. The train was travelling, the driver estimated, at 13 mph, and pulled up 'near the station' where he reported the incident to the station master. Mr Earle was severely cut about the head and body and was taken to his house, where despite medical attention, he died at about 10 pm.

An inquest was held at the Queen's Hotel on the following Monday and driver George Way gave evidence. He had seen the man on the line in the morning. His fireman George Knapman said that he had seen Mr Earle on the line before. The foreman of the jury, Mr Partridge, added that he had seen Millar having his dinner on the line that very day! The doctor said that there were no broken bones but there must have been internal injuries and considered death was caused by shock to the nervous system, 'which might not have proved fatal to a younger man'. The jury gave a verdict of accidental death.

The Coroner said it was a 'frightful warning to the public not to cross the line as a near cut'. He considered that Mr Earle had met his death from his own actions and no-one else was to blame.

Chapter Four

Truly Independent: 1876-1882

One of the original Directors, Walter T.P. Wolston, MD of Edinburgh, Richard's son, resigned before the next half-yearly meeting. He had never seen any return on his 10 shares and probably had decided he never would! Richard Wolston resigned as Secretary becoming a Director in place of Walter, and Charles Ashford, the Assistant Secretary, was appointed Secretary. The interest on debenture loans outstanding was cancelled by issue of 310 £10 Preference Capital shares paying £5 per cent interest to mortgagees (the Directors). These were part of the £9,000 share capital created by the 1875 Act.

The meeting to discuss the results to 30th December, 1875 (one wonders if there was any public discussion as such as the only shareholders seem to be officials!) was held on 29th February, 1876.

Costs for the half year had risen to £1,169 including £215 for repairs to *Queen*, £40 for engine hire and £286 for own locomotive wages and stores. Receipts totalled £889 leaving a deficit on operations of £280. (At this time gross receipts at Brixham station were £1,000 per month which indicates how little the company retained. The fish traffic alone was said to be worth £2,000 a year to the Great Western which at that period did not extend beyond Bristol.) Because of the issue of shares in payment of arrears of interest on mortgages, the general balance sheet had improved to a net deficit of £533, including the figure in dispute with the SDR which had increased to £139. Train mileage run during the period amounted to 6,739 (passenger) and 92 (goods/minerals). It is fairly obvious that the passenger mileage is really 'mixed' because, allowing for a round trip of four miles, only 23 out and back goods trains were run in the whole period.

The May 1876 timetable was less generous than the opening service in 1868.

Brixham to Churston (weekdays): 7.5, 8.40, 10.0 am, 12.53, 1.45, 2.34, 4.37, 6.30, 7.55 pm.
Churston to Brixham (weekdays): 7.22, 9.0, 10.20 am, 1.10, 2.4, 4.14, 5.28, 7.0, 8.47 pm.

Brixham to Churston (Sundays): 7.25, 8.50 am, 7.10, 8.30 pm.
Churston to Brixham (Sundays): 7.45, 9.10 am, 7.30, 8.55 pm.

Running time was still 10 minutes.

In May 1876 the T&B advised the SDR that it was referring the disputed SDR accounts to the Railway & Canal Commissioners.

Immediately the SDR set out to question the right of the Railway Commissioners to consider the matter but, at a judgement delivered on 4th July, 1876, the Commissioners ruled that they had jurisdiction to deal with the complaint. After the taking of evidence the Commissioners decided in favour of the Torbay & Brixham and the full judgement, delivered on 10th August, 1876, is given below:

THE TORBAY AND BRIXHAM RAILWAY COMPANY
V.
THE SOUTH DEVON RAILWAY COMPANY

The railway of the Torbay and Brixham Company is a short line of two miles and one chain from Brixham to a junction at Churston, with the South Devon Railway. It was opened for traffic early in 1868. Rolling stock and a staff for working the railway were provided by the South Devon Company, and that Company through the officials collected the receipts from traffic, and paid out of them the expenses of the line for wages, maintenance, hire of stock, and other services. There was no working agreement in the sense of the Railway Clauses Act, 1863, Part 3, and the arrangement in form seems to have been that the South Devon Company should work and manage the line for and on behalf of the Brixham Company and as their agents. The shares of the latter Company were at first nearly all held by Mr R.W. Wolston, of Brixham, and the terms upon which the line was worked were those to which he individually gave his assent. The various rates and fares charged by the South Devon Company were settled with his concurrence. The rate on consignments of fish by passenger train was made 1s. 8d. a ton, and on station to station goods and minerals 6d., and 4d. per ton respectively at first, and at a later time 8d. and 6d., or 2d. more in each case. In regard to the charge on tonnage goods above 500 lbs. in weight, Mr Wolston acted on the advice of the South Devon Company, who suggested to him that it should be a uniform rate of 1d. per cwt. or 1s. 8d. per ton from Brixham to Churston. Whether these several rates are to be deemed to have included terminals, or to have referred only to carrying, is the subject of difference between the parties before us.

The Brixham line has little, if any, local traffic, its traffic is carried from Brixham to places beyond the line, and at the time we are concerned with was either consigned to stations of the South Devon Company, or passed over that Company's line on to the Bristol and Exeter and other lines. The South Devon, which has now become Great Western, booked the traffic through to its destination, and the railway charge in each case was the sum of the rate or through rate in force from Churston Junction, and of the local rate from Brixham to Churston. But notwithstanding that the traffic was despatched from Brixham, and all documents regarding it prepared at the Brixham Station, the way bills and invoices and the returns to the clearing house were made out as from the South Devon Station at the Churston Junction, and as if the traffic had originated and been booked there, and not at Brixham, and the local rate for the distance between Brixham and Churston, if not paid by the consignor was inserted in a 'paid on' column, and if paid did not appear at all in the advices, and was entered only in a separate account kept by the South Devon Company for the Brixham line. If the traffic went no further than to a South Devon Station, the Brixham Company was credited in that account with their local rate, and all else that was paid as railway charge was retained by the South Devon Company as due to their own line; and if the traffic was partly carried by other Companies, for instance, if it was fish from Brixham to Paddington, the South Devon Company deducted the Brixham share of the joint earnings, viz. the added local rate, account for it separately to the Brixham Company, and returned the rest of the earnings to the clearing house for division amongst the other Companies interested, their own included. The mode in which the clearing house divide is to give, in the first place, out of the receipts to be divided an allowance for terminal services to the two terminal companies - the companies, that is, at either end of the through route traversed by the particular traffic - and to apportion the remainder amongst the carrying companies according to their respective mileages. The traffic from Brixham appearing in the returns sent up to the clearing house by the South Devon Company as traffic from Churston, the South Devon Company received terminal allowances for that end; but as a matter of fact Churston was not a terminal station for Brixham traffic, nor were any terminal services performed there. The services of that kind, such as loading, were done at Brixham, and their cost charged in the expenses of the Brixham line. The Brixham Company say that, in relation to through Brixham traffic, the South Devon Company occupied the position of an intermediate company, and were not entitled to a terminal for themselves, and that the terminals they received ought to be treated as received by them in their capacity of agents of the Brixham Company, and an account rendered of them accordingly. For the South Devon, on the other hand, it is said that the Brixham Company were credited with all the receipts of the line according to the charges fixed for the use of it by Mr Wolston as representing his Company, and that the manner of invoicing the traffic was a matter which they had no title to interfere in.

The Brixham line was opened in 1868, and it was not till 1873 that Mr Wolston claimed that the South Devon Company should allow him terminals on the traffic of his line. But he states that it was not till then that he became aware of the railway practice, that where traffic is carried at through rates by two or more companies, the company at each end of the route receives out of the gross receipts prior to their division by mileage an allowance for terminal services; and he denies that in fixing the tonnage rates of 1s. 8d., or the other rates, he had in his view the handling of traffic which took place at the Brixham Station, or the making of any charge for that or for any service other than carrying. It is true that as regards goods 1s. 8d. for merely carrying would have been at a rate per mile in excess of the authorised maximum for goods of any class; but, as we have said, he adopted that rate at the suggestion of the South Devon Company, and there is no evidence that in so doing he accepted the amount by which the maximum was exceeded as the sum he was to receive for or in lieu of terminals. The South Devon Company say that he could have had terminals if he would have consented that receipts derived partly from his line and partly from other lines should be divided in due mileage proportions, and that he preferred his local rate without a terminal to a terminal, and the same mileage rate as other companies had. But this was denied by Mr Wolston in his evidence, and was not, we think, made out; nor would such a course have been a reasonable one to take, considering the small difference on a line of such short length between its maximum charge per mile, and the charge per mile of any through rate, however low. Mr Wolston seems, indeed, not to have been sufficiently well informed to be able to act for the best in the interests of the Brixham line, but we think it was for the South Devon Company, under the circumstances, to have advised him more clearly and fully than they did, and that as to the matter of terminals they should have allowed him to benefit by their being able to work the Brixham line as regards goods traffic as a through line in connexion with their own line. Nor is there any doubt that had that line been an integral part of their own line, the way bills and clearing house returns they used would not have appeared to emanate from Churston, but would have been headed with the name of the place from which they were in fact issued; and as the South Devon Company were only at the Brixham Station as the agents of the Brixham Company, we think the terminals should go as they would have gone if the way bills and returns had been made out in conformity with the real state of things. We think also that on traffic between Brixham and South Devon Stations, the receipts from which, the South Devon Company working the whole distance, did not pass through the clearing house, the Brixham Company, no agreement to the contrary having existed, and their line being used by the South Devon Company as the agents of its owners, should receive the terminals they would have had supposing their line and the South Devon line had been worked by separate companies on a similar basis of through booking.

In the application it is stated that the terminal on fish received by the South Devon Company was 8s. a ton. But this appears to have been a special terminal agreed to by certain companies, and the allowance to the Brixham Company should be at the ordinary rate for fish traffic conveyed by passenger train and not carted. As regards also the claim in the application to a terminal of 4s. per ton on carted goods, that allowance covers cartage, and the amount for cartage should be deducted, because the South Devon Company, with Mr Wolston's assent, performed or undertook to perform the cartage of traffic at Brixham, and employed an agent for the business at their own expense. With respect to the remainder of that terminal, and with respect to the usual station to station and mineral terminals, we are of opinion that their respective amounts should be accounted for to the Brixham Company; but that so far as the sums already credited to that Company have exceeded their parliamentary maximum rates for carriage, the excess shold be taken as a part payment of the terminals now awarded.

Unhappily the South Devon could not accept this judgement gracefully and attempted to work the accounts in its favour by insertion of entirely new and heavy charges in respect of the use of Churston station. This resulted in the new accounts showing that the Torbay & Brixham owed it a large sum! A further application to the Railway Commissioners resulted in the South Devon again being overruled by a judgement given on 29th March, 1877, detailed below. The SDR had to part with no less than £2,135 5s. 9d., less £350, the amount advanced by them on the security of *Queen* in 1868; thus *Queen* was restored to the Torbay & Brixham at the same time.

THE TORBAY AND BRIXHAM RAILWAY COMPANY
V.
THE SOUTH DEVON RAILWAY COMPANY

By decision which we gave in the Torbay and Brixham Railway Company, against the South Devon Railway Company, in the beginning of August last year, we decided that it was not fair to the Brixham Company that through traffic which originated or ended at the Brixham station should be treated as it had been treated as traffic originating and ending at Churston, which was a station at some distance off and upon the line of the South Devon Company, and we ordered that the South Devon Company, which had received terminals out of the receipts on that through traffic, where it had been sent to the line of a third company, as, for instance, in the case of fish sent to Paddington, considering that it worked the Brixham line as the agent of the Brixham Company, and as their advisers and councillors in matters of rates and charges, should account to the Brixham Company for the terminals they had so received, as also for terminals on traffic between stations on the Brixham line and stations on their own line treating the two lines as separate lines, although happening to be worked by one and the same company. That decision of ours, as I have said, was given in August last and we have now before us accounts which have been prepared with a view of carrying out that order. These accounts show what the total tonnage of the through traffic was in the eight years ending the 31st January, 1876, and this total tonnage has been distributed into various classes according to the classification adopted in the Brixham Company's Act of 1864.

For the year 1875 the division of classes is in accordance with the actual state of things, and for the other years it has been assumed that the tonnage of the different classes bore the same proportion to each other as they were found to bear in 1875. 1 do not think that any better course than that could have been taken, it is agreed to by the Brixham Company, and we have therefore the total tonnage of through traffic carried to and from this Brixham station, and that total tonnage, multiplied by the proper terminals, namely, 1s. 8d. in the case of fish, 1s. 6d. for non-carted traffic, 9d. for minerals, and 4s. less 2s. 6d., for carted traffic, after deducting according to our directions any sums that were charged and paid over to the Brixham Company in excess of its maximum Parliamentary rates, would be the amount that would be payable to the Brixham Company as for terminals under our order.

What then is the reason why this sum should not have been paid over at once to the Brixham Company? The reason appears from these accounts; the South Devon Company have considered that our order had the effect of cancelling altogether the old accounts which had been rendered by them to the Brixham Company for the working of their short line, showing the receipts and the expenses, and that they might prepare new accounts, introducing items which had not been entered before.

The old accounts were not very favourable to the Brixham Company, because the result of the eight years' working was an excess of expenses over receipts to the amount, I think, of £117, but according to these amended accounts, even after allowing the Brixham Company for the terminals granted by us, the working expenses exceed the receipts by more than ten times that amount, or by a sum of £1,323. This is due to various counter-claims and sets-off which are made by the South Devon Company, and as to which we have now to decide whether they should be allowed or not.

The claims made to charge the Brixham Company a percentage upon the cost of the engine for interest and depreciation -

Mr Saunders: Those claims are for the present withdrawn.

Sir F. Peel: I know they are, and I was about to say that as the claims to charge this company a percentage on the value of the engine, and also to charge them for the use of the Churston station, are entirely new charges, are not admitted by the Brixham Company, and are charges of which we know nothing at all, the withdrawal of them was a proper course. If there is anything in them they can be made the subject of a separate application, but they afford no reason whatever why anything due to the Brixham Company in respect of terminals should not be paid in accordance with our award.

The other points are with reference to the rates for carriage for fish and goods generally. What we allowed by our decision to the Brixham Company was their maximum Parliamentary rates for carriage, and we stated in our decision that the rate upon consignments of fish by passenger train was 1s. 8d. per ton, and 1s. 8d. a ton also on goods above 500 lbs. in weight; and in another part of the same decision we said that as regards goods 1s. 8d. for merely carrying would have been at a rate per mile in excess of the authorised maximum for goods of any class, meaning it to be understood that we did not consider 1s. 8d. for consignments of fish by passenger trains to be more than what the Brixham Company had power to charge. The South Devon Company have acquiesced in what we have said as to that matter, and the only point in dispute in regard to fish is upon what tonnage the Brixham Company should be allowed charges for carriage at the rate of 1s. 8d. per ton on its total weight should, for the purposes of these accounts, be treated as an over-payment. We think, looking to the terms of our decision last August, and to their letter of the 19th February, they ought to be content with the tonnage upon which they will receive a terminal being taken to regulate what should be allowed for carriage of fish, at the rate of 1s. 8d. a ton.

Then with regard to goods, as I have said, we allowed any payment in excess of the Parliamentary maximum rates for carriage to go in diminution of the sum payable to the company for terminals. By the Brixham Act the Brixham Company have a short distance clause, which enables them to charge for their two miles and one chain as for a distance of three miles, and it is only when there is a working agreement made in pursuance of the Brixham Act, section 37, that their line and the line with which theirs is in connexion are to be treated as one line, and only actual distance to be charged. Now in our opinion no such agreement has existed as would come within that 37th section. We think the Brixham line did not cease to be a separate line, and that in accordance with the provisions of their Act the Brixharn Company could charge rates of carriage as for a distance of three miles. With these directions there will be no difficulty in finding out what is the sum due to the Brixham Company, and we think that that sum ought to be paid within a month from the present time. [The T&B was awarded half its costs.]

The skirmish with the South Devon before the Railway Commissioners is usually hailed as a great victory for the Torbay & Brixham. It is certain that without the award of £2,135 the Torbay & Brixham could not have continued and would have been taken over earlier or closed. But when one totals the amounts paid for the use of Churston station post-1875 (£1,706) and adds it to the £500 the company had to shell out to the South Devon following a court case in 1877, backdated to cover use from 1868 to 1875, it will be seen that the cash award was cancelled out. But the Torbay & Brixham did get its independence from the grasping South Devon and was able to charge rates more satisfactory to itself in the future, so it was certainly the only course it could take.

Because the line was now independent the Directors appointed a Manager in the first half of 1876, H. Cecil Newton of Totnes, previously an Auditor of the company's accounts. Henry Cecil Newton had been appointed the previous summer as the Secretary of the Buckfastleigh, Totnes and S. Devon Railway at the relatively young age of 23. His previous employer had been the GWR (probably in a clerical capacity) and his home was in Notting Hill, London. Attempts were made to get the GWR to work the railway but these were unsuccessful.

The Great Western Board on 8th June, 1876 approved a new Agreement with the Torbay & Brixham Railway, relating to its independent working, *see Appendix Five*, but a suggestion, presumably from the T&B, that the latter should be allowed a rebate on its traffic was declined. One wonders how it could be justified that the T&B pay for one half of the cost of working Churston station. The hire of the necessary rolling stock cost about £60 for the half-year at first, as against the £33 10s. 6d. charged by the South Devon, but this reduced considerably in later years. It was also necessary to issue Bye-laws and these were sanctioned by the BoT on 23rd November, 1876.

The break with the South Devon Railway led to an immediate improvement in finances and in the half year to 30th June, 1876 traffic receipts were £150 higher than the same period of 1875 at £885 plus £13 miscellaneous, a total of £898, against costs of £602, an operating profit of £296. However, after taking account of the arrears of interest on debenture loans, the general balance sheet recorded a small loss of £107, still a big improvement on the previous six months. Mileage run during the period was 6,800, all mixed.

For the only time the accounts included an interesting break-down of passengers by class and this is appended below:

1876	1st	2nd	3rd	Parly	Total
January	80	1043	3936		5059
February	58	974	2800		3832
March	85	1804	3027		4916
April	80	1043	3936		5059
May	75	1149	3532		4756
June	51	640	2947	1410	5048
	429	6653	20178	1410	28670

[January and April are exactly as printed in the original]

The results for the second half of 1876 included the £1,785 (net) received from the South Devon Railway. This is a bit strange as the appeal by the T&B against the accounts drawn up by the South Devon Railway after the first judgement was not heard until March 1877. However, the Torbay & Brixham accounts for July-December 1876 are dated 16th May, 1877 and it was presumably felt in order to include the settlement as if received in that period. This enabled payment to be made of one year's interest on the preference shares at £5 per cent and a half year's dividend on the ordinary capital at £2 per cent, for the first time. The company was so flush for funds that it was able to make a five guinea donation to Brixham Regatta! The difference the Railway Commissioners' judgement made to the revenue kept by the Brixham company can be seen in the receipts for the period - passengers £598, parcels and fish £638, goods £208, mails £20. After the addition of the SDR money operations showed a healthy £1,836 surplus of income over expenditure. The latter included a charge of £140 for the use of Churston station for the year for the first time, and £57 for engine hire when *Queen* was under repair. A new fish shed had been erected at Brixham, the passenger buildings cleaned, painted and put in good repair. The general balance sheet showed assets of £3,630 including rolling stock and shares.

The Chairman said that the T&B earned throughout the year about £20 per mile per week which was about double the average earnings of other branches in Devonshire. He expressed the opinion that the concern would become one of the best railway properties in the West of England. He had lately been visiting various Cornish fishing ports with the Fishery Commissioners and there appeared to be very few resident trawlers on that coast; the bulk of the fishing was done by Brixham men who went down as far as St Ives. As a result the fish came back to Brixham; there was 'no place comparable with Brixham as a trawling station'.

In seconding a vote of thanks to the Chairman, Mr Spark (who was also a member of the Harbour Commissioners) let slip some remarks which the *Dartmouth Chronicle* picked up: '. . . the old ship was really drifting on the rocks when Mr Ellis took the helm, but owing to his able and skilful management she might now be said to be going before the wind with a valuable freight on board'. - (hear, hear).

At the beginning of 1877 the Torbay & Brixham did threaten to close the line and replace the trains by two horse-drawn omnibuses, for parcels and passenger traffic. This was as a result of the loss of some fish traffic to road because of the higher charges imposed for the use of Churston station. Fortunately the threat was not carried out and, as will be stated later, rates for fish traffic were subsequently reduced.

There was some better news for the company when it received a letter dated 1st January, 1877, from the GPO's Surveyor at Exeter, stating that the Postmaster General had approved an increase in the mail contract from £25 to £40, backdated to the previous January.

The *Dartmouth Chronicle* of 2nd February, 1877 reported that at the annual supper of T&BR employees 'Friday evening last', between 20 and 30 persons sat down to an excellent spread at the Queen's Hotel. H. Cecil Newton was in the chair and stated that the Directors would give a bonus of 5s. to each man next

pay day. It was hoped they would appreciate the spirit rather than the value of the gift as the railway up to the present time had made a considerable loss. A toast was drunk to Mr Wood, 'superintendent of the line'.

In January 1877 the Torbay & Brixham purchased a second engine from the Great Western, an ex-South Devon Railway Avonside-built 0-4-0T called *Raven*, No. 2175. This little engine cost the T&B £1,450 paid in two instalments; her statistics were as follows:

Wheelbase: 7 ft 6 in., wheel diameter: 3 ft
Cylinders: 14 in. x 18 in.
Tank capacity: 450 galls
Boiler: 10 ft x 3 ft 5 in. containing 115 1⅞ in. tubes
Heating surface: 500 sq. ft
Firebox heating surface: 65.3 sq. ft
Grate area: 9.28 sq. ft

Although *Queen* was withdrawn immediately the GWR absorbed the company in 1883, *Raven*, which had been built in 1874, continued in GWR service until 1910, then being sold to the Wantage Tramway where it lasted until 1920. It would be interesting to know how much time *Queen* spent in traffic after purchase of *Raven*; judging by the amount spent on hiring engines whilst *Queen* was the only engine, she was not very reliable and with her small tank capacity must have needed several refills during a turn of duty.

Raven cannot have been too much help in her first few months on the Brixham line for £62 was outlaid in the six months up to June 1877 on the hire of an 'auxiliary engine'. The report and accounts for this period say that:

. . . a considerable sum was also paid for the hire of locomotive power but now that the new engine is in full working order your Directors hope that this charge which has always formed a large item in the Accounts will disappear.

In consequence of the Commissioners' award and the improved receipts, the company was also able to spend quite a considerable sum putting the permanent way into good order, about £1,000 being expended in the *twelve* months to June 1877.

Traffic receipts for the half-year January-June 1877 were £170 up on the corresponding period in 1876 at £1,057. Because the high level of expenses previously mentioned there was a deficit on operations of £786 but sufficient funds remained for a half-year's interest on the 5 per cent Preference shares. The general balance sheet showed asset value of £1,464 including rolling stock and stores. Some 7,000 miles of mixed train mileage was run during the period.

H. Cecil Newton, having recently become the Manager, resigned the office of auditor and Mr T.F. Robinson of Totnes was elected in his place. In the last half-year £852 had been expended on maintenance of way and works:

The average cost of maintaining the way and works throughout the kingdom was about 10 per cent of the receipts, while in the last half-year that expense on the T&BR had amounted to no less than 80 per cent of the receipts. The reason was that while the railway was under the control of the SDR there was never sufficient revenue . . . to maintain the line in first class condition and consequently a great portion of timber in the permanent way became worn out at the same time . . . by charging the whole expense to revenue [in the last two half-years] they had entirely got rid of the exceptional drain on their income . . . no small line had a better train service. There were 12 trains each way every day, and five each way on a Sunday . . .

The improvement in the service since the SDR ceased to work the line, and consequently the T&B had more money available, should be noted. Only a year earlier, in May 1876, the last timetable which we noted, there were but nine trains each way on weekdays and four on Sundays.

The *Dartmouth Chronicle* of 1st June, 1877 reported that 'the men connected with the station had recently been supplied with new clothing made by Mr Prowse of this town'.

It will be recalled that in the case before the Railway Commissioners the South Devon Railway stated that they had credited the Torbay & Brixham with everything to which that company was entitled under the original agreement with Mr Wolston. The SDR presumably felt that the rates negotiated were sufficiently generous to allow any terminal expenses to be paid out of them. However, the Commissioners overruled the SDR who had to pay the relevant terminals allowances. The SDR must have felt that they had in effect paid twice and in 1877 decided to take the Torbay & Brixham to court to obtain payment for the use of Churston station during the disputed years 1868-1875. Here the South Devon won the day and the Torbay & Brixham had to pay £500 'in settlement of old claims for the use of Churston station and other matters'. They were, of course, paying twice yearly for the use of the station after 1875.

A short piece in *The Railway News* for 24th November, 1877 noted the very gratifying increase in earnings since the T&B became independent. At the end of 1875 average receipts per mile per week were £15 4s. 5d.; from February to May 1876 (under GWR management) they increased slightly to £16 13s. 10d. per mile. 'Since that time . . . under its present management, the receipts have shown a progressive improvement, until the average weekly earnings for the month of September last were £26 5s. 3d.'

Less happy for the T&B was a report in the *Dartmouth Chronicle* of 18th January, 1878 that an attempt by the company to get the judgment on Churston station referred back to the Railway Commissioners was refused by the High Court.

The *Dartmouth Chronicle* for 25th January, 1878 carries a report of the T&BR annual dinner, again at the Queen's Hotel. A fine turbot of 20 lb. weight, the gift of J. Salter, fish merchant, was a 'prominent feature in the entertainment' (a quaint way of saying it was eaten!) The company had purchased 'a powerful engine [*Raven*]'. A bonus was declared for the staff.

In 1877 the Directors of the T&B bowed to pressure from the fish merchants and reduced the rates for conveyance of fish. The new charges averaged about one penny per package. As a result during the half year July-December 1877 160 tons *more* fish were conveyed than in the same period of 1876, but revenue *dropped* from £638 to £389. This generous gesture, 'for the purpose of developing the traffic to the utmost', was not justified by future results.

There were increases in the other categories of traffic: 4,387 more passengers, 215 more parcels and 905 extra tons of goods were conveyed compared with the second half of 1876. However, because of the reduction in fish receipts, traffic revenue was £77 lower. Total revenue exceeded costs by £189 and it was possible to pay interest on the loans but no dividend on the shares. The general balance sheet was in the red again to the tune of £1,400 due to the second payment of £725 on *Raven* falling due. Train mileage, all mixed, showed a big increase to 9,873.

To reduce the expenses, instead of cutting the men's wages, the Directors and officers agreed to accept less remuneration for their services. The debentures had been renewed at four per cent instead of five per cent, thus saving interest [and *another* cut in the Directors' income].

Mr A.C. Wolston was elected one of the auditors in place of Mr Robinson who had left the district.

In moving a vote of thanks to the Chairman, Richard Wolston had to listen to another thinly veiled reference to his days in charge when the seconder, R.T. Campion, referred to 'the unsatisfactory position in which the line stood until Mr Ellis joined the Board of Directors. Under his judicious management they might look with much satisfaction to the future . . .'

Henry Ellis, who had steered the company through the South Devon crisis, died in 1878. The new Chairman, Arthur H. Wolston of Exeter, Richard's brother, said that it was to Henry S. Ellis's 'untiring zeal and energy (that) the improved position of the Railway is mainly due'.

This year also the Manager, H. Cecil Newton, accepted a railway appointment in London but was permitted to retain the management of the Brixham line and would 'visit Brixham and inspect the line as occasion may require'.

The expenses for the half year to June 1878 were exceptionally high and included the £500 ordered by the Court to be paid to the SDR, previously mentioned. Passengers continued to increase but fish and goods declined somewhat during this period, with parcels about the same. The following details were included with the half-year report.

January-June 1877		£	*January-June 1878*	£
Passengers	33,345	505	36,883	534
Fish (tons)	782		734	
		241		232
Parcels	2,967		3,038	
Goods (tons)	2,824	311	2,572	301

Operating costs exceeded revenue by £859 during this period and the general balance sheet was slightly better, in deficit to the tune of £926 after issue of £720 worth of shares. Train mileage was lower at 8,878, all mixed. The report and accounts said that:

> . . . since July 1876 about 12,500 feet of the best creosoted longitudinal timber and 450 transomes have been put into the railway besides a large number of new rails.
> The accounts for the half-year . . . show that notwithstanding the continued depression which has so seriously affected Brixham, there has been a slight increase in Revenue . . . the depression in trade had been very severely felt; the shipbuilding, which was to them a most important item of traffic, had been almost at a standstill . . .

There had also been a strike by the fishermen, which was now over.

As well as the £500, the accounts also included a year's payment in respect of Churston station - £245 13s. 10d. - and many other items of special expenditure.

The amount to be paid to the GWR for the use of Churston station . . . was a serious item of expense and they were endeavouring to get it reduced; considering the amount of work performed for the GWR by the T&B company servants it was not unreasonable to expect that some reduction would be made.

During the period the T&B had attempted to negotiate a working agreement with the GWR but had been unable to persuade its neighbour to do so.

The costs of going to law in the 1870s must have been considerably less (as a proportion of a person's wages) than they are now, because the *Dartmouth Chronicle* of 28th June, 1878 carried a report of a very minor action. George Way, engine driver, and George Pook, porter, were summoned by William Ray, formerly a ganger on the T&B for stealing his potatoes which were growing in a plot alongside the line.

Apparently Mr Ray was allowed to plant garden produce on certain plots by the sidings, and then having had an altercation with the station master, Mr Wood, he was dismissed, 'leaving in the ground certain vegetable productions which had not come to perfection' [what wonderful journalistic prose!]. Mr Wood, thinking that the property in the ground belonged to the company, ordered the two defendants to dig the potatoes.

The case was dismissed, but the defendants' claim for costs was not allowed.

The second half of the year was always better for passenger carrying but in 1878 this fell off badly with a decrease of 2,605 over the same period in 1877. A stagnation in trade had affected Brixham badly, particularly ship building. Fish traffic also was down, mainly due to bad weather in the autumn; this had been general in the South West.

July-December 1877		£	*July-December 1878*	£
Passengers	45,600	671	42,995	623
Fish (tons)	1,352		1,220	
		388		360
Parcels	3,249		3,565	
Goods (tons)	2,534	307	2,375	294

Raven had proved expensive involving an outlay of £132 in repairs and alterations and £55 for hire of a replacement engine. This latter outlay indicates that *Queen* was probably stored out of use, too small and inefficient to cope with the traffic adequately. Although operating revenue exceeded costs by £1,031, to try and reduce the outstanding trading deficit the Directors went without fees and £820 share capital was raised (almost certainly amongst the Directors!). The general balance sheet went further into the red with a deficit of £1,057. Train mileage, all mixed, was higher at 9,085.

Mr Newton said that the GWR had 50 branch lines under its management at rates varying from 50 to 52 per cent of the gross receipts. If the GWR would consent to work this line for 55 or even 60 per cent, there would be sufficient traffic to pay the shareholders a dividend. [Regular readers of newspaper railway meeting reports had to wait until June 1880 and the report of the half-year to 31st December, 1879 for Mr Newton to reveal that the GWR was taking no less than 78 per cent of the Brixham gross receipts!] He also considered that the charge for Churston station, which worked out at about 10 per cent of the gross revenue, should not be more than 1 or 2 per cent.

From 1879 onwards, the half-yearly reports which had been quite comprehensive became much more abbreviated, consisting almost solely of figures and little comment. It is as if the Directors realised that they were on a slowly sinking ship and that it was pointless describing each increase in the list in detail! No more dividends were paid on the shares and by the date of amalgamation with the GWR the unpaid interest on debentures stood at £1,145.

Rather than merely list the financial details of each half-year for the remaining years of the line's independent existence, the more important facts are summarised and the reader is referred to *Appendix One* where the revenue and traffic results from 1868-1882 will be found.

The first half of 1879 saw revenue static but just exceeding costs by £16. The general balance sheet continued in the red at £1,037. Mixed train mileage totalled 8,990. Once again the Directors took no fees.

One of the GWR's engineers had told Mr Newton that the T&B line was maintained in very good order. From here on, there was generally a plaintive cry at these meetings for the GWR to take over the line.

In the second half of the year revenue was £41 up on 1878 and a profit of £312 was made on the working for the period. However, unpaid interest and other debts continued to rise so that by the end of the year the general balance sheet deficit had increased to almost £2,300.

In announcing another increase in fish and goods traffic at this meeting, Mr Newton highlighted some of the problems in dealing with the former.

Sometimes fish, which had to go off by the 'perishable' train at night, did not arrive at the port until ¾ or ½ an hour before the train went, and did not all the men employed on the line work with a will it would not get sent off in time. There had never been a case where the fish was kept back overnight and missed the morning market . . . But there was no doubt they were hampered for want of proper facilities for bringing the fish from the market to the station. It had been intimated to him . . . that the company might adopt similar arrangements to those in use at Grimsby and Lowestoft, but as he said to his GWR friends, 'it is very easy to advise, and very well to suggest these improvements, but we must leave this *until you come into your inheritance and adopt the Brixham line as part of the Great Western system.* We recognise the importance of the improvements but we have not the means to carry them out' . . . It was not fair when they considered that their company only received one 99th part of the fish receipts and that [the GWR's] working expenses were 78 per cent, 18 per cent above the average . . . He could not help feeling that they held the line really in trust for the GWR; and he hoped when amalgamation came they would recognise this and deal as liberally as they possibly could [a forlorn hope, it transpired].

It is as well to stand back for a moment, away from this paperchase of statistics and reports, and just consider for a moment what this tiny company was called upon to do. In 1879 they had booked over 77,000 passengers, forwarded 7,000 parcels, 2,042 tons of fish and over 4,700 tons of general goods.

All of the fish and general goods had to be hauled to the station, up a horrendously steep hill, using horses and carts. The fish, in particular, was often late arriving and must not be delayed. Fish is not particularly weighty - just think what 2,042 tons equates to in the terms of individual packages. And all this done with a tiny staff, probably less than a dozen, in a station on a windswept hill with very little shelter. Not until GWR days was a decent fish platform built. It was quite an achievement, particularly as the shareholders (i.e. the Directors) went without dividends, and often without fees. One hopes the people of Brixham appreciated it.

In 1879 J.C. Wall 'on behalf of the chief proprietor Mrs Ellis' suggested to the GWR that it might lease the T&B for £840 pa, or buy it for £20,000 of GWR 4 per cent Preference stock, and that he thought an offer of less than £18,000 could not be entertained. This the GWR declined: the terms were 'so much in excess of the estimated value of the property'. Shortly afterwards the T&B suggested a lease in perpetuity starting at £862 pa (35 per cent of gross receipts in 1878), increasing by 1 per cent per annum until in year 10 the figure of £1,109 was reached, at which it would remain. This offer was similarly declined by the GWR. In view of the contents of Appendix Three, Mr Wall's involvement is interesting!

During the first half of 1880 *Raven* was repaired and thoroughly overhauled at a cost of £103 and auxiliary engine hire of £36, leading to an operating loss of £92, although traffic revenue was £82 up on 1879. By borrowing £500 from loan capital the general balance sheet deficit hovered at about the same level as before. Mixed train mileage was 8,974.

Mr Newton said that he was sometimes asked what was a fair price for a line of this sort. Recently a small line, which from its opening had been in the hands of a receiver, had been sold to a large company at the rate of £10,000 per mile. On going into the matter, he found that the purchase was carried out on the principle that where a line earned £20 per mile per week it was worth £10,000 per mile. He might say that the Brixham line earned considerably more than that and had never been in the Court of Chancery. Regrettably, as we shall see, even when it was sold, the Brixham line was not treated fairly.

In the 23rd July, 1880 edition of the *Dartmouth Chronicle* there was a report that William Bluebeard had broken into Brixham station 'overnight Wednesday', ransacked the booking office, but took nothing. He also broke into the refreshment room, where he stole some coppers, 2 lb. of biscuits, some cigars and some sponge cakes and drank some brandy, whisky and beer! He was apprehended (rolling drunk?) at 2 pm next day. The following week's paper gives his name as 'Bubeer' and describes him as 'a young man of very ungainly appearance'. He was committed to Exeter Assizes. The report is useful in that it gives some indication of what the refreshment room on a small railway had to offer. George Philip of the Queen's Hotel was also licensee of the refreshment rooms.

In the second half of 1880 a decrease in fish and goods traffic more than outweighed an increase in passengers and revenue was £41 down on 1879. However, there was no engine hire this period, permanent way expenditure was down (new rails and crossings had inflated the costs of that department in the first half) and so an operating profit of £284 was made. The deficit in the general balance sheet continued at £2,200. Mixed train mileage was 9,218.

Mr J. Daw was elected a Director, to fill the vacancy caused by the death of Mr Ellis. He had a very large interest in the company. Another reason he had accepted was because of the impending resignation of Mr Newton. Noting the reduction in fish traffic, 221 tons, Mr Spark stated that many of the Brixham boats traded with Plymouth, thus that traffic was lost to the line.

Mr Newton, in reviewing his time with the line since 1876, said that then the line was in a very bad way and only earning about £8 or £9 per mile per week*. Now the receipts were something like trebled. Within the last three or four years the line had been practically relaid. He had frequently spoken to Mr Grierson, the GWR General Manager, about Churston station on which they now paid 12½ per cent of their net income; this was altogether out of proportion for the services rendered and most unusual in the railway world. The GWR had built special vans to convey fish to London 'in a perfectly sound and fresh condition'.

At a subsequent meeting of the Directors, John Daw was elected Chairman of the Board, in place of Mr A. H. Wolston.

(This is the last full report of a T&B meeting in the paper.)

In January 1881 there was a tremendous gale and snowstorm which caused terrific damage to ships in the harbour, four were lost and 25 sustained damage. One vessel, the schooner *Whin*, was driven on to The Strand where it lodged its jib boom through the slated front of the second storey of a house and brought down stones round the windows and chimneys. On Tuesday 18th January all the shops were closed and many of the houses had 8-10 ft of snow in front of them; most of the streets had 2-3 ft of snow. On Thursday a team of men was clearing the snow from the branch line [which had probably been closed since Tuesday although the paper does not say so] and about noon the engine was dug out. In some places the snow was 6-7 ft deep for nearly ¼ mile. Traffic was resumed on Friday, 'before which the mails, etc. were conveyed to Churston by vehicles'. The total cost of the damage in Brixham, including shipping, was estimated at £4,000.

During 1881 Mr H. Cecil Newton, the Manager, was appointed Secretary of the London Tilbury & Southend Extension Railway and resigned his appointment at Brixham. As he had been resident in London for several years it is doubtful that many of the users of the line, or possibly the staff for that matter, noticed the difference! He also resigned as Secretary to a proposed Totnes, Paignton & Torquay Direct Railway Co., which in 1882 collapsed when the GWR refused it any assistance.

Locomotive repairs were again quite substantial at £49 during the first half of 1881, with a further £66 going on hire of replacement engine power. In January, as we have seen, the railway had been snowed up and exceptional expenditure of £7 7s. 9d. was recorded against this event. But otherwise costs were kept right down (there was not even a line of entry 'Directors fees' in the annual report now!) and an operating profit of £53 was made, despite receipts being £83 down on 1880. The balance sheet deficit was almost identical to the previous half year. Mixed train mileage was somewhat reduced at 8,498.

---

* His figures for 1876 do not agree with the *Railway News* analysis of November 1877.

Brixham in broad gauge days. The platform here has not yet been extended over the road bridge and the building has its original canopy. Lighting on the

The GWR Board minutes of 20th July, 1881 record that the General Manager had met Mr Newton recently; the latter had proposed that the GWR should lease the T&B for £400 pa, rising in the third year to £650 pa, and terminating in the purchase of the line for £16,250. The Board would not agree to these terms but made an offer of £12,000 to purchase the line. (Why were they so mean when they knew the value of the fish traffic it carried?) The following Board, on 11th August, heard that the T&B had agreed these terms and the GWR had taken over the working of the line immediately. The necessary powers for purchase would be applied for within two years, pending which the GWR would pay rental of £450 pa.

The second half of 1881 was, as usual, better than the first. Revenue was £118 up on 1880, all departments except parcels showing an increase and a healthy operating profit of £331 ensued. The locomotive had again proved costly (£70 repairs, £56 engine hire) but with effectively only one engine available, needed in traffic day in, day out, and considering the rudimentary nature of the machine, it was probably inevitable. The balance sheet deficit was creeping inexorably upwards and had reached £2,500. Mixed train miles totalled 9,252; the rolling stock certificate was signed 'H. Wood, Superintendent' for the first time (previously Mr Newton had signed it).

Discussions with the GWR continued behind the scenes and on 12th April, 1882 the Secretary of the Torbay & Brixham, Charles Ashford, notified the shareholders of a special general meeting to be held at Exeter on Friday 5th May, 1882 to submit to shareholders:

First Bill in Parliament to be entitled 'An Act for conferring upon the GWR Co., further powers . . . for vesting in the Company the undertaking of the Torbay & Brixham Co., and for other purposes' and secondly
Amendments to be made in the said Bill for vesting the undertaking of the T&B Co., in the GWR, upon certain terms to be therein specified.

The meeting to discuss the half-year results ending December 1881 (detailed above) was held at the end of June 1882 and there are a couple of significant points in the press reports of the meeting. John Daw, the Chairman, said that 'it was well known that they had sold their property to the GWR at a very insignificant price because they wished to wind it up'. And, 'he wished they could have made more equitable terms with the GW Company but they were anxious to get the thing off their hands and had given way'. In fact the selling price, at £12,000, was only half of the cost of construction. Even then £1,000 of the purchase price was to be invested in consols in the names of the GWR Secretary (Saunders) and the T&B Solicitor (Campion) for *10 years* in case of any claims against the GWR, for example for land without proper title. After 10 years the money would be split between Mrs Ellis and Arthur Wolston. The remaining £11,000 would be paid on 1st January, 1883 and an Agreement dated 19th May, 1882 set out how it should be applied, all debts (except debenture debts) being paid off first. There was no buying out of shares or exchange of T&B shares pro-rata for GWR ones as often happened in these takeovers - the GWR got a healthy source of regular traffic at a real bargain price.

The Bill received the Royal Assent on 24th July, 1882 and 1st January, 1883 was set as the date of amalgamation.

For its last year as an independent concern the half-yearly reports were issued as usual. In the first half of 1882 there was a £180 improvement on 1881, passengers in particular being over 5,000 higher than the first six months of that year. An operating profit of £277 was made but the deficit on the general balance sheet stood at nearly £2,700. Mixed train mileage was 8,944. The final meeting of the proud little company was held on 12th July, 1883, showing a decrease of £39 by comparison with 1881. Costs had risen also, particularly in the locomotive department where £51 of repairs had been necessary, together with £44 expended on engine hire. Nevertheless, a small operating profit of £77 had resulted and 9,104 mixed train miles had been run. Its final account showed a balance sheet deficit standing at £2,743.

On the absorption of the T&BR from 1st January, 1883, 15 years to the day from the small company's ceremonial opening, the GWR records list the names of the staff taken over.

Name	Grade	Age	Entered service	Weekly wages
Wood Henry	Station master	57	January 1847	46s.
Pook George	Foreman porter	40	November 1865	25s.
Hayward Reginald	Goods porter	36	May 1865	25s.
Hatherley William	Guard	39	December 1865	22s.
Parker Walter	Porter	27	October 1876	19s.
Woolaway S.	Porter	48	January 1878	20s.

Mr Wood's name would be placed on the Register of clerks; it was his intention to join the Superannuation Fund. All were members of the Provident, Pension, Widows & Orphans Funds apart from Woolaway who was too old to join.

Until the T&B became truly independent of the SDR in 1876 the staff were provided by the latter company. Hence the dates before 1876 in the above table refer to SDR service. Some SDR establishment records for 1873/4 show that Henry Wood (described as 'booking constable') earned 24s. 6d. per week in 1873 and 26s. in 1874. R. Hayward, goods porter, was on 19s. and 20s. respectively. George Pook ('acting guard on branch') earned 18s. and 19s., and William Hatherley, then goods porter, 18s. in both years. So all the men had had wage rises in the years up to 1883, but Henry Wood far more than the others. The table poses an interesting question: why were the T&B driver and fireman not taken over?

So Richard Wolston's railway, his brainchild and the result of his efforts in promoting its Bill, raising its capital, building it and, together with a few relatives and close friends, looking after its interests (and from 1876, running it), passed from this close family circle to one of the biggest railways in the land - the Great Western Railway. It had cost him his fortune, resulting in his bankruptcy in 1870, so his feelings for his creation must have been mixed. He did not survive long after its sale, dying intestate in Weston-super-Mare on 10th April, 1883 at the age of 83. He left a personal estate of just £62 10s., his daughter Maria being granted administration.

Chapter Five

No Steam without Water

When the First Edition of this book was written, the author had no idea of how different things were in Brixham, and particularly on the railway, in the days before mains water was readily available. Since then some files kept by the CME Department at Swindon, specifically on the subject of water matters have been found. There was a file kept for each station, it seems. Those found for Brixham cover a long period, from 1881-1936, while that for Churston is from 1902-1922. The files for other dates were not found. The files were very dirty and dishevelled, having been stored by folding in half and then in half again to take up the minimum of space, bearing in mind that there were hundreds if not thousands of these files covering the whole GWR. But the information they contained was well worth the inconvenience; many interesting snippets were revealed of early life on the branch. Having decided that they were no longer of use, and not being wanted by the PRO, many hundreds of these files were dispatched by BR to the County Records Office at Trowbridge (Wilts). The whole of this chapter is based on these files, and they have also thrown up some hitherto unknown facts about R.W. Wolston.

When the GWR was negotiating to buy the T&B, it was concerned to find that its purchase price did not cover an annual payment to Mr A.H. Wolston, one of the Directors, of £25 pa for the supply of water. The General Manager wrote to William Dean (locomotive & carriage superintendent) asking if the company could provide water cheaper than this. The matter was passed to J. Luxmoore, the Newton Abbot locomotive superintendent, who replied as follows (29th November, 1881):

> The town of Brixham lies in a deep valley between two hills, houses being also built at various levels up each hill.
> The water is pumped up from the valley by means of a water wheel about 8 ft in diameter and three pumps (self-acting) of about 2½ in. diameter.
> The station is nearly on the summit of one of the hills, and the line from Churston to Brixham runs along the top of this limestone hill. I walked over the line but could see no water anywhere nor is there any to be obtained at our station at Churston without pumping as Churston is the highest summit on the Torquay branch.
> I cannot see that we could obtain water at Brixham cheaper than the present arrangement.
> I noticed a pipe leading from the pumps to supply a large house or garden just by. [Was this to Wolston's former property at Parkham Wood?]
> The pump and wheel are not on the railway premises but down in the town and care should be taken that we have a right of way to it and to the stream which turns the wheel.

Mr Dean concluded that £25 was a reasonable outpayment in the circumstances, despite the GWR average being about £15 pa for the same amount of train mileage. However he asked to see the Agreement first. This does not survive on the papers, having been returned to Paddington, but

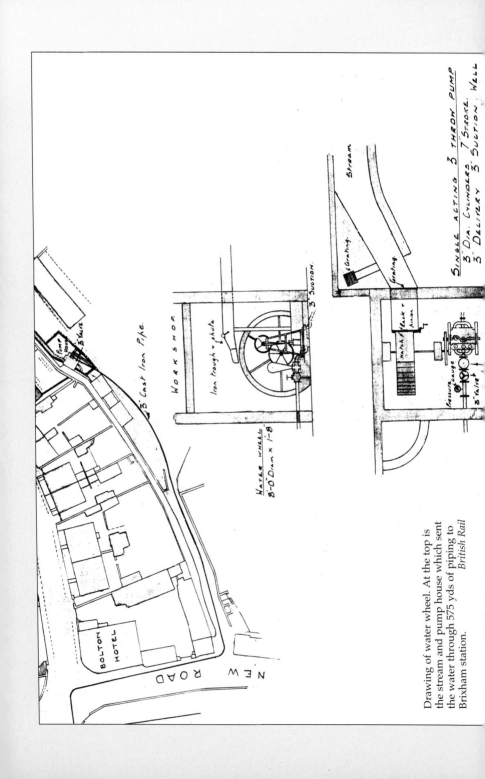

Drawing of water wheel. At the top is
the stream and pump house which sent
the water through 575 yds of piping to
Brixham station.
British Rail

fortunately Swindon wrote out some extracts while the Agreement (dated 5th June, 1880) was in their possession. This had the history of the ground and the water.

On 7th June, 1834 part of the land known as Parkham Wood had been 'granted' by Indenture to Richard Wolston, and on 6th June, 1839 the remainder had been granted. (Without sight of the originals it is not clear whether this grant involved payment.) On 29th September, 1868 he had acquired by grant the neighbouring grounds of Tinkers Wood with its stream and built an aqueduct, water wheel and pumps so as to convey the water to Brixham station. (From Glenmore Road the piping was laid under New Road, Market Street, Higher Street and Station Hill.)

Here things become complicated and the extract of the Agreement, handwritten in a cramped style, is not sufficient to tell the whole story, although it has more than has been recorded up to now. On 24th March, 1866 R.W. Wolston and his wife Maria had agreed to grant Parkham Wood to Isabella S. Reid of Plymouth and Charles Langley of Chudleigh 'subject to redemption by R.W. Wolston on payment of £4,000 and interest on 24th September, 1866' (outstanding mortgage?). It does not appear that Richard Wolston released the property, but on 27th December, 1870 filed a petition for bankruptcy and a Thomas Andrews of Bedford Circus, Exeter was appointed Trustee. On 15th April, 1871 elder brother Arthur Hill Wolston, a T&B Director, took over the whole of Richard's real and personal estate on payment of 2s. 3d. in the pound to the creditors, but, the document notes, no conveyance of Tinkers Wood (with the stream and water wheel) or 'equity of redemption' on Parkham Wood (which had been called for in the 24th March, 1866 document) had been made by A.H. Wolston. [Richard Wolston's iron mine and paint business were sold about 1872.]

On 5th June, 1880 the strip of land in Tinkers Wood, stream and associated works, with full rights of access for maintenance in perpetuity, were sold by A.H. Wolston (with agreement of Reid and Langley) to the Torbay & Brixham Railway for £25 per annum, to be paid in equal half-yearly instalments.

If Isabella Reid and Charles Langley granted the mortgage for Parkham Wood, they may never have received their money directly from the Wolston family. A.H. Wolston died on 15th July, 1883 and there is an extract on the file of an auction of the Parkham Wood properties on 13th August, 1884, with the Tinkers Wood property of the (now) GWR suitably protected.

On 17th May, 1882 the General Manager sent a wire from the House of Commons to Mr Dean: 'We are closing the Agreement with the Torbay & Brixham are you happy with the water agreement?' Mr Dean wired back that he was happy as long as the company's solicitor was. The Agreement to sell the T&B to the GWR is dated 19th May, 1882.

Following A.H. Wolston's death the GWR declined to purchase the rent charge on the Tinkers Wood ground and it was purchased by a Brixham grocer, Mr J. Bartlett, for £550. Bearing in mind that the GWR/BR was paying the £25 pa right up to the 1950s, this seems remarkably short-sighted.

On 29th November, 1884 Mr Luxmoore wrote to Mr Dean stating that the water tank at Brixham, built of wood (12 ft x 8 ft x 4 ft) and holding only 2,400 gallons, was in a dilapidated condition and a larger tank, holding at least 6,000 gallons, should be put up next year. There is nothing on file now until 30th April, 1887 when Mr Luxmoore repeats his request, modifying its size to 5,000 gallons, 'as the present tank is in a very shaky condition'. He also complains of their water course being used as a rubbish tip, having recently noticed a barrowload of old parsnips in the water.

There now ensues some lengthy correspondence about the Queen's Hotel, close by Brixham station. Mr Luxmoore finds that there is a branch pipe just before the station leading to the hotel. At times of water scarcity, almost guaranteed in hot summers, the level of water was insufficient to work the water wheel. It was necessary to hire a horse to work some apparatus which worked the pumps. He had had to hire a horse on 23rd July, 1887 for 4½ hours and therefore objected to the Queen's Hotel having water in times of drought. The hotel owner was George Philip of Harborne, Birmingham, but he had let it to a brewer who had sublet it to a Mr Charles Atkins.

As nothing was known of this arrangement Mr Dean wrote to H.C. Newton, former Manager and now Secretary of the London, Tilbury & Southend Railway, and told Luxmoore to make local enquiries. Mr Newton referred the matter to Charles Ashford, former Secretary, who in turn referred it to Henry Wood, former station master. Mr Wood had no information but did say: 'When the pipes were being laid in, the owner of the hotel may have asked Mr Wolston to allow the hotel to be supplied, and Mr Wolston may out of good nature have ordered it to be done, he was just the sort of person to do such a thing'.

Referred again to Mr Ashford, a letter from Mr Luxmoore to Mr Dean dated 13th October, 1887 says that 'Mr Ashford has looked through his letter books and Minutes of Directors' meetings but can find no trace of the matter'. This in itself is interesting because these books were never passed over to the GWR and their absence is part of the reason that information about the T&B is so limited (mainly to newspaper reports); where are the books now?*

Mr Ashford also remarks that George Philip was also tenant of the station refreshment room up to Michaelmas 1880, latterly at a rental of £16 pa. He points out that Mr Philip will soon have enjoyed these water facilities for 20 years which would mean he would then be entitled to them.

This last point was drawn to the attention of the company's Secretary at Paddington in November, but nothing having been done, on 19th January, 1888 Mr Luxmoore asks if he should cut the water off. Contact was made with the Secretary who said that he had written to Mr Philip, but no reply had been received and the water should be cut off on 28th January (exactly one month before the railway's 20th anniversary). Meantime Mr Luxmoore had written to the Queen's manager with this ultimatum. Strangely enough the Town Council was now laying down water pipes to Furzeham but no water would be available until April.

(A waterworks was completed in Higher Brixham at a cost of £4,000 in 1875. In 1888 the supply was extended to Furzeham where a large reservoir was built, water being pumped to it by steam power.)

Enquiries of the Queen's Hotel revealed that the water was only used for washing up as it was somewhat dirty. Rain water was used for all other

---

* The author's personal feeling is that after the way they were treated by the GWR, and its ridiculously low purchase price, the Directors passed over as little as possible to the new owner.

purposes. There were difficulties in actually finding the branch pipe in the road and it was only on the second visit that it was located and was cut off on 28th January; no response was ever received from Mr Philip.

The horse gear itself came under notice shortly afterwards when the ground on which it stood was sold to a Mr Hazlewood, a local builder. Originally owned by Mr Wolston, the ground was adjacent to, but not part of the Tinkers Wood property for which the company paid £25 pa. Fortunately Mr Hazlewood was prepared to let it stay there on payment of 10s. per year for a lease of seven years. In the same letter to Swindon (24th November, 1888), Mr Luxmoore reminded them he was still waiting for his locomotive water tank at Brixham, some four years after his first request! On 1st January, 1889 Mr Luxmoore wrote that the Town water company *could* now supply the station, having erected a tank, but it would have to be pumped 'and no doubt would be very expensive'.

At last patience was rewarded and on 7th January, 1889 a works order was issued for a 5,000 gallon pillar tank. There was a change of plan and it was decided to erect a 5,500 gallon square tank, spare at Launceston, instead.

On 15th March, 1889 Mr Luxmoore said that a contractor, Mr E.P. Bovey of Torquay, was about to start building the Board School (now Furzeham School) in a field alongside the station and had applied for a supply of water for his portable engine which worked his mortar mill. It worked at 20 psi and had a boiler 6 ft x 2 ft 10 in. and grate 2 ft 6 in. x 1 ft 10 in. Mr Luxmoore thought 240 gallons per day would suffice and suggested a charge of £1 per quarter. All these seemingly trivial matters took several letters to finalise; eventually a charge of 3s. a week was agreed, but on 22nd June it was necessary to cut off Bovey's supply because of shortage. However Mr Bovey agreed to provided a horse, at his expense, to work the pumps in the town and his water was restored.

On being asked in 1896 about the renewal of the lease of the horse gear, Mr Luxmoore said:

> . . . the horse wheel has occasionally been used in times of drought but owing to the distance and height to which the water has to be pumped this method has been given up and a small upright boiler has been put up at the engine house at Brixham station and, by means of an elevator, water sent down from Newton in a portable tank in time of drought is lifted up into the stationary tank.

However, he suggested that the land be retained for access purposes to the water wheel, etc., and in a later letter said the land should be purchased if possible to maintain access and that it was an oversight that it had not been: 'I scarcely think that the Loco Dept could have been consulted on the subject'.

Some true operating matters now come into the correspondence. On 18th September, 1897 J.T. Robinson was now the locomotive superintendent (after at least 15 years of Mr Luxmoore), and wrote to Mr Dean following a request from the Exeter traffic superintendent for a water column on the platform ramp at Brixham. At this time Swindon men were on site erecting a new engine shed, originally located at Stenalees in Cornwall, and it would be an ideal time to do the work 'to avoid the branch engine having to run so frequently from the station to the shed tank . . . There is no doubt but what [sic] it would overcome a great many delays in having to unhook and go to the shed . . .' There was no water at Churston (still), all water being taken from Brixham. However, Mr Robinson, who obviously knew a thing or two about the operators and their way of blaming his department added:

> I question very much whether the cost of fixing a new crane at the station would overcome the few minutes delay if such is the case in taking water at the shed. The delays in taking water in my opinion are attributable to the engine in the first place being detained almost to train time doing yard shunting then being released to the shed for water and should the train be a minute or two late in starting it is put down to waiting engine, taking water.

Mr Robinson must have been a 'caretaker' because by 22nd December Mr B. Giles was in the superintendent's chair (remaining there until the end of 1918). A new broom, he queried why he was paying £25 pa for water when, from early June until now it had been necessary to send a tank of water to Brixham every other day because of shortage. Swindon sent details of the water agreement, but said it was the first they had heard of a shortage and asked Mr Giles to check that the water had not been diverted.

Mr Giles did a full investigation and his reply of 12th January, 1898 has many interesting facts. There had always been a shortage in the summer months and a horse was hired at 1s. per hour to work the pumps. To save this expense, in 1893 a wooden water tank was placed in a truck to convey water from Newton Abbot. The engine pit at Brixham was cemented and made water tight and the water tipped into it, from which it was elevated to the permanent tank by an elevator worked by steam from a vertical boiler. In August 1895 water tank No. 31, holding 3,000 gallons, was received from Swindon and replaced the wooden tank and truck. From early June until 9th December, 1897 the tank had made daily journeys to Brixham, where consumption was about 2,500 gallons daily. He had cemented the walls of the aqueduct and made other adjustments and did not consider diversion was occurring. But some water was lost because the Brixham Urban Authority used the water higher up the stream to work a larger water wheel than the GWR one; in summer the water was impounded and when it was released 'the water comes down faster than our wheel can take it, overflowing at the weir into the natural bed of the river'. There was now a plentiful supply of water and Mr Giles promised to keep a special watch on the situation in future with a view to reducing water supplied from Newton Abbot. Such was the range of matters that a GWR locomotive superintendent was required to be knowledgeable about!

On 14th November, 1902 the divisional engineer, Plymouth asked if the company's steam roller, working at Churston, could have water from the locomotive tank there, not realising there wasn't one! It was agreed that three tenders of water would be sent from Newton Abbot at 3s. per tender.

In August 1905 Brixham was suffering its customary summer shortage and the Regatta Committee asked if they could be supplied with water on 25th and 26th - Hancock's roundabouts were the principal attraction (obviously worked by a steam engine). This request went right up to Mr Churchward's office and a price of 10s. per tank per day was agreed. 'This may appear to you to be a high charge , but it is purely a nominal figure as we should have to run a tender tank

When writing about Hancock's roundabouts at Brixham Regatta in 1905, the author had no idea that an illustration existed. But here is Burrell traction engine No. 1740 *Cornishman* of 1894 descending Overgang towards the harbour with Hancock's of Bristol centre truck containing part of a 4-abreast set of 'Gallopers' in 1910.   *D.K. & M. James Collection*

from Newton Abbot to Brixham, and when I tell you that the rate is 3s. 6d. per ton up to 20 miles, you will see that I am treating you liberally'. Four tanks were supplied. The action was repeated for the 1906 Regatta. (For interest, the first *typewritten* letter appears on file in 1906.)

In 1908 some lengthy correspondence ensued about a water supply for Churston station. By this time the town of Brixham was being supplied with water by Paignton, who also supplied Teignmouth, and had been connected at a point north of Churston, with a reservoir in Brixham. The latter was prepared to supply water at 1s. 6d. per 1,000 gallons which Swindon thought too high. All Churston had was a well; 'although during dry seasons this becomes much becoloured the supply has never failed'. This correspondence went backwards and forwards for months, Swindon regarding the cost as exorbitant; they suggested 9d. per 1,000 gallons as a fair price. Newton Abbot pointed out that in 1908 they had supplied 100 tanks of water, each containing 3,000 gallons, to Brixham - no less than 300,000 gallons! The Brixham locomotive had now been fitted with pumping gear and about 2 cwt of coal was used in pumping each tank, about £6 per year (they accounted for every penny in those days).

This was all referred to the General Manager as the cost of a 3,000 gallon pillar tank would be £255. The GM asked if the price of water could be reduced and they did manage to get Brixham UDC to reduce the price after the first 250,000 gallons (in a year) had been supplied to 1s. 3d. per 1,000 gallons. Finally in March 1909 the GM decided he could live with this charge, for what was intended to be an emergency supply when Brixham dried up, 'as this would be more advantageous to the company than . . . taking water by tanks from Newton Abbot to Brixham'. He authorised the pillar tank.

B R I X H A M.

Estimated Cost of supplying one new Water Wheel
8'0" diameter x 1'8¼" wide.

Drawing No. 61204.   *28th. June 1921.*

	C.	Q.	lbs.	£.	s.	d.
12 C.I.Segments.	3.	0.	0.			
2 C.I.Wheel Centres.	2.	3.	0.	14.	0.	7.
12 C.I.Spokes.	3.	1.	20.			
1 C.I.Spur Wheel. 2'6"	1.	2.	11.			
1 " " " 1'6"	1.	0.	4.			
1 Steel Shaft.	1.	1.	14.	3.	11.	8.
Steel Bar for Bolts.			16.		5.	0.
Steel Keys. 3 ea.					7.	6.
Iron Plate.	6.	2.	0.	11.	7.	6.
Bolts and Nuts.		1.	6.	1.	1.	3.
2 Plummer Blocks.				5.	2.	0.
2 C.I.Pedestals for Plummer Blocks.	1.	0.	0.	1.	3.	9.
				36.	19.	1.
WAGES.						
Painting complete.				3.	0.	0.
Marking off etc., Fitting and Erecting complete, and Machining.				115.	3.	4.
Punching and Shearing etc.				1.	19.	7.
Pressing Buckets.				4.	3.	9.
				£161.	5.	9.

Say £200. 0. 0.

Patterns not included or fixing.

In May 1909, the superintendent at Exeter wanted to join the fun and asked if he could take advantage of this water with a supply to Churston station for drinking and for the toilets. Of course this took much extra paperwork, and once the price got to an extra £45 the GM took fright and wanted to limit Churston's enjoyment to one tap fixed at the north end of the station buildings (or even at the foot of the pillar tank) and nothing for the lavatories! However, once the Engineer pointed out that only £15 was an additional cost, most of which related to 87 yards of piping from tank to building), the other £30 being connected with drainage, he relented. On 25th October, 1909 the Board approved expenditure of £301 for a new tank and water to the station building at Churston, almost a year from the start of the correspondence! By Christmas Eve the tank had not been started, due to 'more important work' involving the Works Manager's staff who did the erecting. On 3rd May, 1910 the Works Manager told Mr Churchward's office 'we are now commencing to erect this pillar tank' (Great Western wheels could grind exceedingly slowly sometimes) but at last it was brought into use on 11th June, 1910. There can't be many water tanks for which the exact date of 'opening' is known.

On 23rd June, 1910 Mr Churchward's office directed that Churston water must only be used in emergency, 'it must only be used to save the cost of carrying water from Newton Abbot to Brixham'. By the end of September 1910 already 91,000 gallons had been used for locomotive purposes and 1,000 gallons by the station, so Brixham must have been in its customary dry state.

In 1921 the water wheel at Brixham was dismantled and sent to Swindon for repairs. There is an indignant letter on file from the Works Manager, by now W.A. Stanier, to Mr Churchward dated 14th May, 1921 saying that the wheel was completely derelict and fit only for scrap and that he was not inclined to carry out any repairs. The cost of a new wheel was estimated (the estimate is included here as an illustration) and the General Manager asked to approve £200 for a new wheel. This was approved on 6th July and a works order issued for a new wheel, 8ft diameter by 1 ft 8½ in. wide. On 7th July the Newton superintendent, now Mr E.G. Wainwright, asked that it be completed speedily as the branch engine was taking all its water at Churston. On 10th September he was told that a new wheel had been sent 'on Wednesday 7th loaded in GN wagon No. 56720'.

A few days later, on 6th October, the CME's office was quizzing Mr Wainwright as to why the water used at Churston for the quarter ending September had gone up from 360,000 gallons, for the same quarter in 1920, to 428,000 gallons this year. Doubtless repressing his true feelings he merely replied that it was due to a shortage of water at Brixham and Kingswear. He reported to Mr Churchward on 17th November that the new wheel had been fixed, but there was insufficient water to work it at present.

In August 1923 there was a general water shortage, so much so that Paignton shut off Brixham's town supply which led to much indignation in the local papers. This shut down Churston's supply so once again tenders were sent from Newton Abbot to Brixham (as the stream had also dried up). This continued into September.

In July 1925 Brixham UDC told the GWR that water would have to be cut off to the Churston tank between 7 am and 11 pm because of shortage, and so Mr Barker (now the Newton superintendent) sent a mobile tank to Brixham as a precaution.

In 1927 the supply of water to Churston was transferred from Brixham to Paignton which meant that the GWR lost its privileged rate over 250,000 gallons, all water now being charged at 1s. 6d. per 1,000 gallons. In December Mr Christison (now Newton superintendent) received his customary 'please explain' from Swindon about Churston consumption and pointed out that there had been a scarcity at Brixham and Kingswear that summer, plus the tank at Torre had been out of action on several occasions. It seems that Churston had again saved the day - it had been truly 'money well spent'. A similar reply was given in December 1929 - 'no water being available at Brixham during the period ending September 1929'.

In 1930 Newton Abbot arranged for the branch fireman to oil the water wheel on a weekly basis for which he was paid one hour's overtime. In June 1934 there was another shortage at Brixham.

From March 1936 the cost of the GWR's water supply from Paignton dropped to 1s. 5d. per 1,000 gallons after the first 10,588 gallons per half-year had been taken. That December Mr Christison was answering his customary 'please explain' from Swindon and said that in this instance the increase at Churston 'was due to the annual cleaning of the leat at Brixham, also it is understood the springs did not break as early as usual at Brixham, causing a shortage'.

Here the file ends so far as day to day matters are concerned. But it is fairly obvious that from what we have seen that Brixham's water supply was very unreliable and that its £25 annual outpayment for the rights to the stream water brought little benefit. Without the Churston tank after 1910 there would have been an extremely regular flow of water tanks from Newton Abbot to Brixham, almost every summer.

There are a couple of later letters on a separate file dealing with the rent payable to Mr Bartlett. In 1907, his daughter Mary Stoddart Bartlett had inherited the rent charge in his will. On 31st July, 1944 the GWR's Secretary records a failure to reach agreement with Miss Bartlett on the 'commutation of the charge' (probably payment of a lump sum to buy it out); 'we have no alternative but to continue the annual payment' (which by now had cost the GWR over £1,500). In June 1947 the papers state that the facilities are no longer used and the GWR Secretary asks the Solicitor whether they can be abandoned. The latter agrees, although the company must maintain the works to avoid flooding, etc. but points out that title to the land cannot similarly be abandoned. The last letter on file is dated November 1954 but gives no clue as to whether the agreement with Miss Bartlett has finally been paid off. It may well be that mains water was supplied to Brixham tank by 1947, or just that Churston's supply was sufficient on such a short line, but unfortunately the papers after 1936 were not available.

Chapter Six

'An insignificant Great Western Branch' 1883-1947

'An insignificant Great Western branch' is how MacDermot's *History of the GWR* describes the Torbay & Brixham after its amalgamation with its huge neighbour, and of course to that great company it was insignificant, just a minor appendage contributing to the well being of the whole body. No longer were accounts published or statistics available to tell the people of Brixham how their little railway was doing. But to Brixham the railway continued to be important, its outlet to the rest of the Kingdom, at least until the 1920s or 1930s when the motor vehicle began to bite into the railways' monopoly. In the case of Brixham, with the station high up above the town involving an inconvenient and tiring climb to catch a train, buses, once established, had the advantage of easy accessibility. But substantial quantities of fish in truck loads continued to be conveyed right to the branch's closure and, unlike passenger traffic, without much seasonal variation.

The timetable for March 1884 is shown overleaf. No goods trains are shown so presumably all trains were capable of being 'mixed'; the branch was worked under the 'One Engine in Steam' principle. The engine working the branch was shedded at Brixham and naturally the first train of the day was from Brixham, whilst the last service finished at Brixham. Trains were timed to connect, normally, with both up and down trains at Churston. However, there were two late trains on the main line, 10.05 pm Kingswear to Newton Abbot and 11.11 pm Newton Abbot to Kingswear which did not have a Brixham connection. On Sundays, as will be seen, there were two long gaps in the service but only one train on the main line did not receive a connection, namely the 10.50 am Newton Abbot to Kingswear (Churston 11.24 am).

The summer timetable, July 1884, showed an increase of one train each way on weekdays, 6.09 pm ex-Brixham and 6.25 pm ex-Churston. The Sunday summer service was identical to the winter one. In October 1884 the 11 train weekday service was restored, as in March. On Sundays the only difference was that the 7.30 am ex-Brixham left five minutes later at 7.35 but as departure from Churston remained at 7.44, this gave only a two minutes' turn round which must have been impossible to achieve and was probably altered the next time the timetable was reissued.

The first expenditure on new works at Brixham by the new owner to be found in the files is that on 17th November, 1886 the Board agreed to erect a new office for the goods clerks at a cost of £57. On 9th January, 1889 the Board were told that Brixham's water supply was normally pumped by waterwheel, but in dry seasons this had to be supplemented by horse power. The ground on which the horse gear stood had recently been purchased by Messrs Hazlewood Bros, who asked for rent of 10s. per annum, which the Board agreed subject to the firm granting a lease on the land.

Note: Some staff in this Chapter are only identified by initials because the PRO embargoes other than basic details for 75 years. Information on those persons fully identified has been obtained elsewhere.

BRIXHAM BRANCH.—Week Days.

Up Trains.	Miles	STATIONS.	1	2	3	4	5	6	7	8	9	10	11
{	2	Brixham	a.m. 7 12	a.m. 8 41	a.m. 9 40	a.m. 10 49	12 30	1 30	3 0	4 16	5 14	6 53	8 18
	1	Churston	7 19	8 48	9 47	10 56	12 37	1 37	3 5	4 23	5 21	7 0	8 25

Down Trains.	Miles	STATIONS.	1	2	3	4	5	6	7	8	9	10	11
{	1	Churston	7 25	……	……	……	12 45	1 45	3 55	4 30	5 33	7 44	9 10
	2	Brixham	7 32	……	……	……	12 52	1 52	4 2	4 37	5 40	7 52	9 17

Sundays.

STATIONS.	1	2	3	4	5
Brixham	a.m. 7 30	a.m. 8 40	p.m. 1 20	p.m. 6 50	p.m. 8 18
Churston	7 37	8 48	1 27	6 57	8 25
Churston	7 44	9 4	1 35	7 7	8 35
Brixham	7 51	9 10	1 42	7 14	8 42

March 1884 Working timetable.

BRIXHAM BRANCH.

Single Line, worked by Train Staff. No Block Telegraph. Only one Engine in Steam allowed on this Branch or two coupled together. All Trains must stop dead before passing the underbridge on the Churston side of Brixham Station and at the overbridge on the Brixham side of Churston Station. The Train must afterwards be steadily drawn to the Platform.

WEEK DAYS.

DOWN TRAINS.

M	C	STATIONS.	1	2	3	4	5	6	7	8	9	10	11 D	12 D	13	14	15	16
			A	D Goods	A	Mixd.	A	A	A	A	A	A	Goods R.R.	Goods R.R.	A	A	A	A
		Churston	A.M. 7 18	A.M. 8 10	A.M. 9 3	A.M. 10 7	A.M. 10 58	P.M. 12 47	P.M. 1 46	P.M. 3 30	P.M. 4 58	P.M. 5 48	P.M. 6 25	P.M. 7 10	P.M. 8 3	P.M. 9 23	…	…
2	1	Brixham	7 25	8 25	9 10	10 15	11 5	12 55	1 53	3 37	5 5	5 55	6 35	7 20	8 10	9 30	…	…

SUNDAYS.

M	C	STATIONS.	1	2	3	4	5	6
			A	A	A	A	A	A
		Churston	A.M. 7 50	A.M. 9 17	P.M. 1 40	P.M. 7 0	P.M. 8 27	…
2	1	Brixham	7 57	9 23	1 47	7 7	8 34	…

UP TRAINS.

M	O	STATIONS.	1	2	3	4	5	6	7	8	9	10	11 D	12	13 D	14	15
			A	D Goods	A	A	A	A	A	A	A	A	Goods R.R.	A	Goods R.R.	A	
		Brixham	A.M. 6 55	A.M. 7 40	A.M. 8 37	A.M. 9 35	A.M. 10 40	P.M. 12 10	P.M. 1 27	P.M. 2 25	P.M. 3 55	P.M. 5 30	P.M. 6 5	P.M. 7 12	P.M. 7 40	P.M. 8 30	…
2	1	Churston	7 2	7 50	8 44	9 42	10 47	12 17	1 34	2 32	4 2	5 37	6 15		7 50	8 37	…

SUNDAYS.

STATIONS.	1	2	3	4	5	6
	A	A	A	A	A	A
Brixham	A.M. 7 35	A.M. 9 0	P.M. 1 25	P.M. 6 46	P.M. 8 10	…
Churston	7 42	9 7	1 32	6 52	8 17	…

Above: October 1894 Working timetable. *Below:* July 1896 Working timetable.

BRIXHAM BRANCH.

Single Line, worked by Train Staff. No Block Telegraph. Only one Engine in Steam allowed on this Branch or two coupled together. All Trains must stop dead before passing the underbridge on the Churston side of Brixham Station and at the overbridge on the Brixham side of Churston Station. The Train must afterwards be steadily drawn to the Platform.

WEEK DAYS.

DOWN TRAINS.

M	C	STATIONS.	1	2	3	4	5	6	7	8	9	10	11 D	12 D	13 D	14	15	16
			A	D Goods	A	D Goods	A	A	A	A	A	A	Goods R.R.	Goods R.R.	Goods R.R.	A	A	
		Churston	A.M. 7 18	…	A.M. 9 3	A.M. 10 10	A.M. 10 55	P.M. 12 47	P.M. 1 50	P.M. 3 30	P.M. 4 55	P.M. 5 53	P.M. 6 30	P.M. 7 10	P.M. 7 40	P.M. 9 30	…	…
2	1	Brixham	7 25	…	9 10	10 15	11 2	12 54	1 57	3 37	5 2	6 0	6 40	7 20	8 10	9 37	…	…

SUNDAYS.

M	C	STATIONS.	1	2	3	4	5	6
			A	A	A	A	A	A
		Churston	A.M. 7 50	…	A.M. 9 17	P.M. 1 30	P.M. 6 35	P.M. 8 7
2	1	Brixham	7 57	…	9 24	1 37	6 42	8

UP TRAINS.

STATIONS.	1	2	3	4	5	6
	A	A	A	D Goods	A	A
Brixham						
Churston						

ne broad gauge 2-4-0ST *Prince* standing alongside the fish dock at Brixham about 1890. The
ods shed can be seen at right.   *Real Photographs*

Prince at Brixham platform about 1891; apparently cab doors were quite a luxury at this period!

Former T&B employee George Pook died in February 1889, aged only 46. Henry Wood, former station master, who had retired on 7th August, 1887, died on 28th September, 1890, aged 65. Edward George Tripp followed Henry Wood, the station master with the longest stay at Brixham, by being the station master with the shortest stay here. Becoming SM at Brixham in August 1887 at £100 pa, he was promoted to chief clerk in the station superintendent's office, Paddington at £110 pa in October 1888. Later, in 1903, he was made station master at Uxbridge.

William Henry Pomeroy, who had come from a porter's position at Torquay to be foreman porter at Brixham in October 1889 was disciplined for an accident on 9th January, 1891 which caused damage to the engine and the coaches to come 'off the road'. He resigned his position in April 1892.

An engine shed had been in use at Brixham since the line opened. This was sited just beyond the platform slope at the Churston end of the station, and on the downside. In August 1890 a coaling platform, 12 ft by 9 ft 6 in., was constructed beneath the large watertank (provided in 1889) which was supported on four legs.

A fascinating document headed 'Memo as to Meal Times. Light Branches, Loco & Carr. Dept Swindon 4th June, 1891' shows that *a single set* of enginemen worked a 15 hour day at Brixham at that time (this was common practice on rural branch lines, there are 26 other similar lines listed). At Brixham they made 22 trips starting at 7.12 am and finishing at 9.17 pm 'Total time (with 1 hour added) 15 hours 5 mins'. The '1 hour added' is presumably to prepare the engine. The meal times (doubtless not paid for) are 7.33-8.41 am, 1.52-3.00 pm and 5.57-6.48 pm. It notes: 'Both men go to dinner daily and morning and evening alternate days'. I take the latter comment to mean that they took it in turns to have the morning and evening breaks. The 15 h. 5 m. day is one of the longest listed, but the record for one set of men was Marlborough at 16 hours 32 mins. It would seem this practice ended about 1896, after which more than one set of men was based at Brixham.

1891 was the year of The Great Storm - a blizzard which swept the West Country from Monday 9th March to Friday 13th March and is described in great detail in the various issues of *The Western Morning News*. Torbay did not suffer as badly as the GWR and LSWR main lines between Exeter and Plymouth which were blocked for several days.

On the first day the wind increased in force at Brixham until by 7 pm it was at hurricane force with the snow falling heavily. By daybreak on Tuesday there was two feet of snow in the open whilst in the lanes and against hedges the snow had drifted 10 feet deep! Great difficulty was experienced in getting the branch engine from the shed to work the 7.12 am train. However, at last this was done and the first train ran but the engine became derailed at Churston. Fortunately there was another engine at Churston and this was used thereafter, the train running backwards and forwards 'to keep the way open'. The cold state of the poor enginemen can only be guessed at but a glance at the photograph of *Prince* which was taken at Brixham in 1891 will indicate the lack of shelter enjoyed by those worthies. (When the photograph was displayed in *The Locomotive* magazine in 1941, that journal commented that it was unusual even to have cab doors at this period!) The service ceased at 4 pm on Tuesday.

Snow continued to fall overnight and it was not possible to resume the service on Wednesday morning although the sun came out in a cloudless sky and melted a quantity of the snow. Workmen were employed all day long in clearing snow from the track to enable service to be resumed by Thursday.

The roads between Brixham and Paignton and Torquay were closed between Tuesday and Saturday morning and, due to damage to the telegraph system, all telegrams had to be taken to Torquay by train for onwards transmission.

The thaw started on Friday 13th March and over the weekend rain fell. During the entire period Torquay was not cut off from Exeter or London by rail, although it was not possible to get to Plymouth. The breakwater at Brixham was severely damaged by the gale, 200 ft being destroyed.

On 13th August, 1891 the Board agreed to extend the fish shed at Brixham and provide a platform and roadway at a cost of £188. At the same meeting, Brixham was allocated £1,976 12s. 6d. for improvements during the narrowing of the gauge. The minutes note that the separate expenditure on the fish platform was to be proceeded with immediately.

The conversion of the Brixham branch from broad to standard gauge took place on the weekend of Friday night 20th May to Sunday night 22nd May, 1892, in company with the main line between Exeter and Penzance and six other branch lines including Newton Abbot to Kingswear. The Brixham engine and coaches were conveyed to Swindon by the 12.45 am special empty stock from Kingswear on Saturday. On the Sunday the line was surrounded by onlookers. At 9 pm a special service was held on a railway bridge for those workers who wanted to attend, plus anyone else who wished to join in. The service was conducted by Revd A. Stewart Sim (Vicar, All Saints, Brixham), Revd A.J. Best (Curate, All Saints), Revd J. Voisey (Curate, St Peter's, Brixham) and Revd L.S. Brown (Curate of Churston). The new standard gauge rolling stock having been sent down from Exeter early that morning, the passenger service resumed on Monday 23rd May with freight restarting the following day.

In 1892 there were seven postmen in Brixham, all of whose work was done on foot. The conveyance of mails to and from the station was done by a contractor, who also acted as luggage contractor for the GWR, and mails and luggage were carried on a flat cart hauled by a mule. Given the steepness of the hills, once imagines the poor mule did not have a very long working life.

In February 1893 the GWR traffic committee agreed to appoint an additional porter at Brixham. A year later, in May 1894, an additional 'signal porter' was approved by the same body (*see below*). This post was necessitated by the opening of Brixham signal box in that year. This brick-built structure situated above the southern boundary wall was visited by Major Mandarin of the Railway Inspectorate on 12th October, 1894:

Brixham. At this terminal station there is only one platform with exceedingly poor accommodation for passengers which ought to be improved. The platform has been somewhat lengthened, the sidings have been rearranged and interlocking has been introduced. The new cabin contains 17 working levers correctly interlocked and 6 spare levers. Requirements: the working of the levers to be made less stiff. Approved subject to the immediate satisfaction of this requirement.

W.B. started as a porter at Brixham on 28th November, 1892. Unfortunately a series of minor misdemeanours retarded his promotion out of the basic grade. He caused the door of a box truck to be broken during shunting in July 1893, 'improperly weighed three consignments of fish for Paris' in February 1894 and the following month caused a fish truck to leave the rails at self-acting points. Two days before Christmas in 1895 he was cautioned for coming on duty late. In March 1897 he became foreman porter, but resigned in February 1901.

On 29th January, 1894 John Penwarden, destined to be station master many years later, joined the staff at Brixham as a porter at 15s. per week. On 14th October, 1895 he became foreman porter (although junior to W.B., possibly because of the latter's record) and on 19th November, 1896 goods checker. On 27th March, 1895 he was fined 2s. for damage caused to the goods shed doors when shunting by failing to check they were open. On 2nd May, 1906 he apprehended three boys who had broken into a case in the goods shed and stolen lozenges, for which action he was complimented. He was still checker in 1907, by then at 29s. per week, but was promoted to be station master at Bampton (Devon) in 1908 for 30s. a week. He remained there for 19 years, returning as station master at Churston in 1927. At this time Henry Fear was station master at Brixham, and the date of his retirement is not recorded in the *GWR Magazine*, but in either 1931 or early 1932 Brixham and Churston were combined under one station master and it is reasonable to assume that Fear retired then and Penwarden took over both stations. John Penwarden retired in 1935.

Samuel Foster was appointed signal porter at Brixham on 13th August, 1894 (the date the box opened?) at 19s. per week and remained until 3rd October, 1895 when he was appointed signalman at Grampound Road. New Year 1895 was not very happy for him; he derailed a coach on New Year's Day and was fined 2s. 6d. (From 1st January, 1920 the grade was renamed the more familiar 'porter-signalman'.)

The timetable for October 1894 was headed by the instruction:

All trains must stop dead before passing the underbridge on the Churston side of Brixham station and at the overbridge on the Brixham side of Churston station.
The train must afterwards be steadily drawn to the platform.

The timetable is reproduced on page 60. As can be seen there were now separate goods trains most of which were 'RR' - run as required. The last trains to and from Newton Abbot again called at Churston after the branch closed and so no connection was available. On Sundays the 10.50 am Newton Abbot to Kingswear (Churston 11.24 am) still had no connection to Brixham - all in all not very different from 10 years before. (The July 1894 timetable had been identical.)

In December 1894 the GWR traffic committee debated and agreed a package of train mileage savings proposed by the General Manager. This included one train each way withdrawn on the Brixham branch (the trains were not identified). In June 1895 traffic committee voted £100 for alterations to the Brixham station building.

The July 1896 timetable (also on page 60) was similar to 1894, except that the morning goods trains were now 9.35 am ex-Brixham and 10.05 am ex-Churston and the former passenger services at similar timings (in 1894) had been withdrawn, and were probably the ones withdrawn in December 1894.

BRIXHAM BRANCH.

Only one Engine in Steam allowed on this Branch or two coupled together.   Single Line, worked by Train Staff.   No Block Telegraph.   All Trains must stop dead before passing the underbridge on the Churston side of Brixham Station on the down journey and at the overbridge on the Brixham side of Churston Station on the up journey.   The Train must afterwards be steadily drawn to the Platform.

DOWN TRAINS.

WEEK DAYS.

M C / 2 1	STATIONS.	1	2	3D	4	5D	6	7	8	9	10	11	12D	13D	14	15	16
		A	A	Goods RR	A X	Goods RR	A	A	A	A	A	A	Goods RR	Goods RR	A	A	
		A.M.	A.M.	A.M.	A.M.	A.M.	P.M.	P.M.	I.N.	P.M.	P.M.	P.M.	P.M.	P.M.	P.M.	P.M.	
2	Churston	7 15	9 0	9 55	10 45	11 35	12 50	1 50	2 40	4 10	4 55	6 0	6 30	7 10	7 50	9 35	....
1	Brixham	7 22	9 7	10 5	10 52	11 45	12 57	1 57	2 47	4 17	5 2	6 7	6 40	7 20	7 57	9 42	..

SUNDAYS.

M C / 2 1	STATIONS.	1	2	3	4	5	6
		A	A	A	A	A	
		A.M.	A.M.	P.M.	P.M.	P.M.	
2	Churston	8 0	9 27	1 15	6 35	8 0	....
1	Brixham	8 7	9 34	1 22	6 42	8 7	..

UP TRAINS.

WEEK DAYS.

X Mixed.

M C / 2 1	STATIONS.	1	2	3D	4	5D	6	7	8	9	10	11	12D	13	14D	15	16
		A	A	Goods RR	A	Goods RR	A	A	A	A	A	A	Goods RR	A	Goods RR	A	
		A.M.	A.M.	A.M.	A.M.	A.M.	P.M.	P.M.	P.M.	P.M.	P.M.	P.M.	P.M.	P.M.	P.M.	P.M.	
2	Brixham	6 50	8 35	9 35	10 15	11 5	11 55	1 27	2 15	3 45	4 30	5 30	6 15	6 50	7 30	8 25	....
1	Churston	6 57	8 42	9 45	10 22	11 15	12 2	1 34	2 22	3 52	4 37	5 37	6 25	6 57	7 40	8 32	..

SUNDAYS.

M C / 2 1	STATIONS.	1	2	3	4	5	6
		A	A	A	A	A	
		A.M.	A.M.	P.M.	P.M.	P.M.	
2	Brixham	7 45	9 10	12 50	6 20	7 45	....
1	Churston	7 52	9 17	12 57	6 27	7 52	..

October 1898 Working timetable.

In 1896 the station master at Brixham, Mr Higginbottom, gave details of passengers arriving at Brixham in 1895 compared with 1891 as a measure of the use of the line. These figures excluded the very large number of people who arrived with tourist or return tickets of which no record was kept:

1891   42,725
1895   56,274

The original engine shed, which was constructed in wood with a slated roof and measured 37 ft by 21 ft, was demolished in 1896 and replaced the following year by a corrugated iron structure standing on dwarf walls. The new shed was slightly longer at 40 ft, but narrower, at 17 ft, and had previously been at Stenalees in Cornwall.

On 7th May, 1896 Arthur Metherell was appointed signal porter, staying until 3rd June, 1897 when he was promoted signalman at Fowey. On 23rd March, 1897 he was cautioned for an error in working the points, damaging an engine and coach. Strangely, a successor, Robert Oliver (signal porter 24th May, 1897 to 24th March, 1898) also went to Fowey on promotion. The signal porter's post only paid between 17s. and 19s. per week and was obviously regarded as a stepping stone - to be stepped off as quickly as possible. No reference has been found to a 'signalman' during this early period, so possibly the nature of the post did not justify such an appointment. Porter Walter Parker, a former T&B employee who had started in October 1876, died in September 1896, aged only 40.

On 1st August, 1897 engine turner (a low grade of driver) Thomas Ellery (aged 28) was watering the coal on his engine at Brixham when the india rubber pipe flew off the union and scalded him on his left thigh. He resumed work on 12th August.

A few days later, on 18th August, fireman W.J.R. (who had come to Brixham as shunting fireman (the lowest grade) in November 1896), failed to keep a proper look out during shunting operations at Brixham and the movement came into contact with a horse and cart fouling the siding. He and his driver, acting engineman J.B., were suspended for one day. The fireman was promoted to 3rd class fireman at Neath in October 1897.

Fireman W.J.B. had a long association with Brixham. Born in October 1879 he started as a cleaner at Newton Abbot in September 1896, coming to Brixham as shunting fireman on 3rd January, 1898. On 19th January, 1899 he fell asleep while on duty, resulting in a late start, due to shortage of steam. For this he was suspended for one day. He was promoted to 3rd class fireman at Wellington in February 1900. Later, while based at Bristol, on 25th June, 1911 fireman B. was firing the 11 pm excursion from Wolverhampton to Bristol when the signalman at Henley-in-Arden turned it into the bay platform, thinking it was a local train. The engine, 'Atbara' class 4-4-0 No. 3382 *Mafeking* was turned on its side and both driver and fireman were severely scalded. Eleven passengers were injured, mostly not seriously; there were only 33 passengers on the train. The engine was afterwards scrapped. The records are not clear, but B. may have been off work for a lengthy period, because when he was promoted to 3rd class engineman at Brixham on 17th April, 1916, the records state that future pay rises will be based on a seniority date of 11th September, 1911, on which he would have been made driver, but for his accident. On 26th July, 1920, while standing at Churston he used his brake whistle to alert an engineman on the main line that he was backing into an occupied siding, thus averting a collision with a fish truck; the other man thought he was still on the main line. For this engineman B. was commended. Although he remained at Brixham for the rest of his career, it would appear that illness caused him to be replaced by another driver in 1931; unfortunately the public records are unclear on this aspect.

On 30th March 1900 William Casley began his railway service as porter at Brixham at 15s. per week. On 17th October, 1903, by then earning 18s., he damaged the shed doors during shunting, and just a few days later, 26th October, damaged two coaches by not checking there was sufficient room for them to pass over some points.

Mark Dymond was signal porter at Brixham from 13th October, 1900 to 12th March, 1901, when he went to Lifton in the same grade. Early in his short stay , on 1st November, he was cautioned for turning a pair of points and derailing a truck.

In June 1899 traffic committee authorised expenditure of £31 to provide electric train staff working on the Brixham branch (it was introduced with the October 1899 timetable). This was a more flexible system of operation as it permitted another train to leave Churston for Brixham once the previous train had arrived at Brixham and its staff had been returned to the machine. The January 1903 timetable compared with that for October 1898 (*page 66*) did not show any great increase in service as a result.

January 1903
Churston to Brixham (weekdays): 7.15, 9.05, 9.55 (Goods), 10.45 (MXD),
    11.30 (Goods) am, 12.20 (FO), 12.50, 2.40, 4.07, 4.50, 6.0, 6.30 (Goods), 7.10 (Goods), 8.05,
    9.35, 10.23 pm. (FO = Fridays only)
Brixham to Churston (weekdays): 6.50, 8.25, 9.35 (Goods), 10.15, 11.05 (Goods), 11.50 am,
    12.32 (FO), 2.15, 3.45, 4.25, 5.30, 6.15 (Goods), 6.50, 7.30 (Goods), 8.20, 10.05 pm.
Churston to Brixham (Sundays): 8.05, 9.37 am, 12.50, 6.50, 8.35 pm.
Brixham to Churston (Sundays): 7.50, 9.20 am, 12.25, 6.33, 8.15 pm.

The four goods trains each way were all 'RR' - run as required. The first pair (9.35/9.55 am) were specially qualified by a footnote 'Mr Hill must arrange for these trains to run when required in order to clear the mileage traffic at Churston' (Mr Hill was the station master at Churston). The branch engine had to be available to shunt Churston Yard between 8.30 and 9.30 pm each weekday to reduce the shunting that Kingswear line trains were called upon to do. The July 1905 timetable was very similar, except that the Fridays-only services had been replaced by daily services at 3.30 pm ex-Churston and 3.45 pm ex-Brixham. The two evening goods trains each way had been reduced to one each way: 7.10 pm from Churston and 7.30 pm from Brixham. Timetables tended to vary little in those days.

Brixham signal box opening hours in May 1903 were 6.40 am-10.40 pm weekdays and 7.40-8.20 am, 9 am-1 pm and 6-9 pm Sundays.

In August 1904 traffic committee approved expenditure of £909 on the following work at Brixham:

Provision of siding for timber traffic
Raising roof of station building
Extension of verandah covering
Improvement of WC and urinal accommodation

which seems a lot of work for a little money. In the event, the final cost was £972. The 'timber siding' must have been the single siding at the west end of the yard; it does not appear on the 1906 Ordnance Survey but it is shown on the 1910 track plan. The verandah roof replaced an earlier roof at ceiling level which was only affixed to the building for about two-thirds of its length (*see picture on page 46*). Work was complete by December 1906.

Fireman F.E.W., born in December 1877, started on the GWR at Bristol in November 1893 and came to Brixham as a 1st class fireman on 7th April, 1902. On 4th April, 1903, while acting engineman, he got the engine off the line at catchpoints at Brixham, for which he was cautioned. On 11th July, 1904, again acting as engineman, he allowed his fireman to move the train at Churston without himself being on the footplate, resulting in slight damage to buffers of coaches and fish trucks. For this his promotion was deferred three months, and his fireman was cautioned. On 1st October, 1904 fireman W. was attempting to pass between '517' class 0-4-2T No. 1443 and a wagon in Brixham loco yard, in order to couple up, when he was caught between the buffers and the lower part of his abdomen injured. He was conveyed by ambulance to the cottage hospital 'with serious internal injuries' (according to the *Totnes Times*). He did not resume work until 6th November. He was promoted to engine turner at Newport on 1st June, 1906.

Fireman R.H.S. was born in May 1885 and started as a cleaner at Newton Abbot in July 1900. He came to Brixham as shunting fireman on 2nd June, 1903. On 4th July, 1905 he fell asleep while on duty, resulting in a late start to the branch train because of shortage of steam. Another shunting fireman, E.G.C. who had started at Brixham on 24th February, 1903, was blamed for not seeing there was sufficient firewood for lighting up the engine, which contributed to that late start. Both firemen were cautioned. Fireman S. resigned 'to better himself' on 22nd March, 1907, refusing to tell the company what he intended to do - obviously a man of spirit! Fireman C. was promoted to 3rd class fireman at Cardiff on 29th April, 1907. It is obvious that there was a constant turnover in firemen at Brixham, as 'shunting fireman' was the lowest grade of fireman available, and used as a stepping stone. As other grades of fireman are mentioned at Brixham, possibly the chief duties of this post were care of the engine overnight, including lighting-up, plus filling in for sickness, holidays, etc.

On 4th June, 1906 the GWR introduced a bus service from Paignton to Brixham. Intended to supplement the train service, it actually extracted rail traffic and was withdrawn on 30th September of that year and was not reinstated.

The July 1906 *Magazine* announced the promotion of parcels porter Charles Edward Lake, who had been appointed parcels porter at Brixham on 16th September, 1896, to be station master at Hemyock.

The station canopy dates this as post-1905, and was possibly an 'official' picture taken to record the work for posterity. The rails are still laid on longitudinal timber baulks, as they would have been in broad gauge days. Because of inadequate room adjacent to the main running line, the u starting signal controlling movements from fish dock to platform, and its lower bracke applicable to movements onto the loop line (on which the cameraman is standing), is separate from the line it controls by two intermediate sidings. The platform sign opposite the engine reads 'Refreshments'.

Lens of Sutto

We know that 4-4-0T No. 13, originally a 2-4-2T and converted in 1897, worked over the Brixham branch in the years 1904 to 1907, so this old postcard was probably composed in that period Here the locomotive heads an open fishtruck and three carriages with outside footboards, abo to leave for Brixham. The 'Railway Hotel' is prominent in the background.

D.K. & M. James Collectio

Churston Station & Ho

A 'List of Passenger Train Engines' Failures' (regularly produced by the CME) for July 1906 records that the unique locomotive No. 13* was hauling the 9.08 am from Churston on the 23rd of that month when the vacuum pipe broke, causing 13 minutes delay. Presumably temporary repairs were made. Strangely enough, at almost the same time the 8.53 am from Kingswear to Newton Abbot, out of which the Brixham train would have connected, suffered an 8 minute late start because of 'broken brake apparatus' on '1076' class 0-6-0T No. 1245.

Some more minor expenditure at Brixham was agreed by traffic committee around this time. First of all, in February 1907 £120 was authorised for a general waiting room. Then in August 1908 a 'cartage establishment' was approved:

	£
4 horses at £55 each	220
4 sets harness at £6 each	24
1 parcels van	61
4 lorries at £51 each	204
erect 6 stall stable	454
	£963

It was necessary to employ one foreman and four carmen, and their annual costs were estimated at £591 2s. 5d. The luggage contractor will have been bought out at this time, unless his contract ended then.

The next available timetable for February 1908, shows the last two trains, 10.05 pm Brixham-Churston and 10.23 pm Churston-Brixham as Wednesdays and Saturdays only. This timetable also indicates the addition of an extra mid-afternoon service in each direction running running each weekday. This gave a total of 12 trains in each direction, 13 on Wednesdays and Saturdays.

There was an unusual accident at Brixham on 4th February, 1909. The 12.10 pm train to Churston was required to pick up fish trucks about 16 yards to the rear of the last coach. The brakesman who was in charge of the train released the handbrake in the coach next to the engine and signalled the driver to set back. However, the reversing movement was somewhat faster than expected and the fish trucks and four wagons were pushed up hard against the buffer stops, one going over the top (from which there was a drop of 30 or 40 feet to the road beneath!). Examination of the footplate revealed the reason - it was empty! In fact both enginemen were off the footplate when the brake was taken off but the regulator was slightly open, causing the train to move. Such mishaps were dealt with seriously and the driver received four weeks' notice, the fireman's promotion being deferred by six weeks.

On 13th, 14th and 15th October, 1909 the Brixham branch was closed for relaying and GWR buses substituted for the trains.

By April 1910 another train had been added to the weekday service (7.30 am from Brixham, 7.53 am from Churston) making 13 each way, 14 on Wednesdays and Saturdays. (In the summer timetable the Wednesdays & Saturdays trains became daily.) On Sundays, however, the first trains (7.30 am from Brixham, 8.05 am from Churston) were withdrawn, presumably due to insufficient patronage. This meant the first Sunday trains now left Brixham at 9.10 am and Churston 9.30

---

* See Appendix Six.

Brixham from the Battery

Looking to the harbour from the Furzeham side of Brixham. The station can be seen on the skyline, *right*, with the goods shed prominent, as usual. The GWR's extension has been added so dating this sometime after 1886. It would appear that the retaining wall at the end of the line is being built or rebuilt. The chimney of Wolston's Bench Works where he produced rust inhibiting paint can just be seen bottom left. Observe the steep hill from harbour to station, up which all traffic for dispatch had to be dragged by animal power in the pre-motor age.

D.K. & M. James Collection

A fine view of Brixham from the air with Brixham station clearly visible at the top of the picture. Under a glass, the goods shed, station, stables, engine shed and signal box can all be seen. The engine appears to be half-in and half-out of the shed. A 4-coach train stands at the platform and the yard is full of traffic. Again the effort of getting fish from the harbour to the station is obvious. This card is dated 1929.

D.K. & M. James Collection

am, but by way of compensation there was an additional early afternoon return working, 2.20 pm ex-Brixham and 2.45 pm back from Churston.

The last surviving original member of staff, who had probably been employed by the T&B from its opening, William Hatherley, first goods porter and later brakesman (guard), retired at Brixham in 1911 after 46 years service. Having been a guard since August 1882 there can't have been an inch of track he was not familiar with. On 14th June he was presented with a cheque for £21 7s., subscribed by his colleagues and the public.

A 2-day national rail strike in August 1911 reduced the service temporarily to 10 each way, the last train leaving Brixham at 6.50 pm.

Bradshaw for October 1911 (reproduced overleaf) indicates another extra train and the first time in the timetables seen that two trains were scheduled at Brixham justifying the provision of the electric staff system. Normally the trains were worked from the Brixham end, out and back, but if this timetable is studied it will be seen that after the 10.45 am from Churston reaches Brixham, the next train is also from Churston, with no equivalent 'balance' from Brixham. This was the 10.55 am Railmotor Paignton to Brixham which left Churston at 11.12, reached Brixham at 11.18 and returned at 11.25 as a through train, unusually, to Torre, calling at all stations including Preston Platform. Torre was reached at 11.55. After a quick reversal the motor was away again just five minutes later at 12 noon to Kingswear (calling at Churston 12.25 but with no connection to Brixham). The 6 pm from Brixham, with its 10 minute running time, was obviously 'mixed'.

In 1912 expenditure of £107 was authorised to renew facing point lock and point connections 20 years old (i.e. put in new when the broad gauge was abolished).

The timetable for May 1913, which is from the Working book, shows two additional late trains which ran on Wednesdays and Saturdays only: leaving Brixham at 11 pm and returning from Churston at 11.23 pm. However the Sunday service had reduced to three each way, in the afternoon only, commencing with the 2.20 pm from Brixham. The 'Y' and 'Z' notes at the head of the timings for the 6.50 pm from Brixham and the 10.47 am from Churston respectively indicate that station trucks were conveyed by these services. These were used for the conveyance of small consignments which did not warrant exclusive use of a truck. The October timetable was identical.

Fireman S.H. was born in January 1884 and started work as a cleaner at Exeter in November 1900. He was promoted to 1st group fireman at Brixham on 1st April, 1913. On 3rd March, 1914, whilst acting engineman, he did not check that the road was clear before running round coaches at Brixham and consequently struck them. His punishment was having his name placed below four others in the same grade, promotion being based completely on seniority. On 12th August, 1915 he committed a similar error at Churston, running round in the main line platforms, although this time the signalman was also to blame. On 19th April, 1916 he transferred in the grade to Newton Abbot, at his own request.

In GWR days much correspondence was used, years later, by writing on the other side and all sorts of interesting facts can be gleaned unexpectedly in this way. For example, the backs of old signalling notices were used for correspondence in World War II. On the back of some 1945 correspondence, the author found the following interesting snippet from a 1914 Auditor's report:

October 1911

DOWN

Week Days

Mls		Mrn	Mrn	Mrn	Mrn	M	aft	aft	aft	aft	aft	aft	aft	aft	aft	H
–	Churston dep.	7.00	7.53	9.08	10.45	11.12	12.55	2.36	3.30	4.15	5.00	5.45	6.30	8.05	9.40	10.23	.....
2	Brixham arr.	7.07	8.00	9.15	10.53	11.18	1.02	2.43	3.37	4.23	5.07	5.52	6.37	8.12	9.47	10.30	..

Sundays

	Mrn	aft	aft	aft	aft
Churston dep.	9.15	12.50	2.45	7.20	8.45 .....
Brixham arr.	9.22	12.57	2.52	7.27	8.52 ..

UP

Week Days

Mls		Mrn	Mrn	Mrn	M	aft	aft	aft	aft	aft	aft	aft	aft	aft	H
–	Brixham dep.	6.40	7.30	8.25	10.15	11.25	12.10	2.15	2.50	3.45	4.35	5.18	6.00	6.50	8.23	10.05 .....
2	Churston arr.	6.47	7.37	8.32	10.22	11.32	12.17	2.22	2.57	3.52	4.42	5.25	6.10	6.57	8.30	10.12 ..

Sundays

	Mrn	aft	aft	aft	aft
Brixham dep.	8.55	12.25	2.20	6.40	8.20 .....
Churston arr.	9.02	12.32	2.27	6.47	8.27 ..

H – Wednesdays and Saturdays   M – Motor Car, one class only

May 1913

DOWN TRAINS

WEEK DAYS

STATIONS		B	B	K	B	B	B	B	B	B	B	K	B	B	B	B	B	B	X	X		SUNDAYS B	B	B
		Pass	Pass	Goods	MXD	Pass	Pass	Pass	Pass	Pass	Pass	Goods	UV	Pass	Pass	Pass	Pass	Pass	Pass	Pass		Pass	Pass	Pass
M C		AM	AM	AM	RR	Z	AM	PM	PM	PM	PM	PM	PM	PM	RR	PM	PM	PM	PM	X	X		PM	PM	PM
– –	Churston d.	7.00	7.53	9.08	9.55	10.47	11.55	12.55	2.36	3.30	4.15	5.00	5.47	6.36	7.10	8.05	9.40	10.23	11.23	.....		2.45	7.20	8.45
2 1	Brixham a.	7.07	8.00	9.15	10.05	10.55	12.02	1.02	2.43	3.37	4.22	5.07	5.54	6.43	7.20	7.17	8.12	9.47	10.30	11.30	..	2.52	7.27	8.52

UP TRAINS

WEEK DAYS

STATIONS		B	B	K	B	B	B	B	B	B	B	B	K	B	B	X	X		SUNDAYS B	B	B
		Pass	Pass	Goods	Pass	Pass	Pass	Pass	Pass	Pass	Pass	Pass	Ety Goods	Pass	Pass	Pass	Pass		Pass	Pass	Pass
M C		AM	AM	RR	AM	AM	PM	PM	PM	PM	PM	PM	PM	Y	UV	PM	X	X		PM	PM	PM
– –	Brixham d.	6.40	7.30	8.25	9.35	10.15	11.40	12.10	2.15	2.50	3.45	4.35	5.18	6.10	6.50	7.30	8.23	10.05	11.00	.....	2.20	6.30	8.20
2 1	Churston a.	6.47	7.37	8.33	9.45	10.22	11.47	12.17	2.22	2.57	3.52	4.42	5.25	6.17	6.57	7.37	7.40	8.30	10.12	11.07	..	2.27	6.37	8.27

RR – Runs when required   U – Suspended   V – London Excursion, runs Fridays only July 12th–September 13th
X – Wednesdays & Saturdays   Y – S.T.374   Z – S.T.10

Brixham (Loco) Leading engineman performs the necessary clerical work.

Coal All coal traced. The authorised form of wagon book should be sent to this station. Firemen coal their engines in their own time and are paid at the rate of 2½ d. per ton.

Water Great increase in consumption due we were informed to the fact that very little water of late had been obtained from the leat in consequence of a slide having been fixed to the top of the leat which has prevented the water being pumped into the tank at the station.

In the summer of 1914 a special train (not in the timetable) left Churston for Brixham each Saturday morning between 4th July and 19th September at 4.30 am, after connecting with an excursion from Wolverhampton to Kingswear. The empty stock for this would have left Brixham about 4.10 am. After unloading, it returned empty immediately at 4.40 am (this time in the timetable) to connect out of a London excursion to Kingswear, leaving Churston for Brixham at 5 am, again on the same dates. After this burst of very early morning activity, it remained at Brixham for the first normal train of the day at 6.35 am, except on Saturdays 12th, 19th and 26th September when yet another empty run was made to Churston at 5.30 to form a 5.50 am from there, connecting out of a London excursion. (This may not have operated, for by then the war was on.) The remainder of the summer service was very similar to that shown for May 1913, with the addition of a late 10.40 pm Brixham to Churston on Mondays and Fridays only, which returned empty from Churston at 11 pm. At this time Brixham had a train service truly worthy of the name. In the winter 1914 service there were 14 trains each way (16 on Wednesdays and Saturdays), as in 1913.

On Friday 26th March, 1915 eight Brixham schoolboys stood in court accused of damaging telegraph insulators on the Brixham branch line on 22nd February. As the paper reported, making it sound like a capital offence:

Mr I. Pengelly, prosecuting on behalf of the Railway Company, said that considerable damage had been done to the telegraph wires and insulators between Churston and Brixham. Even in ordinary times the damage caused great inconvenience, but at the present time, when the management of the railways was under State control, and the railways were required for national purposes in case of emergency, the offence was all the more serious for the reason that by damaging the insulators, cutting the telegraph wires, and thus making short circuits, the whole telegraphic arrangements were disorganised. Where trains and messages were required urgently it would be a serious matter if means of communication from one terminus to another were destroyed . . . One of the lads told the policeman that he was throwing stones at some pigs; one does not generally find pigs disporting themselves on telegraph wires (laughter) . . .

Apparently William James Honeywill, the GWR ganger, had examined the line on Sunday 21st February and found all in order, but when walking the branch the following morning between 6 and 8.30 am had found 16 insulators broken, to the value of £1. They were in different places between Brixham station and the first mile post. The lads, having pleaded guilty were each fined 2s. 6d. and warned that they might have done serious harm to the country. If they were ever again summoned by the company's officials 'they would be severely punished'.

The late Fred Park's memories of the Brixham branch date back to the period of, and after, World War I.

My introduction to the railway was when I used it to go to and from Torre station while attending Torquay Secondary School (now Torquay Grammar School) during the four years up to July 1920. There were always about 12/20 Brixham boys and girls attending.

The railway was the only link in those days and I regularly left home in Heath Road (then Soper's Lane) to catch the 8. 10 from Brixham. I can honestly say I did not miss the train once. Getting back we aimed to catch the Torbay Limited but this was not always possible.

The bully boys always claimed a corner seat and any intruder was soon hauled out. I can remember having to pay 7s. 6d. for a broken door window. It was not my fault, someone pushed me back into it.

Newton Abbot market was, as now, on Wednesdays and local shopkeepers would attend to make purchases. There was one old lady, we called her Mother Kennar, who always arrived at the last minute and so regularly that the staff kept a door open for her until the last moment. On many occasions she was too late to buy her ticket and did so at Churston. Often the train would be moving out and would then stop to take her aboard. Once the train even reversed back into the station to pick her up (!)

The demands of World War I for fighting men denuded the railways of staff and a number of the smaller stations closed from 1917 for the duration of the war. Others lost their Sunday services and amongst those was the Brixham branch which closed on Sundays from 1st January, 1917; these trains were not restored until October 1922. The basic weekday service also reduced to 13 each way.

In January and February 1918 £224 was agreed to be made available for the extension of the fish platform and other accommodation for fish traffic.

The first motorbus competition for Brixham traffic was the South Devon Garage and Motor Touring Co. ('Grey Torpedo cars'), which commenced a service between Paignton and Brixham in 1914 until 1916, and then withdrew for the remainder of the war. They again ran on the route between 1920 and 1922.

In 1919 (possibly August, *see below*) Paignton Motors (W.H. Dalton, prop.) started a service between Paignton and Brixham. This ran for two years until the firm went into voluntary liquidation in early 1922.

In March 1919 the Torquay Tramways Co. gave notice of its intention to start a bus service to Brixham. This firm was responsible for the tram service in Torquay and between Torquay and Paignton, but also ran buses and its competition would have been much more of a threat to the railway. From early 1921 to July 1922 buses were operated between Paignton and Brixham by Torquay Tramways; in July 1922 the tramway company purchased Devon General and the bus operations were continued under that name; three buses were licensed. Devon General operated to a timetable.

In 1922 and 1923 various small operators ran one vehicle each but not to a given timetable and the vehicles could be diverted to more profitable work if the occasion arose. In 1924 licences were granted to Devon General (two buses), W.H. Dalton, G.W Heath, S. Cooper, W. Tucker, G.H. Marks ('Paigntonian') and Soul & Sanders ('Redcliffe Cars') - 1 bus each.

In 1925 a proper timetable was operated, under the title 'Associated Bus Services'. W. Tucker sold his business to a Devon General subsidiary but Paignton UDC would not allow his licence to be transferred. In 1926 (the year of the General Strike) additional operators came on the scene: J. Geddes, Brixham ('Burton Cars'); B. Rutter & J. Mills, Brixham ('Blue Ensign Car'); D. Prout, Churston ('Jolly Roger'); F. Slatter; and A. Swiggs. In 1927 Marks was replaced by R.G. Rutter; after 1928 Swiggs and Heath withdrew and J. Low, Paignton came in. Other changes may also have occurred.

On 31st March, 1931 the eight remaining one-vehicle operators on the route (Prout, Mills, Geddes, Low, Cooper, Soul & Sanders, Dalton, Slatter) were bought out by Devon General for £150 each, which did not include any vehicle purchase. Devon General continued the route, which was a real moneyspinner in the summer, for the remainder of the branch line's existence. Today it is run by Stagecoach. Burton Cars (Geddes) maintained a Brixham-Kingswear service jointly with Devon General until 1988, now also run by Stagecoach. Thanks are recorded to Les Folkard and Roger Grimley for much of the above 'bus' information. Readers are directed to the latter's *A Pint of Beer or a Return to Brixham* for more about the buses during this early period.

The unlikely source of the GWR Suggestions Committee files gives us some interesting first-hand information about the very early days of bus competition with our branch line. All suggestions were kept anonymous from the officers (so that no-one could be penalised for what they said) so we don't know the suggestor's name or where he worked. On 18th September, 1919 he wrote as follows:

> A motor service was started on August 18th between Paignton and Brixham by a private firm. I have watched (its) loading with great interest, and I find it loads exceedingly well, frequently passing with 20 passengers. The charge is a shilling each way and the distance five miles. The bus is an old army lorry fitted up . . . I am in favour of Sir Eric Geddes scheme that roads and railways should be controlled by one body, and here offers a good opportunity for one of our buses to run from Paignton to Brixham and catch the people that otherwise would have travelled by train [presumably he was not a member of Brixham station staff!]. May I suggest that this matter be dealt with quickly with a view to cutting the other people out, as the first with the covered-in bus will get the passenger.
>
> The bus runs from 9 am from Paignton and every hour until 9 pm from Brixham.

So here we have an *open* Army lorry with seats extracting passengers, purely on the grounds of greater convenience, not cost, as the railway charged 7½d. The GWR declined the suggestion on 22nd December.

On 19th April, 1920 the suggestor wrote again.

> Some time ago I made a suggestion . . . and I was surprised the Company could not adopt it. There are at present three buses running and they load exceedingly well and make a considerable difference to the passengers carried by train. I have watched the number falling each day [so he was obviously very local] and I would suggest that the Company give it re-consideration and start a service as they have a garage at Paignton and charge 7½d. the same as by train and make the train tickets available by bus when I am convinced they will carry all the passengers.

This time the GWR only took until 17th May to turn it down.

Our suggestor was nothing if not persistent and a year later on 30th April, 1921 wrote:

I beg to inform you that there have been five different companies' buses running today and they have been loaded nearly all the time. This is a fine route for carrying passengers as so many people stay at Torquay and Paignton, and I hope the Company will further consider the running of our own buses. If the Co. ran buses some of our branch trains could be dispensed with.

This final plea was dismissed on 20th June, with the comment: 'Not considered desirable for the company to compete at present'. So in the space of two years one old army lorry had grown to five different companies competing for the Brixham traffic, and apparently finding enough to continue running.

During the national railwaymen's strike in 1919, which ran from 26th September until work resumed on 6th October, the Brixham branch was closed.

A minor domestic matter which reached the superintendent of the line at Paddington in October 1919 was a claim from 1st class parcels porter C. R. Ashton at Brixham to be regraded to parcels foreman. He claimed that his duties were practically all clerical, and that for the month of September the cash accounted for totalled £1,235. He gave his duties as rendering of all returns, preparation and balancing of traders accounts and parcels monthly accounts, dealing with claims and general correspondence, 'assistance being given me by 1st class parcels porter Ousley'. For this Ashton received 28s. per week and Ousley 26s.

Mr Patey, district traffic manager Exeter, looked at the matter. The statistics he sent to Paddington have unfortunately not remained with his letter, but he states that the parcels traffic 'is pretty considerable'. There were only two parcels foremen in the district, at Newton Abbot and Exeter, both with a much larger staff. He could not recommend that a 'one-over-one' situation justified foreman's rank, particularly as the station master supervised the work. Naturally the superintendent of the line did not disagree with him.

Traffic Committee were approached in December 1919 for the small sum of £85 to adapt the refreshment room at Brixham 'for traffic purposes'. There are no details of what form this adaptation took but in the 1950s the room was a waiting room. The 13-train service was still in operation in December 1919.

Signalling also needed renewals by this time. First £128 was authorised in 1920 to renew some signals over 20 years old. Then in 1921 £250 was authorised to replace the electric staff instruments, also over 20 years old; somewhat more than the original expenditure of £31 in 1899! Electric Token working was introduced in the first half of 1923. The January 1921 timetable is reproduced overleaf.

On 17th June, 1921 station master Mayland made a presentation to engineman W. Matraves, recently retired after 50 years service, the last 16 of which had been as a driver at Brixham.

The GWR-wide census of staff for 31st December, 1922 shows the following authorised staff:

BRIXHAM BRANCH.

Single Line, worked by Electric Train Staff. All Down Passenger Trains must stop dead at the Down Home Signal for Brixham and all Down Goods Trains must stop dead opposite the Up Advance Starting Signal for Brixham—All Up Trains must stop dead at the Home Signal at Churston. The Train must afterwards be steadily drawn to the Platform.

DOWN TRAINS.   WEEK DAYS ONLY.

Distance	Station No.	STATIONS.	Ruling gradient.	Time Allowances for ordinary Freight Trains			1	2	3	4	5	6	7	8	9	10	11	12	13	14	15	16	17	18	19
				Points to Point Times.	Allow for Stop.	Allow for Start.	B	B	B	B	K Goods RR	B	B	B	B	B	B	B	B	B	B	B	B	B	B
				Mins.	Mins.	Mins.	Pass.	Pass.	Pass.	Pass.	Goods RR	Pass.	Pass.	Mixed		Pass.	Pass.	Pass.	Pass.	Pass.		Pass.	Pass.	Pass.	Pass.
M/C							A.M.	A.M.		A.M.	A.M.	A.M.	A.M.	P.M.		P.M.	P.M.	P.M.	P.M.	P.M.			P.M.	P.M.	
—	1655	Churston .... dep.	—	—	—	—	6 50	7 50	..	9 5	9 10	10 45	11 25	1 25	..	2 40	4 35	5 18	5 55	7 25		8 15	8 55	10 15	..
1 26	—	Stop Board	132 R.	3	1	1	—	—	..	—	10P 4	—	—	R	..	—	—	—	—	—		—	—	—	..
1 71	—	Stop Board	82 F.	3	1	1	—	—	..	—	10P 9	—	—	—	..	—	—	—	—	—		—	—	—	..
2 1	1668	Brixham .. arr.	L.	1	1	—	6 57	7 57	..	9 12	10 10	10 52	11 32	1 32	..	2 47	4 42	5 25	6 2	7 32		8 22	9 2	10 22	..

UP TRAINS.   WEEK DAYS ONLY.

STATIONS.	Rpling gradient.	Time Allowances for ordinary Freight Trains			1	2	3	4	5	6	7	8	9	10	11	12	13	14	15	16	17	18	19	20	21
		Points to Point Times.	Allow for Stop.	Allow for Start.	B	B	B	K Goods RR	B	B	B	B	B	B	B	B	B	B	B	B	B	B	B	K Goods
		Mins.	Mins.	Mins.	Pass.	Pass.	Pass.	Goods RR	Pass.	Pass.	Pass.	Pass.	Pass.	Pass.	Pass.	Pass.	Pass.	Pass.	Pass.	Pass.	Pass.	Pass.	Pass.	Goods
					A.M.		A.M.	A.M.	A.M.	A.M.	P.M.	P.M.	P.M.	P.M.		P.M.	P.M.	P.M.	P.M.		P.M.	P.M.	P.M.	P.M.
Brixham dep.	—	—	—	—	6 25	....	8 15	9 35	10 16	11 0	12 10	2 10	3 35	....	4 50	5 33	6 20		7 50	8 30	9 35
Churston arr.	82 R.	7	7	2	6 32	..	8 22	9 45	10 22	11 7	12 17	2 17	3 42	....	4 57	5 40	6 27		7 57	8 37	9 45

R Will stop if required to pin down brakes. See pages 112 and 113 of the General Appendix to the Book of Rules and Regulations.

January 1921 Working timetable.

January 1925 public timetable.

CHURSTON and BRIXHAM.—Great Western.

Down.

Miles		Week Days.							Sundays			
		mrn	mrn	mrn	mrn	mrn	mrn		aft	aft	aft	aft
		mrn	mrn	mrn	mrn	mrn	mrn		aft	aft	aft	aft
—	Churston ....dep.	6 55	7 40	8 59	10 7	11 0	11 40	....	12 55	1 30	2 5	3 25	4 13	5	0 5	5 55	6 40	8 13	5 0	10	5 11	30	1 33	3 53	6 5	6 43	....
2	Brixham ....arr.	7 2	7 47	8 57	10 14	11 7	11 47	....	1 2	1 37	2 12	3 32	4 20	5	7 6	26	4 78	20	10 12	11 37	1 40	4 0	6 12	6 50	....

Up.

Miles		Week Days.							Sundays			
		mrn	mrn	mrn	mrn	mrn	mrn		aft	aft	aft	aft
—	Brixham ....dep.	6 30	7 18	8 5	9 30	10 20	11 20	....	12 18	1 10	1 45	2 53	5 0	4 0	5 3	56	2 53	50	4 40	5 35	6	20	7 30	8 50	10 35	1	50	4 20	6 25	7 15	....
2	Churston 58 arr.	6 37	7 25	8 12	9 37	10 27	11 27	....	12 25	1 17	1 52	2 323	5 7	4 7	5 42	6 27	7 37	8 57	10 42	1 57	4 27	6 32	7 22	....

Brixham	Churston
1 station master (class 2)	1 station master (class 3)
1 booking clerk (class 5)	
1 parcels clerk (class 5)	
2 goods clerks (class 5)	
1 parcels porter	2 ticket collectors (grade 2)
1 porter (grade 2)	4 porters (three grade 2 and a junior)
1 porter signalman	1 porter signalman
2 goods carters	
1 leading goods checker	
1 goods checker	
1 goods porter	
2 signalmen (class 5)	2 signalmen (class 4)
2 passenger guards	
17	10
	(plus 1 extra grade 2 porter in summer)

The summer timetable for 1922 showed an increase from the 16 trains each way (two of which were WSO) of May 1913 to 18 each way (one of which was FO). The first train left Brixham at 6.25 am instead of 6.40 am and the big gap between 8.25 and 10.15 am in 1913 was filled by a train at 9.25 am in 1922. (There was also an unadvertised 'London Excursion', on Fridays only at 8.45 am - passengers still had to change at Churston.) Last trains were normally 9 pm ex-Brixham and 10.15 pm ex-Churston but on Fridays only a late departure from Brixham at 10.35 pm returned from Churston at 10.55 pm. Goods trains were at 9.25 pm ex-Churston and 9.50 pm ex-Brixham. The Sunday service had still not been reintroduced (it was back that October) - there were six trains each way on the main line at Churston on Sundays, two of which terminated at Churston in the down direction returning therefrom to Newton Abbot.

The winter timetable from 2nd October, 1922 restored the Sunday service, last run in 1916, although at first this was a very modest two trains each way:

ex-Churston: 3.53 (from Exeter), 6.39 pm (from Dawlish Warren)
ex-Brixham: 4.10 (to Dawlish Warren), 7.20 pm (to Exeter)

The following April (1923) a third Sunday service each way was provided by extending the 12.25 pm Newton Abbot-Paignton to Brixham (arr. 1.42 pm) and starting the 2.15 pm Paignton-Newton Abbot from Brixham at 1.50 pm.

The late Fridays-only trains were withdrawn with the commencement of the 1922 winter book, but were reintroduced, only three weeks later from 25th October, on Wednesdays and Saturdays only. The return service from Churston was retarded by 30 minutes to 11.25 pm.

In summer 1923 the frequency of the two late trains was made thrice-weekly (Wednesdays, Fridays and Saturdays) rather than twice-weekly (but they always returned to the lower frequency each winter). Also the Sunday service increased to five trains each way (reducing to three in the winter):

Churston to Brixham: 1.33 (a), 3.48 (b), 6.05 (c), 6.42, 7.52 pm.
Brixham to Churston: 1.50 (b), 4.20 (c), 6.25, 7.35, 8.15 pm.

(a) 12.30 pm from Dawlish Warren. (b) From or to Exeter. (c) To Dawlish Warren, arrive 5.36 pm.

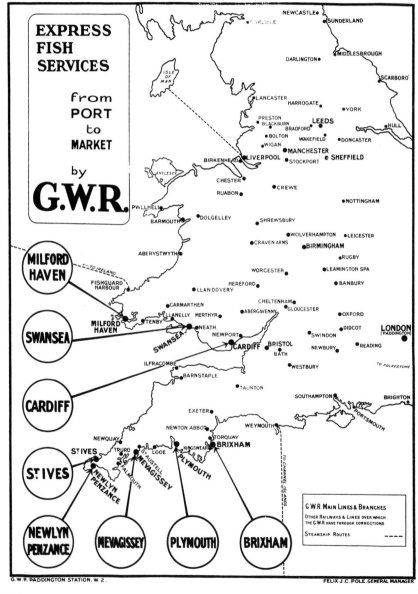

For the summer of 1924 the branch was open 18 hours daily for three days of the week. The first train left Brixham at 6.30 am each weekday. The last passenger train on Mondays, Tuesdays and Thursdays left Brixham at 9.50 pm returning from Churston at 10.10 to form a goods leaving Brixham at 10.30 pm and returning from Churston at 11 pm. On these nights the branch would have shut about 11.20 pm. But on Wednesdays, Fridays and Saturdays the last passenger from Brixham was 10.50 pm which, after return from Churston at 11.25, formed an 11.50 pm goods to Churston which returned from that place at 12.20 am. So the branch would not have closed until after 12.30 am on those nights! There were 20 passenger trains each way with an extra one each way on Wednesdays, Fridays and Saturdays.

For at least one year in 1924, on Sundays during the currency of the summer timetable, Brixham enjoyed through coaches to London! The 1.50 pm Brixham to Newton Abbot was attached at the latter place to the 10.35 am Penzance to Paddington. Notes of a meeting held by the superintendent of the line on 18th December, 1924 under the heading '1.50 pm Brixham to Paddington (Sundays)' state:

Seats were registered [reserved] in this train last summer from Paignton and Torquay, but as is it recommended they should be registered in the 4.35 pm ex Kingswear, it is recommended they should not be registered in the Brixham train next summer.

In 1925 a new 2.25 pm Kingswear-Paddington ran and the 1.50 pm from Brixham only went to Newton Abbot.

At the beginning of 1924 £250 was authorised for the provision of a new goods office at Brixham.

The initial meeting of the Brixham Chamber of Trade was held on 15th January, 1924. Amongst the matters discussed at this first meeting was the abolition of long waits at Churston station! However, at the next meeting this matter was deferred; perhaps there were things closer to home which they could actually have an influence on.

A census of staff dated March 1925 showed that there were still 17 authorised staff at Brixham but some minor changes had been made. The booking clerk and one of the goods clerks were now 'juniors'; the grade 2 porter had become a porter-guard. The census also carried some useful statistics on paybill costs and traffic receipts which were supplemented in manuscript for the following two years:

	1913	1922	1923	1924	1925	1926
Paybill	£951	£2,750	£2,805	£2,764	£2,765	£2,573
Receipts	£18,857	£30,949	£28,425	£26,927	£25,913	£26,190

To take a little of the shine off these excellent 'profits' there was also the cost of the engine establishment, although this was a separate department. One engine, two drivers, two firemen and a shed labourer were authorised and annual paybill costs were as follows:

(1924) £1,094   (1925) £1,066   (1926) £998   (1927) £1,097   (1928) £1,112

At Churston there was now a general clerk (a junior) and the two ticket collectors had been replaced by leading porters; the junior porter had been cut out, so the establishment remained at 10 (the changes took place in 1925 or 1926). There was a much smaller margin here between paybill costs and receipts:

	1913	1922	1923	1924	1925	1926
Paybill	£593	£1,745	£1,742	£1,822	£1,825	£1,557
Receipts	£4,544	£6,937	£6,466	£6,463	£7,202	£6,724

The year 1926 was, of course, a changing-point in the GWR's fortunes. It was the year of the General Strike when the company was caught up in what was basically a miner's strike. I have written extensively elsewhere about its effect on the GWR.* So far as the Brixham branch was concerned, it did not open on the first day of the strike (which had started at midnight 3rd/4th May) and remained closed until Tuesday 11th May, when a service resumed, but no details are known, except that station master Henry Fear worked the signal box and retired driver W. Matraves drove the engine. Although the Strike was called off unconditionally at midday on 12th May, the railwaymen and many others did not return because of what they saw as unacceptable terms of reinstatement by the employers. There was no general return to work on the railways until Saturday 15th May. After the Strike, the shedman at Brixham received a £10 gratuity in recognition of strike services.

Following the Strike, the GWR carried out an extensive survey of branch lines, looking for economies. The Brixham branch looked healthy; receipts for 1925 totalled £25,913 and costs were £7,408, a low 28.55 per cent of receipts (or 37.53 per cent if 'general' charges, etc. were added) as against the GWR average of 83.63 per cent. The only recommendation made was that the branch should be worked by auto-train when available. It was obviously one of their most profitable branch lines, although revenue was down just over £1,000 on 1924 due to 'the effects of road competition on passenger traffic and less fish traffic'.

From 20th August, 1926 the GWR introduced a summer only bus service between Totnes and Brixham enabling visitors to cruise on the River Dart in one direction, the opposite land journey being by rail. This ran again in 1927 and 1928, its final day of operation being 22nd September, 1928. The winter branch service in 1926 was 17 trains each way, plus an extra in each direction on Wednesdays and Saturdays only, an increase of one each way over winter 1925.

The summer 1927 timetable records an increased Sunday service of seven trains each way with even more variety of starting and finishing points:

Churston to Brixham: 12.30 (a), 1.15, 3.40 (b), 4.50, 5.53 (c), 6.50, 8.30(c) pm.
Brixham to Churston: 12.55, 1.50 (c), 4.25, 5.10 (b), 6.30, 7.15 (b), 9.0(c) pm.

(a) 11.10 am from Moretonhampstead. (b) From or to Exeter. (c) From or to Newton Abbot.

Brixham was obviously a popular destination for Sunday excursionists.

Sadly, there was a fatal accident at Brixham station on 31st October, 1928. T.C. May, who was a goods carman, was unloading a sheeted wagon standing a few

* See the Author's *The GWR and the General Strike* published by The Oakwood Press (LP 194).

inches in front of six other wagons in a siding holding eight wagons. Having completed unloading at about 9.40 pm, May drew his vehicle away from the wagons to allow the flap door to be put up and the sheet replaced. The station master meantime called the engine, which was standing nearby, to this wagon to draw it out of the siding. As this took place a cry was heard and May was found to have been caught between the first wagon and the head of the other wagons in the siding; he had been completing the tying down of the wagon sheet.

It was not part of May's duties to assist with wagon sheeting, but it had been his practice to give a hand in connection with this particular wagon previously. The station master was held responsible for failing to check that it was safe to make the movement.

Often these old reports give intriguing snippets of other information, not found elsewhere. This one states that Mr May had come on duty at 8 pm; it was a Wednesday. Was there a night shift at Brixham in the goods department, or had he come on for a special short turn of duty?

The summer timetable 1929 saw the introduction of auto-trains to the branch which meant much quicker turnrounds were possible at each end as it was no longer necessary to run the engine from one end of the train to the other. The special auto-coach provided included a driving vestibule where the driver was located when the coach was being pushed by the engine. The basic service remained at the 20 trains each way of summer 1924, plus an extra each way on certain days, 10.30 or 11 pm from Brixham and 10.45 or 11.35 from Churston, which ran on Fridays only and Wednesdays & Saturdays only respectively. The introduction of auto-train working caused the withdrawal of guards from these trains on the Brixham branch, but not until 1930, the last two guards being Messrs Hedge and Casely.

Brixham engine shed closed on 22nd July, 1929 after which the branch engine came down from Newton Abbot each morning, returning there at the end of the day's service. For example in the winter 1929 service, the engine came down with a 3.25 am Newton Abbot to Brixham goods which arrived at 5.32 am. It returned light to Newton Abbot at 10.30 pm except on Wednesdays and Saturdays when a later train operated in each direction, and it finally left Brixham at 11.50 pm. The Working timetable for the following winter, September 1930, is included overleaf.

After closure of the shed one set of men remained based at Brixham until the end of steam, other men required for each day's duties being provided by Newton Abbot. The other set based at Brixham until shed closure were sent to Newton Abbot, and the shedman went to Kingswear.

A fairly minor matter arose in 1930 which was not concluded for *five* years. Since the withdrawal of guards on the Brixham, Brentford, Clevedon and Fowey branches, post office mails were conveyed in the luggage compartments of the trailers, locked with a normal carriage key. The Post Office was concerned about security and asked for special locks and keys for these compartments. The General Manager suggested that the mails should be secured inside the luggage compartment by chain and padlock. The Post Office was not happy with this and pressed for its first suggestion - special locks and keys - 'similar to those in use on the Company's Brixham-Churston branch line'.

BRIXHAM BRANCH.

Single Line, worked by Electric Train Token. All Down Passenger Trains must stop dead at the Down Home Signal for Brixham and all Down Goods Trains must stop dead opposite the Up Advance Starting Signal for Brixham—All Up Trains must stop dead at the Home Signal at Churston. The Train must afterwards be steadily drawn to the Platform.

DOWN TRAINS.

Distance M. C.	Station No.	Ruling gradient	Point to Point Times Mins.	Allow for Stop Mins.	Allow for Start Mins.	STATIONS		Service	Churston dep.	Brixham arr.
1 26	1655	—	3	1	1	Churston	dep.	Goods (A.M.)	5 20	5 32
1 69½		95 R.	3	1	1	Stop Board			P	P
		79 F.	1	1	—	Stop Board				
2 1	1668	78 F.	1	1	—	Brixham	arr.			

WEEK DAYS — Churston dep. → Brixham arr.

Service	Churston dep.	Brixham arr.
Goods (A.M.)	5 20	5 32
Auto	6 50	6 57
Auto	7 48	7 55
Mixed	8 30	8 40
Auto	10 10	10 17
E'gine	10 48	10 55
Auto	11 45	11 52
Auto (P.M.)	12 27	12 34
Auto	12 58	1 5
Auto	1 30	1 37
Auto	1 55	2 2
Auto	2 38	2 45
Auto	3 10	3 20
Auto	4 5	4 12
Auto	4 42	4 49
Auto	5 27	5 34
Auto	6 0	6 7
Auto	6 45	6 52
Auto (7 16)	7 16	7 23
E'gine	8 50	9 0
Auto	8 18	8 25
Auto	9 23	9 30
Auto	10 10	10 17
Auto Y	11 35	11 42

SUNDAYS — Churston dep. → Brixham arr.

Service	Churston dep.	Brixham arr.
N'wth Abbot Pass. (P.M.)	1 25	1 32
Exeter Pass.	4 6	4 12
Pass. (P.M.)	5 50	5 57
Pass.	6 43	6 50

UP TRAINS.

Distance from Pad'gton M. C.	Ruling gradient	Point to Point Times Mins.	Allow for Stop Mins.	Allow for Start Mins.	STATIONS	
227 2	78 R.	7	7	1	Brixham	dep.
225 1				2	Churston	arr.

WEEK DAYS — Brixham dep. → Churston arr.

Service	Brixham dep.	Churston arr.
Auto (A.M.)	6 30	6 37
Auto	7 5	7 12
Auto	8 10	8 17
Auto	9 30	9 37
Auto	10 28	10 35
Auto	11 25	11 32
Auto	12 5	12 12
E'gine WSX	10 50	10 37
Auto	12 40	12 47
E'gine WSO	11 50	11 57
Auto (P.M.)	1 10	1 17
Auto	1 42	1 49
Auto	2 20	2 27
Auto	2 50	2 57
Auto	4 20	4 27
Auto	4 55	5 2
Auto	5 40	5 47
Auto	6 25	6 32
Goods	8 0	8 7
Auto	8 30	8 40
Auto	9 7	9 14
Auto	9 14	9 55
Auto	10 2	10 9
E'gine WSX	11 0	11 7
E'gine WSO	11 50	11 57

SUNDAYS — Brixham dep. → Churston arr.

Service	Brixham dep.	Churston arr.
Ex'ter Pass. (P.M.)	1 45	1 52
Ex'ter Pass.	4 20	4 27
Pass.	6 5	6 12
Exeter Pass.	7 15	7 22

R Will stop if required to pin down brakes. See pages 163, 185 and 186 of the General Appendix to the Book of Rules and Regulations.

Y—Wednesdays and Saturdays only.

GREAT WESTERN RAILWAY.

NOTICE TO DRIVERS AND FIREMEN.

INSTRUCTIONS TO BE OBSERVED BY DRIVERS AND FIREMEN IN WORKING RAIL MOTORS OR AUTO TRAINS WHEN THE ENGINEMAN IS DRIVING FROM THE VESTIBULE END AND THE FIREMAN REMAINS ON THE FOOTPLATE.

(1)   It is essential that there should be a proper understanding between the driver and fireman as to the working of the engine and the following General Instructions should always be observed.

(2)   The driver should satisfy himself that the fireman properly understands the working of the reversing gear, vacuum brake, lubricator and sanding gear, and the management of the fire and boiler.

(3)   On receipt of a signal to start from the guard, the driver must sound the whistle which the fireman must acknowledge, and the driver must not start until the fireman has acknowledged his signal.   Before acknowledging the driver's signal the fireman must satisfy himself that the brake is off and that the reversing lever is in the correct position.

(4)   When approaching signals or terminal stations, the fireman must be on the look out and be prepared to act in case of emergency from any cause.

(5)   If a fireman discovers any fault in the working of the engine he must inform the driver at the first stopping place, but if the fault is such that it is necessary to stop before reaching the stopping place the fireman must call attention of the driver by applying the vacuum brake.

(6)   The fireman must not leave the footplate or the engine room without the consent of the driver.

(7)   The following is the code of electric bell signals between the driver and fireman and guard :—

1 ring	...	...	To start.
2 rings	...	...	To stop.
3 rings	...	...	Fireman to blow brake off.

C. B. COLLETT.

CHIEF MECHANICAL ENGINEER'S OFFICE,
SWINDON.
October 1929.
Circular No. 4940.

Notice re working of railmotors 1929.

TRAFFIC DEALT WITH AT STATIONS.

EXETER DIVISION. (Branch Lines).

STATION.	YEAR.	Staff — Supervisory and Wages (All Grades) No.	Staff — Paybill Expenses £	Total Receipts £	Passenger Train Traffic — Tickets issued No.	Season Tickets No.	Receipts — Passengers (incl. Season Tickets, etc.) £	Parcels £	Miscellaneous £	Total £	Goods — Forwarded Coal and Coke "Charged" Tons	Forwarded Other Minerals Tons	Forwarded General Merchandise Tons	Received Coal and Coke "Charged" Tons	Received Other Minerals Tons	Received General Merchandise Tons	Coal and Coke "Not Charged" (Forwarded and Received) Tons	Total Goods Tonnage Tons	Total Receipts "Coal and Coke Not Charged" (excluding) Tons	Livestock (Forwarded and Received) Wagons	Total Carted Tonnage (included in Total Goods Tonnage) Tons
Kingswear Branch (contd.) — Churston (‡)	1903	9	415	3,806	48,516	*	1,980	201	263	2,444	—	—	166	2,023	184	2,281	102	4,739	1,452	66	278
	1913	9	593	4,544	52,802	*	2,161	325	172	2,668	16	33	361	1,413	1,964	2,006	472	6,221	1,886	154	295
	1923	11	1,742	6,465	40,960	161	3,511	169	192	3,872	7	—	368	56	1,446	1,462	1,255	4,594	2,598	152	252
	1929	10	1,670	5,633	25,578	114	3,038	365	351	3,754	—	84	207	25	814	888	1,252	3,270	1,879	170	189
	1930	10	1,656	5,464	25,417	101	2,833	379	406	3,618	—	90	153	148	633	981	1,248	3,188	1,846	154	145
	1931	9	1,592	5,234	19,893	84	2,634	387	294	3,215	—	—	123	177	791	904	1,434	3,524	2,019	108	152
	1932	9	1,471	5,886	16,498	120	2,343	357	215	2,915	—	—	155	346	981	1,904	2,140	4,812	2,971	33	232
	1933	9	1,249	5,897	15,774	116	2,311	354	218	2,883	9	6	212	309	579	2,475	1,556	5,140	3,014	27	110
	1934	9	1,296	5,135	15,456	110	2,228	298	171	2,755	—	—	342	280	310	1,218	694	2,845	2,380	16	122
Brixham Branch — Brixham	1903	12	625	17,609	68,765	*	3,861	1,735	4,770	10,166	—	39	1,931	6,409	607	5,629	1,259	15,874	7,443	—	2,807
	1913	15	951	18,587	83,603	*	5,179	1,532	3,924	10,635	—	88	1,652	1,841	898	6,044	5,136	15,798	7,052	—	2,906
	1923	17	2,905	28,425	58,621	703	6,527	1,868	8,174	16,569	73	385	1,453	322	517	4,625	5,108	16,221	11,856	—	2,674
	1929	17	2,672	25,492	58,076	922	5,138	2,331	5,245	12,712	9	809	1,801	948	601	4,647	8,709	17,011	12,780	—	8,086
	1930	15	2,254	29,610	71,281	854	5,270	2,527	5,844	13,141	40	238	2,170	1,823	865	4,065	7,376	16,673	13,409	—	3,235
	1931	15	1,987	22,739	58,625	547	4,365	2,361	3,807	10,517	—	300	1,408	2,338	429	8,460	6,988	16,038	12,222	—	3,123
	1932	14	1,832	21,316	55,108	573	4,082	2,351	4,467	10,910	9	161	1,226	2,827	488	3,272	6,565	14,175	10,406	—	2,722
	1933	14	2,130	18,779	52,735	710	4,024	2,270	2,822	9,116	35	204	1,075	1,693	479	3,272	7,700	14,458	9,663	—	2,610
	1934	14	2,143	19,704	53,222	620	4,085	2,272	2,046	9,303	25	256	1,889	500	190	3,658	9,375	15,303	10,401	—	3,116

* Not available. ‡ Controlled by Brixham.

Staff, paybill costs, receipts and traffic details for Churston and Brixham, 1903-1934.

BRIXHAM—THE HARBOUR.
(GREAT WESTERN RAILWAY)

GWR official postcard of Brixham - this one was posted in 1913.   *Author's Collection*

GWR poster advertising Brixham.   *British Rail*

Great Western Railway

BRIXHAM
TORBAY · SUNNY DEVON
For full particulars and Free Guide Book, write Secretary, Publicity Committee, Brixham

A train from Brixham, pushed and pulled by a 'Metro' tank, approaches Churston in the 1930
It is conveying a fish truck rear, ready for attachment to the back of an up train, probably afte
the train signalled on the down line has left. A trainload of gas coal, unloaded from a ship
Kingswear, and *en route* to Torquay Gasworks, has been stabled in the down refuge siding.

J. Scott-Morgan Collectic

Looking through Churston village to the branch railway bridge in the background.

D.K. & M. James Collectic

This caught Paddington completely by surprise, neither the GM nor the superintendent of the line (SOL) knew about it! It turned out that local arrangements had been made by the Exeter traffic superintendent and the Newton Abbot locomotive superintendent; the handles on the passenger-side communicating doors to the luggage area had been removed and special locks fitted, the keys being held by the Brixham station master. However, while this arrangement was being considered by Paddington, the Exeter Post Office surveyor pressed for the outside doors also to be fitted with special locks, and the SOL was against this as it would set a precedent 'for the fitting of all brake compartments with special locks'. On 8th May, 1931 the Post Office was told that the GWR was prepared to put a bolt on the inside of the communicating doors but would not provide special locks on the outside doors. On 14th May, the SOL suggested to the GM that the Brixham arrangements should be withdrawn and that all cars used on push-pull services without guards should have a throwover catch on the inside of the communicating door. This would do away with special locks and keys and would be impossible to tamper with from the passenger side, would obviate the need for the suggested special outside door locks and would enable the footplate staff to open the door for evacuation purposes in emergency without need for a special key. The GM, referring to his recent letter to the Post Office, said, in effect, 'hold fire' until the latter replies.

And there the matter went dead for three years, apparently forgotten by all concerned (unless the intervening correspondence is missing from the file). But in June 1934, following withdrawal of guards on the Abingdon branch, the matter surfaced again and now instructions went out that all trailer vehicles should have catches fitted on the inside of the communicating doors. On 27th September, 1935 the SOL was able to confirm that the work had been done.

The file reveals that, in 1930, mails were being conveyed on the 10.10 am, 1.27 and 2.20 pm from Churston and the 10.22 am, 1.40, 6.25 and 7.55 pm from Brixham. Mostly it was only to/from Torquay, Exeter or Plymouth, but the 10.10 and 1.27 down and the 7.55 up did carry bags which were conveyed on the Travelling Post Office services.

1931 saw expenditure of £152 on renewal of a facing point connection, 34 years old. On 27th June, 1932 Lt-Col Mount of the Ministry of Transport Railway Inspectorate examined some new works at Brixham (possibly the same job):

Instead of a trailing connection in the adjacent siding with a diamond on the up and down running line, a connection has been laid in the latter with 97½ lb. material on ballast, facing traffic from Churston junction and to serve the existing locomotive shed siding.

From all appearances the siding is little, if ever, used now. The points which are coupled to a single tongue trap are worked from the box, which contains an old frame of 16 working and 7 spare levers. Three additional shunt signals have been provided and the connection has full facing point equipment.

The new work was approved. Despite 'appearances' the siding must have been used sometimes for the engine to take on water or coal even if the shed was now closed. But as we have seen in Chapter Five, the supply of water was unreliable. It was simpler to take water at Churston as the column was on the bay platform.

BRIXHAM BRANCH.

Single Line, worked by Electric Train Token. All Down Trains must stop dead at the Down Home Signal for Brixham. All Up Trains entering the Bay Line must stop dead at the Home Signal at Churston. The Train must afterwards be steadily drawn to the platform.

DOWN TRAINS.

Distance M.C.	Stn. No.	Ruling Gradient	Point-to-Point Times (Mins.)	Allow for Stop (Mins.)	Allow for Start (Mins.)	Station
—	1655	—	—	—	—	Churston …… dep.
26		95 R.	3	1	1	Stop Board
69½		79 F.	3	1	1	Stop Board
2 1	1663	78 F.				Brixham …… arr.

WEEK DAYS

Station	B Goods SO‡	B Auto.	B Auto.	B Auto.	B Mixed.	B Auto.	B Auto.	B Auto.	B Auto. Y	B Auto. SX	B Auto. SO	B Auto. Z	B Auto.
Churston (dep.)	a.m. 5 20	6 5	6 53	7 43	8 30	9 20	10 38	11 40	p.m. 12 15	12 45	1 4	1 27	2 15
Brixham (arr.)	5 32	6 12	7 0	7 50	8 40	9 27	10 45	11 47	12 22	12 52	1 11	1 34	2 22

(Goods: R and P stops shown at Stop Boards. Mixed 8 30: R at Stop Boards.)

WEEK DAYS (continued)

Station	B Auto.	B Auto.	B Auto.	G Auto. Engine & Van SX	B Auto.	B Auto.	B Auto.	B Auto.	B' Auto.	B Auto.	B Auto. SO	B Auto. W80
Churston (dep.)	p.m. 2 55	3 30	4 0	4 43	5 24	5 55	6 30	7 15	8 23	9 23	10 0	11 33
Brixham (arr.)	3 2	3 37	4 7	4 50	5 31	6 2	6 37	7 22	8 30	9 30	10 7	11 40

(G column — Allow for Start 5† 2 / 5+15.)

SUNDAYS

Station	B Exeter Pass.	B Pass.	B Pass.	B Exeter Pass.	B Pass.	B Exeter Pass.	B Pass.	B Exeter Pass.	B Pass.
Churston (dep.)	p.m. 12 25	1 15	2 15	3 35	4 48	5 45	6 29	7 33	8 20
Brixham (arr.)	12 32	1 22	2 22	3 42	4 55	5 52	6 36	7 40	8 27

UP TRAINS.

M.P. Mileage	Ruling Gradient	Point-to-Point Times (Mins.)	Allow for Stop (Mins.)	Station
227 2	—	—	—	Brixham …… dep.
225 7	78 R.	7	2	Churston …… arr.

WEEK DAYS

Station	D Empty Auto SO‡	B Auto.	B Auto. K	B Auto. Newt'n Abbott SX	B Auto.	B Auto.	B Auto.	B Auto.	B Auto.	B Auto. SX	B Auto.	B Auto. ¶	B Auto.	B Auto.
Brixham (dep.)	a.m. 5 50	6 35	7 3	8 10	9 0	9 52	10 20	11 20	11 58	p.m. 12 30	12 50	1 8	2 0	2 35
Churston (arr.)	5 57	6 42	7 10	8 17	9 7	9 59	10 27	11 27	12 5	12 37	12 57	1 15	2 7	2 42

WEEK DAYS (continued)

Station	B Auto.	B Auto.	B Auto.	B Auto.	B Auto. K	Newt'n Abbott Goods SX	B Auto.	B Auto.	B Auto.	B Auto. SO	Engine W8X	Engine W80
Brixham (dep.)	p.m. 3 13	3 43	4 28	4 45	6 13	6 40	6 58	7 25	8 12	9 45	10 25	10 57
Churston (arr.)	3 20	3 50	4 35	4 52	6 20	6 50	7 5	7 32	8 19	9 52	10 32	11 4

SUNDAYS

Station	B Exeter Pass.	B Newton Abbott Pass.	B Pass.	B Pass.	B Taunton Pass.	B Exeter Pass.	B Pass.	B Exeter Pass.	B Pass.
Brixham (dep.)	p.m. 12 55	1 50	1 57	4 30	5 10	6 7	7 18	8 0	8 35
Churston (arr.)	1 2	1 57		4 37	5 17		7 25	8 7	8 42

R—Will stop if required to pin down brakes. See pages 153, 185, and 186 of the General Appendix to the Book of Rules and Regulations. Y—Runs 5 minutes later on Saturdays. Z—Runs 6 minutes later on Saturdays. ‡—Runs 12 minutes later on Saturdays. †—Runs July 27th to September 7th, inclusive. ¶—Runs 12 minutes later on Saturdays.

The summer 1932 timetable showed a 10 per cent increase in trains compared with 1929.

The *GWR Magazine* for September 1934 reported that the company had just ordered 396 motor vehicles at a cost of £156,500 in a continuing programme to replace horse-drawn vehicles by those of a mechanical type. Among the list of depots to be so modernised was Brixham. The former stables was used to garage the motor vehicle.

The intensive service provided during the summer months in the 1930s is demonstrated in the Working timetable for July 1935, here included. To enable freight to be dealt with it was necessary to run a very early goods train at 5.20 am from Churston and, except on Saturdays, an hour has been allowed for shunting and berthing the wagons until the first auto leaves Brixham at 6.35 am. On Saturdays (27th July-7th September), however, any goods or empty fish trucks would have been quickly detached as the engine had to pick up the auto coaches and run empty to Churston at 5.50 am prior to forming a 6.05 am from Churston to Brixham.

At 5.02 pm (SX) an engine and brake van left Churston for Brixham to carry out any shunting necessary to form up the evening goods train to Newton Abbot leaving at 6.40 pm (SX). Incidentally it would have been impossible for this engine to leave at 5.02 pm as the 4.55 pm from Brixham only arrived at Churston at 5.02 pm. The token had to be taken to the signal box and a fresh one obtained for the goods engine which would probably have been standing outside the box. So departure was more likely to be 5.05 pm, but this still allowed 10 minutes for a right time arrival at Brixham - more than enough! Notice that the next auto left Churston at 5.24 pm so after arrival at Brixham at 5.31 pm there were two trains at Brixham on and off until the departure of the goods at 6.40 pm.

The Sunday service was now eight in each direction and three down trains are through from Exeter, whilst there are through trains to Newton Abbot, Exeter and Taunton (one each).

In 1935 consideration was being given to setting up a fleet of 12 steam trawlers in Brixham. Those who opposed the scheme said that expensive alterations would be needed to the harbour, and that it would be necessary to establish hydraulic means of transport up to the station. A drawing showing such a proposal has been found in the Railtrack Great Western archives, but unfortunately it is undated and there is no written material with it to establish its provenance. The scheme came to nothing, although a firm called Brixham Trawlers Ltd was set up in 1936 and employed six, later eight, steam trawlers, formerly at Hull until moving to Fleetwood at the end of 1937. In January 1938 a new, local firm, Torbay Trawlers Ltd, was set up with five, later eight, steam trawlers, but the onset of World War II caused the removal of all but two vessels.

In 1937 Brixham UDC paid the GWR over £900 to remove 3,500 cubic yards of mud from the harbour, using their dredger, and depositing it outside the international limits. This deepened the berths by the inner side of the pier by five feet.

The July 1938 passenger service was very similar to 1935 but the Sunday service had dropped back to seven trains each way. The winter 1938 timetable was on a par with the *summer* 1935 and 1938 ones with a very generous 23 down

A poor image but photographs of staff are rare; in this scene in the Brixham bay at Churston about 1935 are (*left*) driver Albert Shaw (Brixham 1931-1938) and (*middle*) fireman John Richardson (Brixham 1919-1940). The uniformed man to the right is unfortunately unknown.   *Courtesy Mrs R. Crick, Brixham*

(plus 2 SO) and 24 up (plus 1 SO) trains. In the event it was to be the last intensive winter timetable; the last arrival at Brixham was at 11.45 pm on Saturdays. There were four trains each way on Sundays. The Sunday services, back to eight trains each way, ran for the last time in the summer of 1939, although they were briefly restored in 1949 and 1950.

In August 1939 the GWR issued comprehensive instructions for the evacuation from London in the event of war. The movements would take place over the space of four days. The Brixham branch was not much affected; apart from a couple of retimings where trains ran earlier, the only special arrangements involved were that an extra train left Churston at 11.55 pm each night, connecting with an 11. 15 pm special from Newton Abbot, which in turn had connected out of a 5.15 pm from Paddington to Plymouth. The branch engine returned light to Churston at 12.08 am where it was coupled to the stock of the 11. 15 pm down special, returning empty to Newton Abbot and leaving here double-headed.

The winter service *intended* to have been introduced from 25th September, 1939 was as follows (note that for the first time the Sunday service was suspended until May):

Churston to Brixham (weekdays): 6.50, 7.43, 8.30, 10.08, 10.45 am, 12.13, 12.43, 1.08, 1.28, 2.13, 2.52, 3.30, 4.0, 4.40, 5.20, 5.43, 6.27, 7.12, 7.55, 8.34, 9.23, 10.13, 11.37 (SO) pm.
Brixham to Churston (weekdays): 6.33, 7.03, 8.10, 9.33, 10.30, 11.25 am, 12.30, 12.55, 1.18, 2.0, 2.35, 3.13, 3.43, 4.28, 4.53, 5.30, 6.15, 6.38, 7.25, 8.05, 8.55, 9.45, 10.45 pm.
(23 departures from Brixham)
Churston to Brixham (Sundays comm. 5th May, 1940): 1.10, 4.23, 5.45 pm.
Brixham to Churston (Sundays ditto): 1.40, 5.0, 6.30 pm.

The service *actually* introduced from 25th September, 1939 by a special wartime emergency timetable was *weekdays only*, as follows:

Churston to Brixham: 6.53, 7.28, 8.38, 11.04, 11.40 am, 12.35, 1.10, 1.53, 3.10, 4.25, 4.53, 5.20, 6.26, 6.55, 7.35, 9.20 pm.
Brixham to Churston: 6.40, 7.03, 8.10, 9.20, 11.25 am, 12.20, 12.55, 1.40, 2.05, 3.50, 4.40, 5.05, 6.10, 6.40, 7.20, 8.55 pm.
(16 departures from Brixham)

However, the big gap in the morning was filled from December 1939 by trains from Churston at 9.40 and 10.12 am returning from Brixham at 9.58 and 10.48 am, an 18 train service. A further revision in February 1940 added two further trains, making 20 trains each way, cut back to 19 in October 1940, and to 18 in October 1941.

The *Magazine* for February 1940 records the promotion of F.J. Loram, signalman at Brixham, to Torre. He had been at Brixham since the early part of 1922 and had served under four station masters in that lengthy period.

Joe Trethewey was a fireman at Newton Abbot in the late 1930s/1940s working the branch regularly from 1940 to 1942, and he remembers how busy the branch could be in the summer holiday period, when there was an auto-trailer either side of the engine. The only time the fireman saw the driver was when the latter changed ends at Brixham or Churston, or when the crew had their break. He has known times when two or three trips had to be made to Churston to ensure that all the passengers at Brixham caught the last service from Kingswear. Similarly in the heavy part of the fishing season each trip made to Churston during the early evenings conveyed a truck or two to make up a fish special from there, the quantity of traffic being too great to attach behind the regular passenger services from Kingswear. One day, during the sprat season of, it is thought, 1942, 24 wagons were dispatched! On rare occasions at such time of glut sprats were loose loaded with shovels, after placing boards across the bottom of the doors; although Jim Cook never saw this done in the time he was there as branch fireman (1945-1959), he had heard it spoken of.

Northfield Sidings (1940)

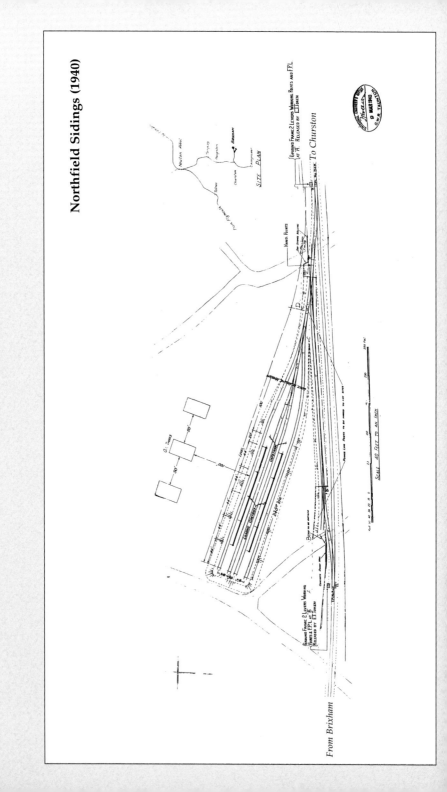

The harbour and the town were at the receiving end of bombs dropped by aircraft on several occasions during World War II, but the railway was not damaged. Ellis's *History* lists 17 occasions when bombs caused damage and death and/or injury. 1942 was the worst year with seven attacks between January and July.

During the war the Torbay Paint Co. (Wolston's old firm) turned over to 100 per cent production of camouflage paint. 'Hedge black' was in 24-hour production and six railway lorries in relays took their loads of 40 gallon drums of this and other colours to Churston station, sometimes as many as 600 drums a day. Churston was used rather than Brixham because the firm was located in New Road, where a new factory had been built in 1937-39, from which it was a relatively straight and direct road to Churston, rather than the excessively steep and winding route to Brixham station. In 1941-2 over 2 million gallons, and in 1942-3, 3¼ million gallons of paint were produced. As things improved for the Allies and the need for camouflage paint decreased, the firm was left with 45,000 40 gallon tanks on its hands - some were sold for use as water storage tanks in rural areas, others were used to store materials for D-Day. A certain amount of naval (inwards) traffic was dealt with during the war although the heaviest loads were handled at Churston.

A fuel reserve depot for the Air Ministry was built at 226½ MP some ½ mile west of Brixham station in 1940. Authorised in April at a cost of £4,304, it opened on 23rd October, the Ministry of Transport being so advised. They got round to inspecting and approving the new layout in June 1948.

The late Fred Park, MBE worked for Esso at Brixham for 49 years and was Manager during the war years. He provided some unique memories of the working of the wartime fuel storage sidings at Northfields Lane which was rail-connected to the Brixham branch. The fuel (for the RAF) was brought in by sea and stored in underground tanks at Berry Head, from where , after blending to convert it into high octane grades, it was piped to Northfields Lane for transfer to rail tank cars. Two loading gantries, each serving two rail sidings holding 10 tank cars, a total of 40 cars, were provided. (The pipe route was via Heath Road, Ranscombe Road, King Street, around the Harbour, Overgang and under Furzeham Green.)

The loading track had to be perfectly level in order to allow accurate measurements of loading the railcars. The loading bar had to be just awash when filled to calibration level.

The railway staff had no access to the blending procedure,* in fact the highly poisonous Tetra Ethyl head came in special barrels with an inner and outer bung and the rail staff were not allowed to transfer the barrels from truck to road delivery vehicle until we had inspected them and certified that they were not damaged. Even the vapour could be absorbed into the skin and could prove fatal.

Our men handling the blending at Berry Head had to have special clothing and gas masks and be examined by a doctor every six months to make sure they were not absorbing the lead.

We had two 500 ton balancing tanks at the Northfields Lane siding to take the two grades (87 octane and 100 octane) from Berry Head. The railcars were usually filled from these tanks, although it was quite possible to fill direct from Berry Head.

Apart from two trainloads sent to Thames Haven when it was considered too risky to send tankers through the Dover Straits, and one load to Micheldever, all the rest went to Islip in Oxfordshire from where it was distributed to local airfields.

* This corrects a statement made in the First Edition.

BRIXHAM BRANCH.

Single Line worked by Electric Train Token. All Down Trains must stop dead at the Down Home Signal for Brixham. All Up Trains entering the Bay Line must stop dead at the Home Signal at Churston. The Train must afterwards be steadily drawn to the Platform.

Down Trains.

Stations, distances and ruling gradients:

Distance (M. C.)	Stations	Ruling Gradient
— —	Churston .... dep.	95 R.
1 28	Stop Board	79 F.
1 69¼	Stop Board	78 F.
2 1	Brixham .... arr.	

Week Days

Class	Type	Churston dep.	Brixham arr.
B	Auto.	a.m. 7 15	7 22
B	Mixed.	a.m. 8 25 R	8 32
B	Auto.	a.m. 9 45	9 52
B	Auto.	a.m. 11 40	11 47
B	Auto.	p.m. 12 50	12 57
B	Auto.	p.m. 2 20	2 27
B	Auto.	p.m. 3 50	3 57
B	Auto.	p.m. 4 25	4 32
B	Auto.	p.m. 5 0	5 7
B	Auto.	p.m. 6 0	6 7
B	Auto.	p.m. 6 55	7 2
B	Auto.	p.m. 7 45	7 52
B	Auto.	p.m. 8 10	8 17

Sundays

Class	Type	Churston dep.	Brixham arr.
B	Auto.	p.m. 8 45	8 52
B	Auto.	p.m. 9 45	9 52
G	Engine & Van ex Newton Abbot R R	p.m. 4† 3	4†10

Up Trains.

Stations, distances and ruling gradients:

Ruling Gradient	Stations
—	Brixham .... dep.
78 R.	Churston .... arr.

Week Days

Class	Type	Brixham dep.	Churston arr.
B	Auto.	a.m. 6 58	7 5
B	Auto.	a.m. 8 3	8 10
B	Auto.	a.m. 9 13	9 20
B	Auto.	a.m. 10 43	10 50
B	Auto.	a.m. 11 23	11 30
B	Auto.	p.m. 12 28	12 35
B	Auto.	p.m. 2 0	2 7
B	Auto.	p.m. 3 28	3 35
B	Auto.	p.m. 4 10	4 17
B	Auto.	p.m. 4 43	4 50
B	Auto.	p.m. 5 38	5 45
B	Auto.	p.m. 6 15	6 22
B	Auto.	p.m. 7 30	7 37
B	Auto.	p.m. 7 55	8 2
B	Auto.	p.m. 8 28	8 35
B	Auto.	p.m. 9 30	9 37
G	Engine.	p.m. 10‖ 0	10‖ 7

Sundays

Class	Type	Brixham dep.	Churston arr.
C	Fish to Newt'n Abbot R R	a.m. 5 30	5 37

R—Will stop if required to pin down brakes. See pages 143, 144, 178, 179 and 180 of the General Appendix to the Book of Rules and Regulations.

May 1942 Working timetable.

We loaded the tank cars (normally 4,000 gallons) and then pulled them out to the engine Stop Board, where the railway staff took over. We had two 5 hp electric capstans off the ends of the loading gantries with large pulleys set in the ground for fairleads, so we were able to pull up to five loaded tanks up or down. We also had 'Easycar Pushers' for individual wagons (6 ft crowbars to 'pinch' the wheels) - quite effective but very slow.

Once the railway staff let one tank car run off the lower end of the loop and two wheels embedded in the ballast, luckily without any spillage. [This was on 14th October, 1941 and resulted in the cancellation of just two trains the following day - 9.20 am ex-Brixham and 9.40 am ex-Churston - when a railway crane was brought in to rerail the vehicle. A Devon General bus covered the trains.]

The loaded cars went out in batches of 10 (the maximum weight for the branch) to Goodrington Yard from about 11.00 am, the last usually by 4.15 pm. No movements took place after dark. The engines used were normally of the '4500' 2-6-2T type.* When the full train was assembled at Goodrington it set off, double-headed, at 5.30 pm. It was always given air cover between Teignmouth and Exeter.

The business gradually slackened off on arrival of jet engines which required so much extra fuel that the Air Ministry decided their depots had to be nearer the aerodromes.

We had 70 tank cars allocated to us and it allowed us to make up a 40-car train at least twice a week. We were supposed to receive the returned empties the afternoon of the day following dispatch, but there were always three or four missing, having been stopped due to 'hot boxes' or other defects. These were repaired by Wagon Repairs Ltd but took up to 10 days to return to us.

Most of our air raids were hit- and-run from the Channel Islands, usually 'been and gone' before the siren sounded. I have watched them coming in at low level and following the contours like horses jumping the fences. Our depots must have led a charmed life.

The OS 1:25 000 Outdoor Leisure Map for South Devon (1978) still shows five storage tanks (they were partially buried) in the ground at the former rail depot. The three nearest the branch line were intended for lubricating oil but never used, the two behind for aviation spirit. The OS map even shows that one of each type of tank is derelict (dismantled).

Joe Trethewey remembers working one of these fuel trains during the war. Whilst travelling along the coast between Dawlish and Dawlish Warren he noticed the wings of an aircraft over the train; suddenly the plane veered away as a group of Spitfires approached and he saw it brought down in the sea off Dawlish beach. Had the train been hit by gunfire or bombing the consequences for Dawlish would have been horrific.

The depot was on the upside of the line; approaching from the Churston direction there was a ground frame (Depot No. 1 GF) at 226 m. 38 ch. giving access to a loop from which diverged a group of four dead-end sidings to hold rail tank cars. At its other end the loop converged into the branch line at 226 m. 48 ch. at which was sited Depot No. 2 GF. These ground frames were released by the token. There were gates at 226 m. 40 ch. and 226 m. 45 ch. on the loop, between which points the loop and sidings were classed as private sidings. Although very busy during the war, by the time of the MoT inspection the depot had been placed on a 'care and maintenance' basis.

The Working timetable for May 1942 (included) shows that Brixham was now surviving on a 16-train service (during the war freight trains were published separately, hence their omission here). The same service was in force in October 1942. Note the 'as required' service on Sundays for fish traffic.

* On one occasion a large tender engine, officially prohibited from the branch, turned up at Churston and special permission had to be obtained by telephone for this locomotive to do the job.

On 23rd August, 1945 '14XX' 0-4-2T No. 1427 prepares to propel two trailers to Churston.
The late H.C. Casserle

Seen on the same day, a view across a deserted platform to the goods shed.
The late H.C. Casserle

Because of a reduction in services between Newton Abbot and Kingswear, the summer and winter 1943 timetables on the Brixham branch showed 15 trains in each direction, weekdays only, with departures from Brixham ranged between 6.58 am and 9.30 pm. This timetable was in operation for the whole of 1944 and spring/summer 1945. The October 1945 service was almost identical but, with removal of one train between 4 pm and 5 pm (there had been two in this hour), the number of trains dropped to 14 in each direction, weekdays only.

Some wartime accident reports have been preserved and give a small insight into actual events on a rural branch line. On 28th January, 1941 a party of passengers alighted from the 1.30 pm Paddington at Churston at 8.10 pm and made their way to the Brixham bay. Remember that wartime blackout conditions meant that nowhere outdoors was well lighted; the night was very dark 'and extremely difficult to discern anything without a light'. The passengers were advised to follow porter Howard who was wheeling a load of luggage to the Brixham train, but another porter (Hunt) noticed that some passengers were going to the left of the barrier at the end of the bay line rather than the right. He called out but was too late to stop a Naval Petty Officer from falling onto the line. Fortunately he only suffered a swollen knee cap which he made light of. The report notes, 'Blue lighting has not yet been installed here'.

On 14th October, 1941 there was the derailment at Northfield Sidings, noted earlier. On 9th December, 1941 at 2.40 pm four empty vehicles were being gravitated into the shed road at Brixham and the porter carrying out the movement did not apply the brakes sufficiently early to avoid a collision with vehicles already there. They moved and caused fairly extensive damage to a lorry belonging to the Brixham Gas Co. standing alongside the adjacent coal siding.

Lightning really did strike twice (metaphorically speaking) on 28th and 29th April, 1943 when two similar collisions occurred in the bay line at Churston. On 28th April the 6.15 pm from Brixham (engine 4827 pushing trailer 160; driver Coombes and fireman Williams) hit the buffer stops at 6.21 pm, having previously been brought to a stand at the home signal as the Regulations required. Damage was done to the buffer stops and the coach; the four passengers on board were 'shaken' and fireman Williams slightly injured but he remained on duty. At 7.05 am the following morning the 6.58 am from Brixham (engine 4827 pushing trailer 167; driver Walling and fireman Gerring) repeated the incident, again having been stopped at the home signal. This time there were 26 passengers on the train, one of whom was thrown against the doorlight (window) causing it to break and the passenger receiving minor injuries and shock. Two battery cells were also broken. All the footplatemen were Newton Abbot men.

A Joint Enquiry was held at Exeter and the conclusion reached was that the accidents were caused by a mechanical defect in the regulator gear on No. 4827. When the leading end gear was coupled to the coach, the regulator would not close by ⅝th of an inch, allowing a slight emission of steam to the cylinders. This defect had been reported on 23rd April but was not 'considered sufficiently serious' and was not attended to until after the second accident. Both enginemen were aware of the defect and were criticised for (not having) 'exercised greater care and judgment owing to the prevailing weather

A view across a well filled yard to the goods shed in August 1946.   *The late C.A. Pearc*

An unusual picture, taken from the signal box, looking towards the engine shed siding and it
water tank. Exit from the siding is controlled by an elevated shunting signal, while the main lin
starting signal, right, is on a concrete post.   *Jack Eveleig*

conditions'. Although this criticism came from the local officials, the CME and the superintendent of the line did not agree, and reported to the General Manager that the essential cause of the accidents was the mechanical defect which should have been remedied as soon as it was reported. 'The matter has been suitably followed up with the staff concerned'. Doubtless the damage to two trailers gave an immediate problem in wartime conditions.

On 29th November, 1943, at 7.53 am during shunting operations at Brixham engine No. 4839 with brake van leading and two trailers in tow went towards the stop blocks on the platform line, so as to run-round a van left in the platform. The train , however, did not clear the points to the loop (No. 11) so the guard called the movement back towards the platform. Unfortunately the signalwoman was not advised of the change of plan and took the driver's whistle as an indication that the points were clear. Reversing the loop points caused No. 4839 to be derailed all wheels. The breakdown vans were ordered from Newton Abbot at 8 am and arrived at 9.52, the engine being rerailed at 10.55. The 8.03 and 9.13 am from Brixham and the 8.25 and 9.45 from Churston were all cancelled, passengers being conveyed by road. The only damage was one rail chair broken.

As the 9.13 am from Brixham ran into the bay line at Churston at 9.20 on 11th September, 1944 (engine No. 4866 pushing trailer 167) it collided with the buffer stops, breaking five battery cells and splitting the buffer stops (again!). There were only two passengers, a boy aged 15 and a girl of 17, who were not injured. This time it was decided the accident happened 'due to an error of judgment on the part of the engineman . . . coupled with the greasy state of the rail . . .'

At about 10. 15 pm on 6th November, 1944, locomotive 4827 (driver Thomas fireman Phillips) pushed the two trailers up to the stop blocks at Brixham for overnight stabling. The locomotive returned to the platform with a supernumary porter who had been acting as shunter riding on the top step on the fireman's side. As he attempted to get off opposite the booking office, his jacket caught in something on the engine and he was dragged between the engine and the platform, although the locomotive stopped almost immediately. He received quite extensive lacerations, and eventually (but not until April 1952 and by then 65) received compensation under the Workmen's Compensation Act because of permanent partial disability.

At about 2.45 pm on 25th November, 1944, the signalman at Churston lowered the signals for the 1 pm Hackney to Brixham freight, worked by 2-6-2T No. 4547 and consisting of five wagons and brake, to leave the down/up main (bi-directional loop) and proceed to the branch. He then had to leave the box for personal reasons. On his return some eight minutes later he observed the track circuit to the rear of the down branch starting signal to be clear and assumed the train to be on its way. He reversed the down/up main to branch points (No. 31) to normal. He immediately afterwards heard a movement start, and looking out of the box, discovered that the goods train had stopped opposite the bay platform water column to take water, and was now proceeding towards Brixham. The two leading wheels of the engine derailed on points 31. The breakdown vans were ordered at 3 pm, arrived at 4.45 and the engine was quickly rerailed (at 5.05 pm). In the meantime all trains to/from Kingswear were worked over the up main loop and Brixham trains worked to/from the up branch home signal, passengers completing the remaining 150 yds on foot. Normal working was resumed on the Kingswear line at 5.20 pm and on the branch with the 6.15 pm ex-Brixham.

On 19th December, 1944 during shunting operations with the 1 pm Hackney to Brixham freight at Brixham at 2.15 pm, another misjudged shunt movement caused a collision with vehicles in the shed road, and once again damage to a lorry unloading coal nearby, this time belonging to Mr Martin, coal merchant. On 12th January, 1945 high winds at Churston caused a 2-wheel barrow to be blown on to the track, where it was run into by the 3.45 pm Newton Abbot to Kingswear.

A sad accident occurred on 28th July, 1945 when a young lady student from Yorkshire on holiday in Torquay, fell out of the 7.30 pm Brixham to Churston some ½ mile from the latter place. The train comprised two trailers being pushed by locomotive No. 4866, and the lady fell from trailer No. 167. The fireman saw her alongside the line as he passed and stopped the train. Some passers-by in the road, including an off-duty railwayman, quickly attended the scene and stopped a passing car which took the lady back to Brixham, where she was admitted to hospital. The doors of the trailer were confirmed to have been shut at Brixham, were in perfect order, and as they opened inwards it was impossible for someone to fall out; it was concluded the passenger had jumped. Fortunately for her she suffered nothing worse than a sprained ankle. She was later admitted to Devon County Mental Hospital.

On 23rd May, 1946, at 10.10 am, during shunting operations in Brixham yard, engine No. 4870 became derailed two leading wheels because the points leading from the long siding to the shed road were not properly closed. The breakdown vans arrived at 12.13 pm and the engine was then used to take up the branch service, commencing with the 1.05 pm from Churston. No. 4870 was rerailed at 12.45 pm and returned to shed with the breakdown vans at 1.25 pm. In the meantime the 10.25, 11.23 am and 12.18 pm Brixham to Churston and the 11.00 and 11.40 am Churston to Brixham services had all been covered by road vehicles.

The easing of wartime restrictions allowed an improvement to a 16-train service in May 1946, with a 30 minute later last departure from Brixham of 9.55 pm, and a late return from Churston at 10.35 pm, restored in October (but still 16 trains).

As has been mentioned before, the water supply to the tank at Brixham had to be pumped from sea level to a height of 135 ft and by a quite circuitous route. Eventually the pipework corroded and the supply of water became unreliable. By the 1940s, if not before, it had become the practice to take water exclusively at Churston, only using the Brixham supply in emergency.

On one occasion during the very hard winter of 1946/47, branch fireman Jim Cook remembers, the supply at Churston froze up and it was necessary to use the Brixham tank, situated alongside the former engine shed spur, just west of the platform. There was normally no reason to use this short spur and, when the locomotive ran up to the tank, the track opened under its weight, derailing the engine. Consternation! There was no way of getting the engine back on the track so the breakdown vans were summoned from Newton Abbot and in the meantime branch passengers were conveyed by road.

The breakdown vans were propelled in from Churston and stabled in the top coal yard. The '45XX' tank engine which had brought them was coupled to the auto-coach and the passenger service recommenced. Because the '45XX' could not be worked by the auto-coach it was necessary to run-round after each journey. It was essential to disconnect the facing points from single line to the engine spur from the box as these were coupled with the catchpoint in the spur, which, of course, needed to remain closed.

Eventually the branch engine was rerailed, the track repaired, and the Newton Abbot breakdown gang returned their packing and lifting tools to the vans. The '45XX' engine uncoupled from the branch coach and returned to its vans. The driver of the branch engine was instructed to run out onto the single line. But then disaster struck! In best Will Hay, rather than GWR, tradition the engine derailed again, this time on the catchpoints which, unfortunately, had not been reconnected to the signal box and had opened under the engine! So the weary breakdown men unpacked their tools once again . . . doubtless all concerned made some overtime that day!

In the last eight months of the GWR's existence, at 9.05 pm on 24th April, 1947 after passengers had alighted from the 8.45 pm from Churston, it was necessary to draw ahead to the fish platform to unload fish from a truck formed at the rear [coals to Newcastle?]. It was then intended to return the truck to the passenger platform, before running round via the loop to detach the trailer. When the driver whistled before setting back, the signalman thought he was whistling for the loop points (No. 11), although no request had been made by the shunter, and reversed the points as the trailer passed over them, derailing four wheels. Our old friend No. 167 received damage to its vacuum pipe and buffer guide and a broken buffer. This became an overtime job, the breakdown vans, ordered at 9.10 pm, arrived at 12.30 am and the trailer was rerailed at 3.30 am. The 9.00 and 9.55 pm ex-Brixham and the 9.20 and 10.35 pm ex-Churston were all cancelled, the report noting 'No passengers for any of these services' which may well have caused eyebrows to be raised at Paddington.

The last summer timetable issued by the GWR, 16th June-5th October, 1947, reflected an increased summer service but not up to pre-war levels. In 1938 24 trains ran (Saturdays excepted) and 26 (Saturdays only) in each direction. In 1947 15 trains were scheduled Saturdays excepted and 18 on Saturdays only. The first departure from Brixham was, as usual, 6.58 am and the last 9.55 pm; this ran each weekday and returned from Churston at 10.35 pm. The branch remained closed on Sundays. The 15-train service continued that winter.

At midnight on 31st December, 1947/1st January, 1948 Wolston's railway and all other parts of the Great Western Railway were transferred to the ownership of the state and became part of British Railways, Western Region. For another 13 years, however, things were to change very little and the Brixham 'Whippet' scampered backwards and forwards to the junction at Churston, as it had since 1868.

CHURSTON AND BRIXHAM. (Week Days only.) (Third class only.)

	a.m.	a.m.		a.m.	a.m.	a.m.			a.m.	p.m.	p.m.	p.m.	p.m.	p.m.	p.m.		p.m.		p.m.	p.m.		p.m.	p.m.	p.m.	
Churston ... dep.	7 15	8 25	...	9 40	10 20	11 0	...	11 40	12 35	12 55	2 35	2 10	3 40	4 22	4 50	...	5 55	...	6 50	7 40	...	8 45	9 20	10 35	...
Brixham ... arr.	7 22	8 32	...	9 47	10 27	11 7	...	11 47	12 42	1 2	2 42	2 17	3 47	4 29	4 57	...	6 2	...	6 57	7 47	...	8 52	9 27	10 42	...

	a.m.	a.m.	a.m.	a.m.		a.m.	a.m.	a.m.	a.m.	p.m.	p.m.	p.m.	p.m.	p.m.	p.m.		p.m.		p.m.	p.m.	p.m.	p.m.		p.m.	
Brixham ... dep.	6 58	8 3	8 55	9 0	...	10 5	10 35	10 45	11 23	12 15	1 3 0	1 48	3 20	4 5	4 34	...	5 30	...	6 15	7 15	8 5	9 0	...	9 55	...
Churston ... arr.	7 5	8 10	9 3	9 7	...	10 5	10 55	10 55	11 30	12 22	1 8 7	1 55	3 27	4 12	4 41	...	5 37	...	6 22	7 22	8 12	9 7	...	10 2	...

Q—Saturdays excepted.   S—Saturdays only.

June 1947 public timetable.

Brixham station, May 1948; (*left to right*): senior porter Edgar Trickey, porter Tom Taylor, drive
Reg Westaway, and fireman Jim Cook on the footplate of '14XX' No. 1439, still in GWR livery
Courtesy Jim Coo

A full line up of the Brixham staff in September 1949 to mark the retirement of Cecil William
Back row (*left to right*): clerk Peter Hall, (?) reliefman, clerk Rod Saunders, clerk 'Nipp'
Widdicombe, relief clerk Stan Cook (later Brixham's last station master 1955-1963
supernumary porter Fowler, fireman Jim Cook, driver Reg Westaway. Front row (*left to right*
porter Tom Taylor, parcels motor driver Percy Wadham, senior porter Edgar Trickey, static
master Cecil Williams, checker Dick Stancombe, goods motor driver Ernest Ash, porter Fran
Payne. *Courtesy Jim Coo*

Chapter Seven

In Decline: 1948-1963

In its first summer timetable British Railways ran 18 trains each way on the branch. The winter 1948 service, from 27th September of that year returned to a fairly lavish level of 19 trains in each direction weekdays only. As usual the first one left at 6.58 am and the late last departure of 10.35 pm each weekday was restored. This returned from Churston at 10.55 pm arriving Brixham 11.02 pm. So, by the time the light engine returned to Newton Abbot, the branch had been open nearly 18 hours.

Although the summer 1949 timetable did not increase this 19-train service, its big surprise was the restoration of the Sunday service, last seen in 1938, and a generous one at that. For this reason the Working Timetable is included. The Sunday service was repeated for the very last time in summer 1950, at which time the weekday service was improved to 20 (SX) and 21 (SO) trains each way.

The timetable introduced from 25th September, 1950 was practically identical to that of 1948. An interesting feature of the relevant working book was that Sunday service was shown, marked 'Suspended', except for the following, which were 'RR' (run as required):

5.45 pm EBV (Engine & Brake van) Kingswear-Brixham arr. 6.05 pm
6.45 pm Fish Brixham-Newton Abbot (at Churston 6.52/7.02 pm)

In February 1951, because of a national coal shortage, the Government insisted the railways reduce their consumption of coal. A supplement dated 12th February, 1951 showed the withdrawal of many trains on Western Region and against Churston to Brixham indicated 'service suspended'. However, it is fairly certain that there was a change of heart on this and that the service was reduced to the following basic seven trains each way, rather than completely shut down:

Churston to Brixham: 8.25, 11.07, 11.40 am, 12.35, 1.28, 3.48, 4.50 pm
Brixham to Churston: 8.03, 10.25, 11.23 am, 12.15, 12.50, 3.15, 4.30 pm

The next supplement (1st April) shows these trains 're-instated' but Jim Cook, who was the Brixham-based fireman from 1945-1959, is certain the line did not close, as he would have remembered having 'a holiday'. It is thought therefore that the above service ran throughout but that it had to be 'reinstated' in April as the previous supplement had withdrawn all trains. The remaining (not yet reinstated) trains in the timetable were shown withdrawn from 1st May, 1951.

The summer 1951 service originally intended to run from 18th June-23rd September, but subsequently cut back to 9th September, reflected the previous standard of service:

Churston to Brixham: 7.15, 8.25, 9.15, 10.00, 11.07, 11.40 (SX), 11.55 (SO) am, 12.35, 1.30, 2.10, 2.40, 3.08(SO), 3.46, 4.17, 4.50, 5.55, 6.48, 7.35, 8.43, 9.15, 10.05, 10.55 pm.
Brixham to Churston: 6.58, 8.03, 8.55, 9.30 (SO), 9.35 (SX), 10.17 (SO), 10.25 (SX), 11.23 am, 12.10, 12.50, 1.45, 2.22, 2.52 (SO), 3.20, 3.58, 4.34, 5.30, 6.10, 7.15, 8.05, 9.00, 9.45, 10.35 pm.

(SX) = Saturdays excepted, (SO) = Saturdays only.

BRIXHAM BRANCH.

Single Line, worked by Electric Train Token. All Down Trains must stop dead at the Down Home Signal for Brixham. All Up Trains entering the Bay Line must stop dead at the Home Signal at Churston. The Train must afterwards be steadily drawn to the platform.

DOWN TRAINS.

WEEK DAYS.

Distance.	STATIONS.	Ruling Gradient.	Time Allowances for Ordinary Freight Trains.			K	B	B	B	B	B	B	B	B	B	B	B	B	B
			Point-to-Point Times.	Allow for Stop.	Allow for Start.	Frght	Auto.	Auto.	Auto.	Auto.	Auto.	Auto.	Auto.	Auto.	Auto.	Auto.	Auto.	Auto.
M. C.			Mins.	Mins.	Mins.					SO			SO		SX	SO		
—	Churston ...... dep.	85 R.	—	—	—	a.m. 5 30	a.m. 7 15	a.m. 8 25			a.m. 9 40	a.m. 11 7			a.m. 11 40		p.m. 12 35	p.m. 1 30
1 26	Stop Board ::	79 F.	3	1	1	P	—	—			—	—			11 55		—	—
1 69½	Stop Board ::	78 F.	3	1	1	P	—	—			—	—			—		—	—
2 1	Brixham ...... arr.		2 17	1	1	5 45	7 22	8 32			9 47	11 14			11 47		12 42	1 37

SUNDAYS.

	B	B	B	B	B
	Auto.	Auto.	Auto.	Auto.	Auto.
Churston dep.		p.m. 12 5	p.m. 1 40	p.m. 3 10	p.m. 3 50
		—	—	—	—
		—	—	—	—
Brixham arr.		12 12	1 47	3 17	3 57

WEEK DAYS. (continued)

STATIONS.		Frght SX	B Auto. SX	B Auto.	B Auto.	B Auto.	B Auto.	B Auto.	B Auto.	B Auto. SO	B Auto. SX	B Auto.	B Auto.
Churston .... dep.		p.m. 1 54	p.m. 2 10	p.m. 4 50	p.m. 5 55		p.m. 6 45		p.m. 7 33	p.m. 7 50	p.m. 8 43	p.m. 9 15	p.m. 10 5
Stop Board		P	—	—	—		—		—	—	—	—	—
Stop Board		P	—	—	—		—		—	—	—	—	—
Brixham .... arr.		2 9	2 17	4 57	6 2		6 52		7 42	7 57	8 50	9 22	10 12

B Auto.	B Auto.
p.m. 10 55	p.m. 11
—	—
—	—
11 2	11

SUNDAYS. (continued)

B Auto.	B Auto.	B Auto.	B Auto.
p.m. 4 35	p.m. 5 20	p.m. 6 45	p.m. 7 40
—	—	—	—
4 42	5 27	6 52	7 47

UP TRAINS.

WEEK DAYS.

M.P. Mileage.	STATIONS.	Ruling Gradient.	Time Allowances for Ordinary Freight Trains.			B	B	B	B	B	B	B	B	B	B	B
			Point-to-Point Times.	Allow for Stop.	Allow for Start.		Auto.	Auto.	Auto.	Auto.	Auto.	Auto.	Auto.	Auto.	Auto.	Auto.
M. C.			Mins.	Mins.	Mins.						SO	SX	SO		
227 2	Brixham .... dep.	78 R.	7	2	1	a.m. 6 58	a.m. 8 3	a.m. 8 55		a.m. 10 15	a.m. 10 25	a.m. 11 23	a.m. 11 30	p.m. 12 15	p.m. 12 50
228 1	Churston .... arr.					7 5	8 10	9 2		10 22	10 32	11 30	10 57	12 22	12 57

SUNDAYS.

B	B	B	B
Auto.	Auto.	Auto.	Auto.
p.m. 1 20	p.m. 2 45	p.m. 3 30	p.m. 4 15
1 27	2 52	3 37	4 22

WEEK DAYS. (continued)

STATIONS.	B Auto. SX	B Auto.	B Auto.	B Auto.	K Newt'n Abbot Frght SX	B Auto.	B Auto.	B Auto.	B G Engine
Brixham .... dep.	p.m. 1 45	p.m. 2 33	p.m. 3 20	p.m. 4 5	p.m. 3 40	p.m. 4 34	p.m. 5 30	p.m. 6 10	p.m. 7 15
Churston .... arr.	1 52	2 42	3 27	4 12	3 50	4 41	5 37	6 17	7 22

B Auto.	Auto.	Engine
p.m. 8 5	p.m. 9 45	p.m. 11 10
8 12	9 52	11 17

SUNDAYS. (continued)

B Auto.	Auto.	B Auto.
p.m. 5	p.m. 6 25	p.m. 7 5
5 2	6 32	7 12

R.—Runs 15 minutes earlier on Saturdays.

Summer 1949 Working timetable with reintroduced Sunday service.

The 10.35 pm ex-Brixham ran for the last time on 8th September; never again was Brixham to have such a late train. Nor for that matter did the 6.58 am ever run again, 'first trains' in future being about 8 am.

In his book *Torbay Story*, published in 1951, Eric Delderfield says that

> . . . for the last ten years (the 'Whippet') had accomplished the trip 23 times daily, carrying an average of five passengers each time. It is regarded by affection by all who have cause to use it.

From 10th September, 1951 the basic seven-train service, practically identical to February-June 1951, was reintroduced. This continued a fortnight longer than in 1951 to 30th June, 1952 when a less generous summer service was introduced, which ran until 14th September:

Churston to Brixham: 8.25, 9.13 (SO), 9.45 (SO), 11.07, 11.40 am, 12.33, 1.28, 1.55 (SO), 2.50 (SO), 3.43, 4.15(SO), 4.50(SX), 4.55(SO), 5.55 (SO), 6.30 (SO), 7.05 (SO), 7.35 (SO), 8.30 (SO) pm

Brixham to Churston: 8.00 (SO), 8.03 (SX), 8.55 (SO), 9.30 (SO), 10.15 (SO), 10.25 (SX), 11.23 am, 12.15, 12.45 (SO), 12.50 (SX), 1.40, 2.30 (SO), 3.15, 3.57 (SO), 4.30, 5.25 (SO), 6.08 (SO), 6.45 (SO), 7.20 (SO), 8.10 (SO) pm

Notice that the SX service was practically the same as the winter, and a far worse service than the 1950 winter service before the fuel cuts.

As might be expected these severe cuts had a dramatic effect on passenger ticket sales. For the years 1939-1945 an average of 607 season and 25,800 ordinary tickets had been sold each year. For 1946-1950 the average was 357 season and 14,600 ordinary tickets. In 1951 season tickets dropped to 300 and ordinary tickets almost halved to 7,700; 1952 was even worse with 210 seasons and 7,241 ordinary tickets. The pre-1951 ticket sales' figures were never returned to in the rest of the branch's life.

That winter (1952) the seven-train service was increased to eight each way and summer 1953 was similar to 1952 with the last departure from Brixham still at 4.30 pm, except on Saturdays. A ninth up train was introduced in winter 1953. Although fairly similar to 1952 and 1953, the 1954 summer timetable is reproduced in full because it is from the working book and shows all movements.

The winter book from 20th September, 1954 gave a slightly improved winter service of 10 trains each way, weekdays only, leaving Brixham between 8.03 am and 4.30 pm. In June 1955 the last train from Brixham (SX) became 5.10 pm, and this became the 'last train' in all subsequent winter timetables until dieselisation.

By the summer period 1957 the train service had been restored to a more reasonable level. On Mondays to Fridays there were 12 trains each way with the last departure from Brixham at a more sensible 6.30 pm (this train had been restored in summer 1956). On Saturdays the service expanded to 17 each way, the last train leaving Brixham at 8.40 pm.

That summer there was a Devon General bus strike. During the seven days in July 1957, no less than 15,192 passengers were carried on the branch, according to figures in Brixham Museum. This is more than would normally be carried in the entire summer service! See accompanying photograph of a train from Brixham during this period conveying three trailers and a parcels van.

BRIXHAM BRANCH.

Single Line, worked by Electric Train Token. All Down Trains must stop dead at the Down Home Signal for Brixham. All Up Trains entering the Bay Line must stop dead at the Home Signal at Churston. The Train must afterwards be steadily drawn to the platform.

DOWN TRAINS.

WEEK DAYS.

Distance.		STATIONS.	Ruling Gradient.	Time Allowances for Ordinary Freight Trains.				K	G	K	Auto. SO SX	Auto. SO	Auto. SO	Auto. SX	B	B	Auto.	Auto.	Auto.		
				Point-to-Point Times.	Allow for Stop.	Allow for Start.			Fr'ght SO	N'ton Abbot Engine SX	Fr'ght SX										
M.	C.			Mins.	Mins.	Mins.		7|5 a.m.	a.m.	a.m.	a.m.	a.m.	a.m.	a.m.	a.m.	a.m.	11 40	12 33	p.m. 1 25		
—	20	Churston......dep.	95 R.	3	1	1	7 0	7|40	8 25	9 15	9 10	9 45	11 0	11 7							
1	69½	Stop Board	79 F.	3	1	1	—	—	—	—	—	—	11 7	—			—	—	—		
2	1	Stop Board	78 F.	1	1	—	—	—	—	—	—	—	—	—			—	—	—		
		Brixham......arr.					7 15	7|47	8 32	9 30	9 17	9 52	11 14	11 14			11 47	12 40	1 32		

n 19th August, 1953 '14XX' No. 1466 waits to leave with the 12.15 pm to Churston. At least one
sh truck is attached behind the auto-coach.   *The late J.W.T. House*

n 12th May, 1954 '14XX' class 0-4-2T No. 1427 hurries past Churston's fixed distant on its way
ere from Brixham with a mixed train (the freight part only consisting of a brake van), likely to
e the 10.20 service. Notice that compared with Peter Gray's photograph of six years later, the
st of the signal is made of wood and the signal itself is slightly closer to Churston, on that side
Elberry Lane bridge.   *Courtesy Brixham Museum*

There cannot have been many occasions in its entire history when Churston had five engines there in steam at the same time (excluding double-headings of course). In July 1954 '45XX' class 2-6-2T No. 5552 arrives with a local to Kingswear, while 'Manor' class 4-6-0 No. 7824 *Ilford Manor* waits in the down refuge with a parcels train for Kingswear and another '45XX' 2-6-2T is in the branch siding with a very short goods (possibly for Brixham). No. 1466 is waiting at the up branch home signal to enter the station, and has a fish truck at rear to be attached to the next up train. It may have already been in the bay, unloaded, and is now waiting for the down train (No. 5552) to clear before attaching its truck to a train from Kingswear. Another goods, with a pannier tank at its head, looks like it has been put away in Churston yard, until it can resume its journey.
The late J.W.T. House

Seen soon after leaving Churston on 8th August, 1955, an auto-train headed by '14XX' class No. 1427 accelerates smartly towards Brixham. The Bridge Road overbridge is just out of sight extreme left.
R.E. Toop

t an unknown date in the 1950s, 0-4-2T No. 1466, hauling two trailers and propelling a fish uck, blows off impatiently as it awaits departure to Brixham. *D.K. & M. James Collection*

his could be just after or just before a school run (two trailers), or it could be a summer's day, ut the platform is almost deserted. '14XX' class No. 1452 was not a frequent visitor, the author nnot recall seeing it at all. Note the shunting pole awaiting its next duty in the roof support llar. The white painted chimneys beyond the coal wagons belong to the Queen's Hotel in S. rzeham Road. *D.K. & M. James Collection*

Although this happened daily, photographs of a mixed train are rare. Here trailer W222W head
a mixed working awaiting departure from Brixham. Note the unusual totem attached to the ga
lamp above the gents' toilets   *David Lawrence (Hugh Davies Colln*

The arrival at Churston of the mixed train, here revealed to be powered by No. 1427, seer
standing at Brixham platform in the top picture. A large amount of luggage and mails has beer
unloaded from the luggage compartment. When it is ready, the freight portion will be shuntec
to Churston yard.   *David Lawrence (Hugh Davies Colln*

4XX' class 0-4-2T No. 1439 receives some admiring looks from schoolchildren as it waits at
'ixham on 20th June, 1957.   *J.R. Bonser*

Brixham train taking water in the bay at Churston on 20th June, 1957.   *J.R. Bonser*

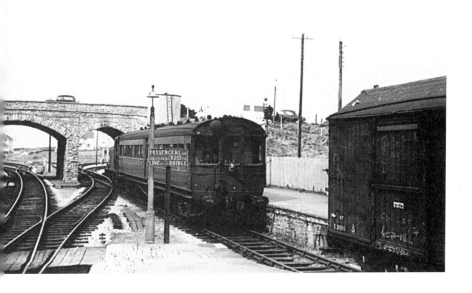

On Saturday 27th July, 1957, during a provincial bus strike, class '14XX' 0-4-2T No. 1466 hurrie
the 12.15 pm from Brixham with its unusually heavy load of three trailers and a parcels va
towards Churston. The leading vehicle is crossing the east end entrance to Northfield Siding
(disused since 1951). Station master Stan Cook leans out of the trailer driving vestibule window
probably wishing it was always like this!   *Courtesy Brixham Museum*

A busy scene at Brixham on 19th September, 1957, following the arrival of the 11.07 am from
Churston, to form the 11.23 departure; 1466 and trailer W240W. If only all the trains had loade
this heavily.   *T. Wrigh*

The winter book showed 11 trains each way, weekdays only, departures from Brixham ranging between 8.03 am and 5.10 pm. During this period the 8.25 am Churston-Brixham and 10.15 am Brixham-Churston were mixed trains, no exclusively freight service was scheduled. Brixham signal box opened at 7.30 am for the day's train service.

In 1958 the Western Region withdrew hundreds of 'lightly loaded and unremunerative passenger services' (from 30th June), but the Kingswear line was almost unscathed and the Brixham branch was completely unaffected. As in summer 1957 12 (SX) and 17 (SO) trains ran each way at practically identical timings.

Between 20th and 26th September, 1958 the electric token working on the Brixham branch was replaced by a wooden train staff and 'one engine in steam' operation, which had been the method used before 1899. Brixham signal box was closed and all signals there removed, except the down distant, retained as a marker. The down home signal was replaced by a stop board at which all trains had to stop dead, before drawing slowly into the station or yard. The engine shed siding was taken out of use and all remaining connections in the main line worked from new East and West ground frames, locked by the wooden staff. This simplification, apart from saving the cost of the signalmen and maintenance of the equipment, meant that it was no longer possible to have more than one train at Brixham at a time.

The winter period of 1958 again adopted the 11-train service, but this time the mixed trains were 7.35 am ex-Churston and 10. 15 am ex-Brixham. In addition there was a 'Q' (ran if required) empty railmotor 5.50 pm Churston-Brixham which returned with a 6.07 pm 'Q' fish train from Brixham to Churston. The summer 1959 timetable was again 12 (SX) and 17 (SO) trains each way. Because of a printing strike that year the winter timetable was not issued until 2nd November but a supplement introduced the standard 11-train winter service from 14th September.

Following this, in October 1959, the 4,000 gallon water tank measuring 12 ft x 12 ft x 6 ft and standing on 19 ft iron columns, and now, of course, inaccessible to engines, was offered for sale. Said to be 'in fair condition except that the bottom has been concreted' and weighing an estimated 7 tons, a Torquay scrap dealer bought it for £4 per ton and the costs (to himself) of its removal.* There is an amusing tailpiece to this story, which will be related when describing the closure of the branch.

In 1959, well before Beeching, the Regions were looking at what they called unremunerative railway services. Surprisingly, a report on the Brixham branch, produced on 7th July, 1959, used revenue figures as old as for the 12 months ended 31st December, 1956. Contributory revenue was counted and passenger traffic in and out earned £21,450 (53,469 journeys), parcels forwarded and received earned £18,915 and freight (pretty well all 'received') £11,986.

The sums were done by balancing the immediate, short term and long term annual savings achieved by closure (£6,653) against the estimated loss of receipts and extra costs elsewhere (£10,729). A discreet inquiry of Torbay Trawlers Ltd (not disclosing the reason for asking!) had indicated that there would be total loss of their traffic, valued at £6,000, to rail if the branch closed.

* Perhaps the concreting had reduced its capacity because it was said to be 5,500 gallons when installed.

For a short while in July/August 1958 an 'auto-sandwich' ran on the Brixham branch comprising 0-4-2T No. 1470 and trailers W222W and W240W (here leading, photographed on Saturday in August 1958). In the yard two single-deck buses, one Devon General the other Burton Cars, await passengers for the holiday camps in Brixham.   *(Both) L.F. Folkard*

On 4th September, 1959 0-4-2T No. 1470 propelling its trailer approaches Churston with the 12.15 pm from Brixham.   *T. Wright*

On 13th August, 1955 the down 'Torbay Express', headed by 'Castle' class 4-6-0 No. 5028 *Llantilio Castle*, makes its penultimate call at Churston, while '14XX' 0-4-2T No. 1427 and trailer W222W await departure with the connection to Brixham.   *R.E. Toop*

On 2nd September, 1959 0-4-2T No. 1470 propelling a trailer and hauling a fish truck forming the 12.15 pm from Brixham runs into the down main platform at Churston. After any passengers have left it will await the arrival of the 12.15 pm from Kingswear, hauled by 'Castle' No. 4037 (*see below*) and attach the truck to its rear.   *T. Wright*

'Castle' class 4-6-0 No. 4037 *The South Wales Borderers* leaves Churston with the 12.15 pm Kingswear to Exeter on 2nd September, 1959. The leading three coaches in BR chocolate and cream will be attached to the 'Cornishman' at Exeter. The Brixham train is out of sight at its rear having attached the fish truck seen in the other photo, and will leave the down main platform at 12.33 pm.   *T. Wright*

The two figures above therefore showed an annual loss to BR of £4,076 if the branch closed, and it was kept open. The Accountant had said that further savings could be made; for an outlay of £14,500 on a single diesel power car, a net annual improvement of £1,939 in working costs would be obtained, and this was recommended [but not implemented, probably because the car was not available, until 1961]. (As a matter of interest, for the reader to make comparison, the replacement costs for the '14XX' locomotive were shown as £8,034 and the trailer £5,963.) Other interesting facts included in the report were that fish traffic forwarded in 1958 had earned £10,000 and that Northfield Sidings had last been used in 1951. The reduction of the signalling from electric token to one engine in steam in 1958 had already reduced staff costs by £879 pa.

The 1960 summer service again adopted the well tried formula of 12 (SX) and 17 (SO) trains but an innovation was the introduction of a 3-car diesel unit for the Saturday service. This was brought down attached to the 6.20 am Newton Abbot to Kingswear, and uncoupled at Churston. After working the last up service from Brixham at 8.40 pm the unit returned empty to Newton Abbot, leaving Churston at 9.05 pm. The winter service 1960, as introduced, was the same as the previous two years.

It had been intended to dieselise the Brixham service from 30th January, 1961 but a temporary shortage of diesel stock prevented this. The last steam passenger train left Brixham at 5.10 pm on Saturday 4th March (locomotive 1470) and a single car diesel commenced operation the following Monday. The 7 am Newton Abbot to Paignton was extended to Churston to form the first branch service leaving the junction at 7.40 am. The former 'Q' paths for fish traffic in the evening became passenger trains from the same date, leaving Churston at 5.50 pm and Brixham at 6.07 pm - this gave a 12-train service in each direction. The single power car returned empty from Churston to Newton Abbot. Now there was no fireman, guards, withdrawn in 1930, were reinstated.

One other consequence of dieselisation was that it was no longer possible to run mixed trains to convey freight traffic, mainly coal, to Brixham and return the empties. Fish vans of course could still be coupled to the passenger trains. A new early morning goods service on Mondays, Wednesdays and Fridays only was introduced. This left Goodrington yard at 5.17 am and after running round at Churston arrived at Brixham at 5.45 am. A variety of motive power worked this trip from 0-6-0 pannier tanks to 2-6-2 tanks and 'D63XX' class diesels. The author who lived right opposite the station can recall many early mornings disturbed by the shunting of coal trucks, particularly when a steam engine was working the freight. Departure was at 6.15 am or when work was finished and, after attaching any empties, etc. at Churston, the junction was left at 6.42 am arriving Goodrington 6.52 am.

The 1961 timetables were little changed but one extra train ran Saturdays excepted during the summer, a 13-train service. A survey taken that July revealed that on Mondays to Fridays during the summer an average of 137 passengers used all the daily trains from Brixham and 172 from Churston. July Saturdays were better, however, with an average user of 245 from Brixham and 379 from Churston.

On 11th March, 1960 '14XX' class 0-4-2T No. 1470 has just passed over the bridge over Elberry Lane with the 11.05 am Churston to Brixham. Churston's up fixed distant is just to the rear of the train. In the background the line curves left towards a cutting and Bridge Road overbridge.
Peter W. Gray

On a fine spring day 0-4-2T No. 1470 is coming off the curve between Churston Road and Bascombe Road bridges and is entering Bascombe Road cutting, about midway between Churston and Brixham, with the 12.35 pm from Churston on 30th April, 1960. *Peter W. Gray*

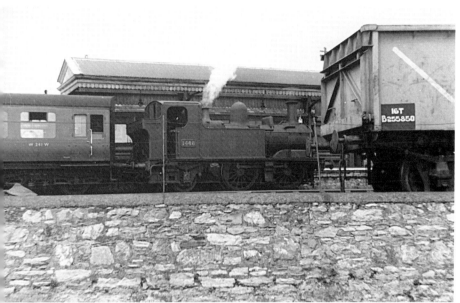

In June 1960 No. 1466 and trailer W241W wait between trips at Brixham.   *Author*

Midway between Brixham and Churston, approaching Bascombe Road cutting 0-4-2T No. 1470 is working the 11.25 am Churston to Brixham service on the last day of steam, 4th March, 1961. This train connected with the up 'Torbay Express' at Churston.   *Courtesy Brixham Museum*

This is Churston at Whitsun 1962, obviously very wet. Although train details are not available the author having consulted the Working timetable considers these are the 8.30 am Paignton t Kingswear 'B set' (down main), 8.35 am Kingswear to Newton Abbot, to which the signalma has just handed the token, up main, with its rear portion for the up 'Mayflower' at Newto behind two non-corridor coaches; both of these trains are hauled by 'D63XX' diesel-hydraulics The 8.50 to Brixham waits in the bay.   *Roger Holmes (Hugh Davies Colln*

On 13th August, 1962 the signalman (thought to be Jim 'Ginger' Brown) prepares to receive th token from the fireman of 'Hall' class 4-6-0 No. 4996 *Eden Hall* arriving with a three coac portion detached at Newton Abbot from an express to Plymouth or beyond. In the up platfor D6338 waits the 'road' with an up freight from Kingswear. The single car for Brixham waits i the bay for connecting passengers. In less than a year such rail connection will no longer exist
R.E. Too

Perhaps the last opportunity for the branch to prove its worth came in the summer of 1961 when Devon General again went on strike, from midday Saturday 5th August. The strike was over the withdrawal of a penny-an-hour bonus for maintenance men. However, because the bus drivers and conductors were traditionally members of the National Union of Railwaymen (because of the links with the railways in the 1930s), higher management was not prepared to run extra trains; the shunters at Exeter had walked out for a time in protest at extra stops in some trains. For that reason 'pleas made by the station master at Brixham to run additional diesel services were refused, as were several others' [Divisional correspondence]. However, the author can recall that the branch trains during this period were exceptionally heavy as it was the only way to reach Brixham, except by the *Western Lady* ferry service or taxi.

Notes made at the time show that in the winter 1961 timetable, diesel single power cars W55000, W55013 and W55019 took their turn on the branch. The driver and guard worked on the branch from 7.40 am-12.27 pm (early turn) and 12.33-6.12 pm (late turn). Any fish trucks for 'local' destinations, Exeter, Plymouth or Cornwall, Bristol or Cardiff usually left attached to the 1.05 pm departure, while fish for London always left attached to the last train, at 6.05 pm.

In February 1962 the Exeter District Unremunerative Railway Services Committee produced its report on the Brixham branch. Its opening statement said it all: 'Proposal - Complete closure'. Average numbers of passengers conveyed daily in 1961 were as follows:

	Winter M-F	Winter Sats	Summer M-F	Summer Sats
Churston to Brixham	43	61	174	381
Brixham to Churston	46	43	141	252

Costs, including staff and train movement came to £9,006 pa and additionally £1,095 pa set against eventual renewal of the diesel car would be avoided. Against this was £3,773 pa estimated loss of receipts and £67 extra cartage costs (parcels deliveries from Churston) giving an estimated net saving of £6,261 by closing the branch. No fish traffic was anticipated to be lost - it would be taken to Churston by the senders. Furthermore £13,155 in repairs to permanent way, buildings and roads would be saved between 1962 and 1966.

Under the heading 'Possibility of making the passenger service remunerative' the report said: 'The branch line is too short and offers little, if any, scope for development in spite of the introduction last year of diesel working. The competing bus service is frequent and far more convenient than rail . . .'

Inwards freight had totalled 4,664 tons in the last 12 months, all but 90 tons of this being coal to three merchants, one of whom had ceased receiving coal by rail in that time. This would all come to Churston in future.

Under 'Recommendations' the report said:

It is doubtful whether this branch line has ever been an economic proposition for the conveyance of passengers only and its survival has been in the past entirely dependent upon the revenue derived from the despatch of fish.

Since 1957 the volume of fish has consistently declined, receipts were £8,645 in 1957 and £4,850 for the last 12 months ended 30th September, 1961.

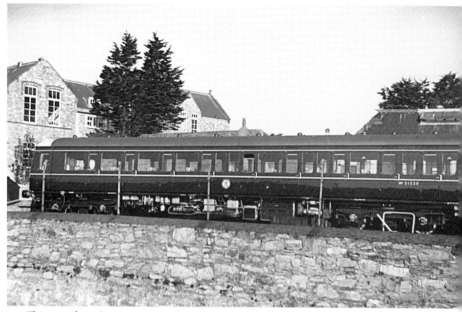

This must have been a summer Saturday as a 3-car dmu is waiting to work the first departure of the day from Brixham (1962). *Author*

Memories! A cheerful group in 1962 (*left to right*): author in unofficial working garb, supernumary porter, porter Stan Goddard, driver (possibly 'learning the traction'), driver Bob Wise in the fairly short-lived green 'Diesel uniform'. *Author's Collection*

The fish would be sent from Churston (there was definite resistance from the wholesalers to take it to Paignton). Why was there such a change from the fish merchants' previous stance? Coal would be unloaded at Churston and the buses could cope with the passengers.

So that was it. What a difference from 1959 when due account was taken of inwards traffic which obviously added to the well being of the organisation as a whole.

Unsurprisingly, on 18th April, 1962 the Western Region Board approved complete closure, despite the fact that the annual net savings were now declared as 'not less than £4,800' rather than the £6,261 of the report (amongst other changes, 'estimated loss of receipts' had increased from £3,773 to £4,504). The case was submitted to the Transport Users' Consultative Committee (TUCC) for rubber stamping ('consideration', officially) by the end of the month. Many written objections were received, one objector suggesting through trains should be run to Paignton in the summer. This would have been quite feasible with the single diesel car, and like the Henley branch today where off-peak trains run through to Reading after many years of running to and from the branch junction at Twyford only, may have helped to halt declining passenger loadings and stimulate fresh traffic. Passengers detraining at Paignton would have been less likely to take the bus, had there been a train to take them direct to Brixham station, from where they could have taken a taxi to final destination (which they had to do at Brixham bus station anyway). But this is all conjecture, we shall never know whether it would have helped.

To their credit, Brixham UDC were completely against closure, Mr W.A. Saxton, Town Clerk, pointing out that the capacity of the roads into Brixham, and possibly the capacity of public road transport, were insufficient, also that the proposed goods termini at Paignton and Churston were 'unsuitable, too distant and too inconveniently sited for the proper service of the public'. A later letter said that people were quoting half-an-hour spent in bus queues at Paignton during May and June that year.

Drew Street Coal Co. said they would take all their sea-borne coal from Teignmouth (port) by road in future, 70 trucks last year, thereby adding to the already overcrowded roads. Another 120 trucks came from the Midlands, etc. collieries and this fuel would have to be roaded from Churston. They wanted coal to continue to come in to Brixham, two or three times a week.

Another objector pointed out that Brixham's population had grown by 22 per cent since 1951. Unfortunately, as BR pointed out in its reply, only ½ per cent of the population were using the train in the winter. Single fares from Brixham to Churston at this time were 7d. by road and 9d. by rail. A table (not part of the papers to the TUCC) showed passenger bookings and revenue from Brixham for 1959-1961:

| | Ordinary | | Season Tickets | |
	No.	£	No.	£
1959	9,100	2,739	76	65
1960	8,509	2,780	69	68
1961	12,402	3,444	71	66

[The 1961 figure was probably enhanced by the Devon General bus strike in August. *Author*]

18th JUNE–9th SEPTEMBER 1962 (Last summer of operation)

Weekdays only (Second class only)

Churston – Brixham (down)

	am SO	am SX	am SX	am SO	am SX	am SO	am SO	am SO	am SO	am SX	am SO	pm SX	pm SO	pm SX	pm SO
Churston . dep.	7.25	7.40	8.10	8.15	8.50	9.15	9.45	10.20	11.00	11.05	11.40	12.10	12.15	12.40	12.50
Brixham....arr.	7.32	7.47	8.17	8.22	8.57	9.22	9.52	10.27	11.07	11.12	11.47	12.17	12.22	12.47	12.57

Brixham – Churston (up)

	am SO	am SX	am SX	am SO	am SO	am SO	am SO	am SO	am SO	am SX	noon SO	pm SX	pm SO	pm SX	pm SO
Brixham... dep.	7.43	7.55	8.36	9.00	‥	9.30	10.00	10.45	11.15	11.55	12.00	12.21	12.30	1.20	1.25
Churston ...arr.	7.50	8.02	8.43	9.07	….	9.37	10.07	10.52	11.22	12.02	12.07	12.28	12.37	1.27	1.32

Churston – Brixham (down)

	pm SX	pm SO	pm SX	pm SO	pm SO	pm SX	pm	pm	pm SX	pm SX	pm SO	pm SX	pm SO	pm SO	pm SO
Churston . dep.	1.38	1.45	2.40	3.08	3.42	3.50	4A22	4B47	5.15	5.45	5.50	‥	7.00	8.28	9.15
Brixham....arr.	1.45	1.52	2.47	3.15	3.49	3.57	4A29	4B54	5.22	5.52	5.57	….	7.07	8.35	9.22

Brixham – Churston (up)

	pm SX	pm SO	pm SX	pm SO	pm SO	pm	pm	pm SX	pm SO	pm SO	pm SX	pm SO	pm SO
Brixham... dep.	1.53	2.40	3.15	3.20	4.05	4B33	5B27	6.00	6.25	‥	7.50	8.40	9.28
Churston ...arr.	2.00	2.47	3.22	3.27	4.12	4B40	5B34	6.07	6.32	….	7.57	8.47	9.35

A = 2 minutes later (SO); B = 3 minutes later (SO)

Also contained in the BR general information not presented to the TUCC was a note that on 18th June, 1962 unemployment in Brixham stood at 7.3 per cent, whereas the unemployment figures for Devon and Great Britain were both 1.8 per cent.

A census carried out during June 1962 showed that tail traffic (of fish vans) was being conveyed by the 7.40 am and 12.40 pm ex-Churston (empty vans) and the 1.05 and 6.05 pm ex-Brixham. During week ending 9th June, 1962 six loaded fish vans were dispatched, one by the 1.05 pm (Mon) and one each day by the 6.05 pm service (Mon.-Fri.).

What was to be the last summer timetable was introduced on 18th June, 1962 (*see opposite*). The Mondays to Fridays service was the same as before but for some inexplicable reason, considering the proposal to close, the Saturday service was increased by one to 18 each way involving a new late departure at 9.28 pm. This continued through to Newton Abbot leaving Churston at 9.40 pm, only nine minutes in front of the 9.40 pm Kingswear to Newton Abbot! This was the latest service Brixham had had since summer 1951. The unit working the service ran as a passenger train, 7.05 am ex-Newton, Mondays-Fridays, and empty at 5.55 am on Saturdays.

The TUCC hearing was held in Brixham town hall on 16th August, 1962 and on 29th October the TUCC wrote to the Minister of Transport that no real hardship would result from closure, providing that Churston station remained open, and that the bus service to/from Brixham was re-routed into the station yard from the main road. However, it strongly recommended that any decision on closure should be deferred until Dr Beeching's full proposals on line closures throughout the country were available. It also agreed with the strong feeling locally that even a small increase in road congestion in the Torbay area was undesirable (having your cake and eating it?).

The now familiar 13-train winter service began on 10th September (*see below*). Whilst waiting for closure to be approved a short section of track had had to be re-sleepered with second-hand materials. This was due to the Minister of Transport deciding that any branch line closures in the pipeline would be deferred until after publication of the Beeching plan. Otherwise the line could have closed in the autumn of 1962.

Churston to Brixham: 7.44, 8.10, 8.50, 11.05 am, 12.10, 12.40, 1.38, 2.40, 3.50, 4.22, 4.47, 5.15, 5.45 pm.
Brixham to Churston: 7.55, 8.36, 10.45, 11.55 am, 12.21, 1.20, 1.53, 3.15, 4.05, 4.33, 4.59, 5.27, 6.00 pm.

Meanwhile the Bristol divisional manager was getting prepared and asked all concerned to draw up a scheme for the recovery of redundant assets. The drawing office at Swindon (CM&EE) said that scrap merchants might be interested in the water tank at Brixham. Other items of scrap were listed, but thought to be of insufficient value to sell (*see Appendix Seven*, 1962 items). Also, while awaiting the Minister's decision, Brixham Chamber of Trade asked that if Brixham closed, Churston revert to its old name of 'Brixham Road'. Brixham UDC said that this had originally been *their* suggestion, not the Chamber's, and would not support the latter's request *now*, because it pre-supposed closure, but

they wrote separately asking that the name be changed anyway as it would increase the publicity of the branch line and soften the effect if the line did 'ever come to be closed (but my Council are not to be taken as assuming that it will be)'. BR declined the request, saying that there would still be reference to Brixham in the timetable, even if the branch closed.

On 22nd March, 1963 the Minister gave his consent to complete closure 'subject to the [bus] operator providing the services [stated] to augment them as . . . necessary on Saturdays in summer and to arrange for a stopping place in the station yard at Churston'. This wording gave rise to some difficulty. Devon General said that it would be impractical to re-route the normal stage carriage service into Churston yard (access being on a very bad corner on the road overbridge and entailing a steep and narrow incline), although obviously a special service on summer Saturdays could start and finish there. Later, the Secretary of the TUCC clarified matters by stating that the diversion into the yard was intended to cater for the summer Saturday traffic.

On 3rd April, 1963 the announcement finally came; the Brixham branch would close from Monday 13th May, 1963, the last train running two days earlier. Apart from the need for emergency relaying, the delay in announcing the closure also scuppered plans for a train-bus connection from Paignton to Brixham involving through ticketing. A condition of closure was that Churston should be the railhead from Brixham (even though it was listed as a station due for closure in the Beeching Plan). A few *hours* before closure, a notice was posted at Brixham saying that on Saturdays 6th July to 24th August a special bus service would be provided for long distance travellers holding through tickets to Brixham, from Churston to Brixham.

As far as freight was concerned, incoming 'less than wagonload' and delivered traffic would go to Paignton, while 'station to station' traffic in wagonloads, such as coal, would go to Churston. Parcels traffic would be delivered from/taken to Churston, and arrangements for luggage in advance collection could be made at Brixham bus station office.

On 9th April, 1963 the divisional manager told the chief civil engineer that it was necessary to give the Ministry of Power (which controlled Northfield Sidings) three month's notice of termination of their agreement, and therefore no recovery of track could take place within that period.

The funeral of the branch was a subdued affair. This is how the *Western Morning News* reported it:

Fog signals exploded, school children shouted, and flags waved as the last train left Brixham's crowded station on Saturday evening. For a brief moment the branch line was *en fête*.

But the demonstrations were short-lived. They had ceased well before the train completed its two-mile journey through uninteresting cuttings to the junction station at Churston. It was the least eventful branch-line funeral so far.

In the words of a railway inspector: 'We are closing ourselves down too quickly for the interest in last trains to be kept up'.

A railway enthusiast who has not missed a single Westcountry 'burial' complained that the epidemic of closures was heavy on the pocket; he had just spent £1 on miscellaneous tickets - many of them in stock since GWR days - for his collection.

KU3/9/2

A1/106

10th June 1963

(WESTERN REGION)

TRAFFIC DEPARTMENT

GENERAL INSTRUCTIONS CIRCULAR

(PASSENGER & PARCELS)

(5)   WITHDRAWAL OF PASSENGER TRAIN SERVICE BETWEEN CHURSTON AND BRIXHAM

The passenger train service between Churston and Brixham was withdrawn on the 13th May 1963 and passengers for Brixham should be booked to Paignton or Churston.   Through bookings to Brixham may be made **on Saturdays only** during the summer service but this will not apply locally and Day Return tickets must not be issued to Brixham.

Frequent direct alternative road services between Paignton Bus Station (adjacent to Paignton Railway Station), Churston and Brixham are operated by the Devon General Omnibus & Touring Co. Ltd., their stage carriage service No. 12.

Passengers in possession of through rail tickets to Brixham arriving at Paignton or Churston on Saturdays, 22nd June, 29th June, 31st August and 7th September will have their tickets honoured on the Stage Carriage service to Brixham and will be issued with Seat Regulation and bus exchange tickets at the Bus Company's Office in Brixham before they return by bus from Brixham to Churston.

On Saturdays, 6th July to 24th August, 1963 inclusive a special bus service for railway passengers holding through tickets will operate to and from Brixham as under:—

In-coming passengers should alight at Churston where on production of tickets to Brixham they will be directed to the special bus.   Intending passengers from Brixham should obtain rail tickets or produce return rail ticket at the Brixham Bus Station Office, when they will be issued with Seat Regulation tickets which will enable them to travel by the appropriate special buses connecting with trains at Churston Station.

	Brixham Bus Station Dep.	Churston Rly-Station Arr.	Churston Rly-Station Dep.	Brixham Bus Station Arr.
SPECIAL	8.00 a.m.	8.15 a.m.	8.25 a.m.	8.40 a.m.
BUS	8.50 a.m.	9.05 a.m.	9.05 a.m.	9.15 a.m.
SERVICE	9.15 a.m.	9.30 a.m.	9.35 a.m.	9.45 a.m.
FOR	9.45 a.m.	10.00 a.m.	10.05 a.m.	10.20 a.m.
PASSENGERS	10.25 a.m.	10.40 a.m.	10.45 a.m.	11.00 a.m.
HOLDING	11.00 a.m.	11.15 a.m.	11.20 a.m.	11.35 a.m.
THROUGH	11.45 a.m.	12.00 noon	12.05 p.m.	12.25 p.m.
RAIL	1.10 p.m.	1.25 p.m.	As required	
TICKETS	3.00 p.m.	3.15 p.m.	3.20 p.m.	3.35 p.m.
	3.50 p.m.	4.05 p.m.	As required	

Parcels and other passenger rated traffic will be collected and delivered from Churston Station at the rates and distances applicable with Brixham.   Parcels traffic addressed " to be called for " will be dealt with at Churston and must be charged thereto.

The present facilities for the collection and delivery of passengers luggage in advance from and to addresses in Brixham will be maintained and collection orders for such luggage will be accepted at the Brixham Bus Station Office.

(EPR.90499 B.)

Upon arrival at Churston, itself now threatened with closure under the Beeching plan, some of the passengers transferred to the Exeter train. But many left the station to rejoin their cars parked in the yard. Even when it comes to performing last rites for branch lines, the finances of petrol companies benefit more than do the railways.

The *Brixham Chronicle* said:

The last Brixham train ran on Saturday. It left the station at 6 pm full of railway enthusiasts from all over South Devon. Cameras clicked and tape recorders whirred as detonators exploded beneath the wheels of the engine (!). The branch from Churston has served the town since the first train ran in 1868. All traffic will now be dealt with at Churston.

In the eight busiest weeks of summer the D.G. Bus Co. will run a Special Saturday service from Churston to Brixham. This will operate from July 6th to August 24th.

To add insult to injury the new timetable for the summer period 1963 showed a service on the Brixham line with an additional Saturdays-only service, making 19 each way! The last Saturday up train would have been at 9.13 pm.

Reverting to the redundant assets saga, on 10th May, 1963 the local M&EE manager at Plymouth told the CM&EE at Swindon that there were no assets at Brixham, 'the water tank, water crane and yard crane having been sold to a local scrap merchant some two or three years ago'. This caused especial concern to the chief civil engineer because they had been included in the contract with the scrap material removal contractor, and the contract would have to be adjusted. The divisional manager, now at Plymouth, was asked to sort the matter out and reply. In his reply on 7th November, the latter said that the water tank and jib had been sold in January 1960, while the elevator, pump and water wheel had been removed in 1957 and the site occupied by the pump house subsequently redeveloped. In a separate letter, a month later, he reported the crane was *still there*. Meanwhile, a few day's later the CM&EE, agreeing that the assets had been removed earlier, apologised to the civil engineer for not keeping his records up to date. And a list from his department dated 17th December, 1963 confirmed the crane had been sold in 1960! In the author's view there must have been many mistakes like this, such was the rush to close branch lines at this period.

The divisional manager, Plymouth replied to a letter from the (railway) district estate surveyor on 16th July, 1963 to the effect that the coal merchants had 'nearly vacated the site' (although they had been allowed until the end of 1963 to do so), adding that 'This is an extremely valuable site'.

It was not quite the end, however, because that summer Michael Winner was filming *The System* in the Torbay area and, under the heading 'Station Re-opened', the *Brixham Chronicle* of 6th September, 1963 reported:

The System, the feature film being shot in the Torbay area, is providing a source of amusement and employment for many residents.

At the weekend the film unit was at Brixham railway station, re-opened and renamed Roxham for the occasion. Scenes involving three of the stars, Jane Merrow, Andrew Ray and Oliver Reed, were shot.

BR provided an engine, coaches and station staff. Local people joined in as extras.

Although a rather gloomy picture it is included because Brixham station is viewed from a rather different angle. It is likely to be a summer Saturday because a 3-car dmu is in the platform; these were introduced in 1960. Note the foundations of the former goods shed in the foreground.

Courtesy Brixham Museum

The scene when the feature film 'The System' (director Michael Winner) was filmed in September 1963. The station has been renamed 'Roxham'.   *Author*

The engine was a 'D63XX' class diesel, and the coaches ordinary main line stock, something that had never happened whilst the line was open, although a 'D63XX' did haul the freight trips after dieselisation.

A letter from the HQ management accountant to the chief civil engineer dated 13th February, 1964 said that formal approval had now been given to the recovery of redundant assets between 225 m. 19 ch. and 227 m. 6 ch. (the buffer stops at Brixham) by J.N. Connell Ltd at a cost of £12,000 (coincidentally the same amount as the GWR paid for it); recovered materials were valued at £20,000, including £6,800 for rails, leaving a surplus for BR of £8,000. To this was added £30, the proceeds from the Ministry of Power Northfield Siding site recoveries, after allowing for costs of recovery.

A review of the special buses on Saturdays in 1963 was carried out early in 1964 and noted that carryings were 'comparatively small'. The divisional manager attempted to get the bus transfer point altered to Paignton, at which point it was felt the ordinary service, augmented as necessary, could cope, without recourse to special hired buses. He wrote to the Secretary of the TUCC asking for the Minister to be approached for a variation to his previous consent. Unfortunately, before such consent was given, he issued separate instructions that passengers for Brixham should change at Paignton. This was objected to most strongly by Brixham UDC and the Chamber of Trade. Paddington became involved and instructed that the arrangements issued re changing at Paignton must be withdrawn and the *status quo* maintained.

In view of the light loadings of the special buses in 1963, surprisingly the 1964 proposals were for an enhanced service of 13 buses from Brixham and 14 from Churston, between 8 am and 7.10 pm, from 4th July to 22nd August. However, steps were being taken to let passengers arriving without through tickets to be allowed on the buses - the previous year they had been simply turned away by the Devon General inspectors, despite the representations of the Churston station master!

A subsequent review of these bus loadings for 1964 provided the following figures (totals for the day shown on *all* buses):

4th July: 44; 11th July: 97; 18th July: 107; 25th July: 102; 1st August: 94; 8th August: 72; 15th August: 114; 22nd August: 92.

In the same way as the summer Saturday figures for the trains used to show, the heavier loadings were always from the Churston end; for example on 4th July only 4 out of 44 were from Brixham and on 18th July only 24 out of 107 used the buses from Brixham. At a meeting of divisional management with Devon General on 20th November, it was agreed to have another go at making Paignton the railhead for Brixham.

However, similar arrangements applied in 1965 with a 12 return journeys' service, although it was run for two weeks longer than before (until 4th September). Loadings for the 10 weeks totalled 897 passengers (722 for eight weeks in 1964). No further details are to be found on the file, but the special service was still running in 1969, a BR/Devon General meeting that July bemoaning the 'extremely low' loadings and this was, in fact, the last year that it ran. (Since April 1966, the main line from Paignton to Kingswear had been

Some of the new houses built at the site of Brixham station, seen in 1986. Furzeham School is still instantly recognisable in the background.   *Author*

operated as a shuttle service the only exception being the summer Saturday through trains but the number of these had been halved compared with previous years.)

The station buildings at Brixham were still standing in 1966 but were finally demolished in December 1966 after attention from vandals in October/November and a severe storm on 17th October blew out all remaining glass in the verandah roof. On 20th December all buildings were demolished except the former stables and a huge bonfire made of everything that would burn. By 29th December the site had been cleared and loads of spoil were arriving. By 20th January, 1967 the foundations of a new housing estate had been laid. This, of course, precludes the station ever being reopened at its old location.

On 15th May, 1998 a plaque was unveiled at the new Saxon Heights flats, built upon the site of Richard Wolston's Parkham Wood house, where he had lived from 1831 to 1870, commemorating the worth of this great benefactor of Brixham for all time.

The signal box nameboard has found a good home at Didcot Railway Centre.
The late J.W.T. House

Chapter Eight

The Line described and operating details

The junction at Churston was a passing place on the single line between Goodrington and Kingswear. Lengthy loops were provided capable of holding 41 wagons plus engine and van, that on the down side was signalled for either down or up trains. The line between Torre and Kingswear opened in stages between 1859 and 1864 and the layout at Churston at first was very simple. In 1892 the platforms were extended and a new 39-lever signal box opened in 1893. This was sited in the 'V' of the junction between the Brixham branch and the main line at the north end of the station. There was then a facing junction between the Brixham bay and the up main line as well as the trailing crossover from down main to Brixham bay which remained until the end. The loop siding on the branch was extended in October 1909.

The 1893 signal box was closed on 9th February, 1913 and a new 48-lever brick-built box opened the same day, situated on the down platform. This was necessary because the platforms and loops had been extended towards Kingswear, the loops by six chains (estimate £4,282). After removal of the first signal box, the refuge siding at the Goodrington end of the layout was extended towards the station. The facing connection, Brixham bay to up main, was removed in the early 1950s (photographs show that it had gone by 1953).

Churston station layout remained unaltered until the closure of the Brixham line when the branch was curtailed at 225 m. 19 ch. (i. e. about ¼ mile beyond Churston station). The branch loop was made into a dead-end siding and the ground frame abolished, the siding later being removed. The down refuge siding was abolished on 31st October, 1965.

Churston lost its *winter* Sunday train service from 4th October, 1964 and its *summer* Sunday trains called for the last time on 17th September, 1967 (at least so far as BR was concerned). From April 1966 the Paignton-Kingswear section was worked as a shuttle service, apart for a few through trains at the beginning and end of the day. There was no longer a need for a crossing loop at Churston and this and the remaining sidings were taken out of use, and the signal box closed, on 20th October, 1968. Summer 1971 was the last year in which Saturday long distance trains ran through to Kingswear. Although scheduled for closure by BR, the section from Paignton to Kingswear was taken over by the Dart Valley Railway Co. on 1st November, 1972 (without a break), and steam trains are run between Easter and the end of October each year. In 1979 Churston's crossing loop was reinstated, with colour light signals operated from a new signal box on the down platform. Subsequently control of the signalling for the whole line (by now known as the Paignton & Dartmouth Steam Railway) was transferred to Britannia Crossing, near Kingswear.

Before the auto-trains were introduced on the Brixham branch in 1929 the 3- or 4-coach trains of ordinary passenger stock occupied the full length of the bay platform at Churston. The auto-trains, when one-coach, just fitted behind the starting signal; trips to the water tank at the end of the platform were often

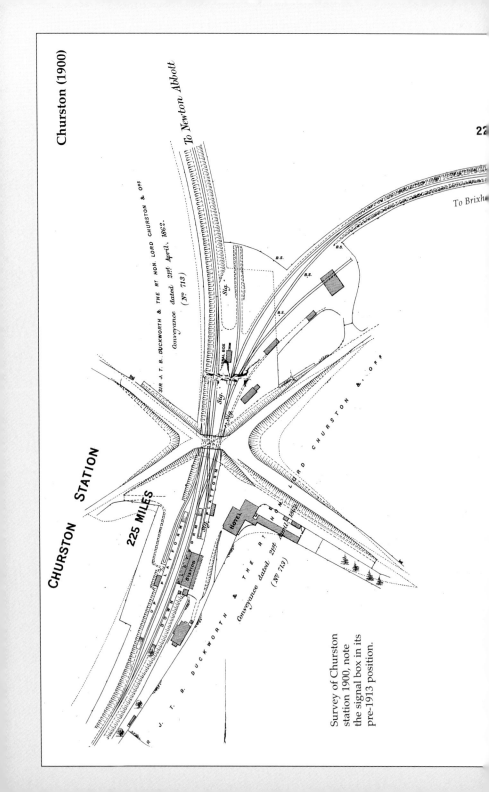

Churston (1900)

22

To Newton Abbott

To Brixh

CHURSTON STATION

225 MILES

SIR J. T. B. DUCKWORTH & THE RT. HON. LORD CHURSTON & OR^{RS}

Conveyance dated 21st April, 1862.

(N° 713)

SIGNAL BOX

HOTEL

J. T. B. DUCKWORTH & THE RT. HON. LORD CHURSTON & OR^{RS}

Conveyance dated 21st April, 1862.

(N° 713)

Survey of Churston
station 1900, note
the signal box in its
pre-1913 position.

G.W.R.
Churston

This must be one of the Sunday trains that came in from far-flung places like Newton Abbot, Dawlish Warren or Exeter and did a trip on the branch before returning whence it came. Unfortunately as no date or other details are available we can only speculate. It appears to be backing onto the branch at Churston before the engine runs round.

Lens of Sutton

L. & N. W. RY.
Brixham

On 19th August, 1953 the fireman heads towards the signal box with the token from Brixham. The next working of No. 1466 and its trailer is the 11.40 am Churston to Brixham. The up 'Torbay Express' is signalled on the (reversible) down main line, which was done whenever no train was due to cross at Churston as this line was nearer the booking office and the signal box. *The late J.W.T. House*

There are several differences here from the 1930s picture at the same location. In this 1950s scene with a train disappearing towards Brixham, the trailing connection in the up main line (the facing connection in the bay line) has been removed and there is a throw-off point, protecting the steep incline towards Goodrington, in its place. The short arm elevated exit signal from the refuge siding has been replaced by a ground disc. Although there is quite a lot of coal on the ground, there are no wagons in the yard. Note Churston's 3 ton yard crane, just to the left of the prominent telegraph pole. This crane, No. FM 3209, cost £191 in 1932 and was sold for scrap, for just £5, in 1960. *C.W. Judge Collection*

Taken from the north end of the down platform, this photograph shows the passenger facilities at Churston and its long platforms. *C.W. Judge Collection*

Churston in a sorry state: the Brixham bay line and up main crossing loop have been recovered and the signal box demolished, thus photographed in the period 1968-1972, before being sold to the Dart Valley Railway. *D.K. & M. James Collection*

Brixham Station (1905)

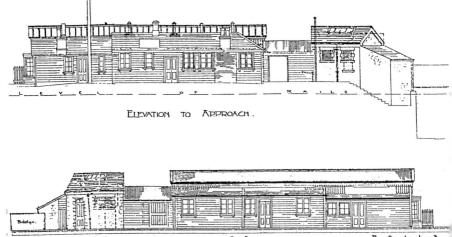

ELEVATION TO APPROACH.

ELEVATION TO RAILS

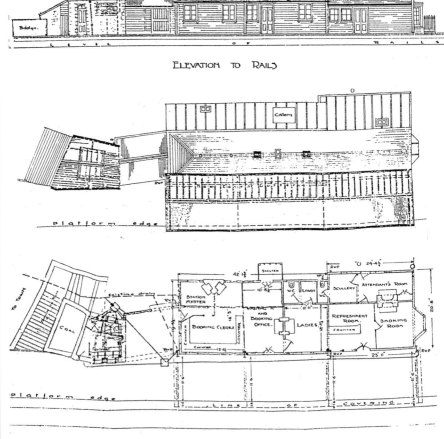

Alterations at Brixham 1905.

British Ra

made without the signal being lowered. On Summer Saturdays two auto-coaches were conveyed for most of the day, sometimes one either side of the engine so then the driver spent nearly his full turn of duty in the driving vestibules, the fireman remaining on the engine on his own.

Leaving Churston the branch train passed underneath the stone-built road bridge at the platform end and immediately began to curve round to the right until proceeding at an angle of about 90 degrees to the main line in a south-easterly direction. Beyond the small goods yard the line entered a cutting and passed beneath a road bridge (Bridge Road); before long the cutting ended and the line ran on a shallow embankment between the fields, in a reasonably straight line. Crossing over an underbridge (Elberry Lane), the attractive tree lined drive (Green Lane) leading to Churston Court, the home of Lord Churston who presided at the line's opening ceremony, could be seen on the left. Now on a steeper embankment the line started to curve to the left and crossed Churston Road leading to Churston Court and Churston Church which came into view on the left. In the other direction the road led through the village of Churston Ferrers to join up with the main Paignton-Brixham road under which the branch passed at Churston station.

Completing its curve the line again changed from embankment to a deep cutting, probably the location of the rock-fall in 1870, passing beneath another overbridge (Bascombe Road) and entering upon a stretch which crossed featureless countryside in a nearly straight line for the next mile. After a short distance the cutting gave way to embankment again, the latter lasting for about ¼ mile, then another short stretch of cutting before becoming level with the surrounding fields.

The line which had until now been nearly level apart from 7 chains at 1 in 95 rising now fell steeply towards Brixham (1 in 79/78). It is odd how the reporting of the gradients on the branch varied. Until July 1923 the service timetables showed the gradient is 1 in 132 rising to 1 m. 26 ch. and 1 in 82 falling thereafter (the gradient quoted in the opening inspection report). But from 1923 onwards it is shown as 1 in 95 rising and 1 in 79/78 falling. 1 mile 26 chains from Churston (just under ¾ mile from Brixham) was a stop board at which all down goods trains had to pin down their brakes. At 226 m. 38 ch. (just over ½ mile from Brixham) the Air Ministry sidings (dating from 1940) diverged to the right, then the line was raised on an embankment to cross Northfields Lane by a bridge, on the approach to Brixham. The embankment steepened, then bridged a road before another, and final, cutting enveloped the line at the end of which was another stop board (1 mile 69 chains from Churston) at which brakes of descending goods trains were lifted. Just beyond was the home signal for Brixham and a facing junction giving access to the sidings. All down trains had to stop dead at the home signal because of the steep gradient approaching the station.

The layout at Brixham was fairly limited as the station site was a narrow one with a high retaining wall on its south side because the level ground had had to be created on the top of a hill. The length of the station/yard area combined was less than ¼ mile and, as will be seen from the track plan, the branch line finished on quite a tight curve. The following measurements and details relate to the track plan (*page 144*), which dates from 1910.

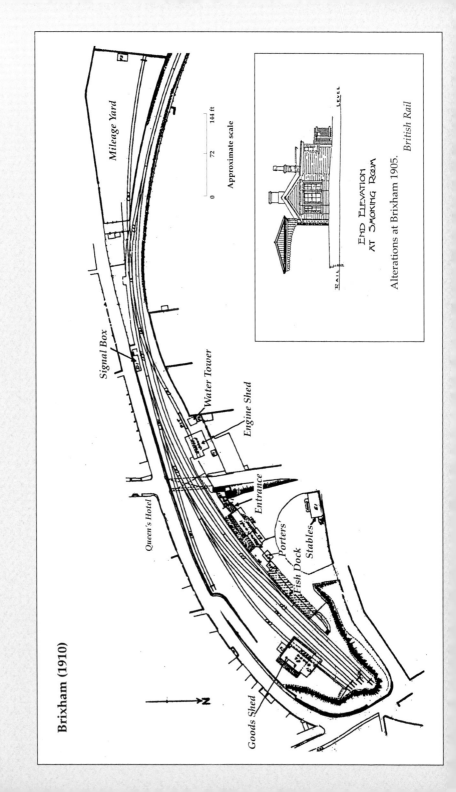

Brixham (1910)

N

Mileage Yard

Signal Box

Water Tower

Engine Shed

Queen's Hotel

Entrance

Porters'

Fish Dock

Stables

Goods Shed

Approximate scale

0   72   144 ft

END ELEVATION
AT SMOKING ROOM

RAIL LEVEL

Alterations at Brixham 1905.

British Rail

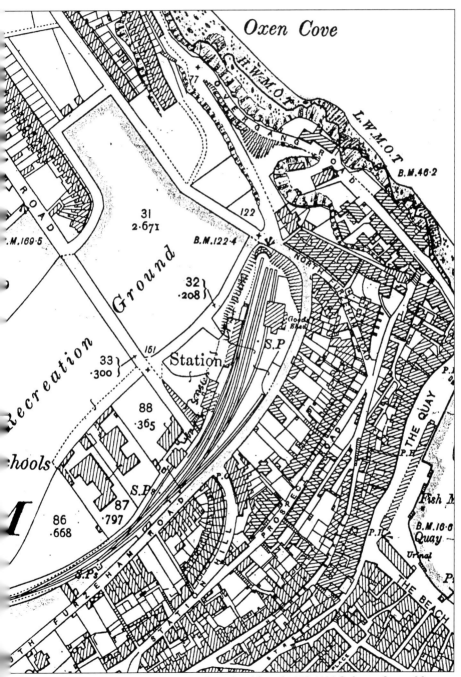

Reproduced from the 25", 1906 Ordnance Survey Map

The west end of the main station building showing entrance to platform; the steps to the main road are at the extreme right, in front of the stone-built gents' lavatory.   *The late I.H. Smart*

The yard side of the main station building (east end).   *The late I.H. Smart*

he fish dock seen from the roadway side.

The late I.H. Smart

ooking through the unique goods shed. Note the loading gauge and yard gas lamp.

The late I.H. Smart

Looking towards the buffer stops at Brixham from the centre of the yard. There is a good supply of empty fish trucks on hand, but very little else. *C.W. Judge Collection*

Looking towards the station from the signal box. The coal truck, seen being manhandled into the platform in the opposite picture, is being unloaded into the coal store and its contents will be used for the various office fires. *C.W. Judge Collection*

Brixham yard, looking towards Churston, after closure of the signal box.

C.W. Judge Collection

A good picture of the station buildings, uncluttered by a standing train, seen on 7th August, 1960. *Left to right*: coal store; gents' toilets with 227 MP affixed; entrance/exit; main building (the doorways were: booking hall, ladies', waiting room, station master's); porters' room (with glazed bricks); senior porter's office (with small window) and fish dock beyond. Note the small luggage scales on the platform by the exit.

R.E. Toop

As the branch train passed the home signals to enter the station it ran alongside the only west-facing siding, that marked 'Mileage Yard' on the plan on page 144, which, in the author's experience in the 1950s, was used only for coal traffic. This could accommodate 12 wagons; alongside was a 6 ton crane. As the train slowly squealed round the last curve it crossed the connection from the yard loop to engine shed (in 1931 this connection was made a facing one from the branch single line) and passed the small brick-built signal box. Both of these structures have already been described in Chapter Six. The train slowly crossed the road bridge over Station Hill and came to a stand in Brixham platform. This was 203 ft long with a 132 ft extension at its eastern end which was used for loading fish.

In 1910 the platform buildings were as follows (from west to east)

Coal store
Gentlemen's toilets (newly built in 1905), a stone structure separate from the main (wooden) station building
Booking clerk's office with station master's office behind
Booking office hall and waiting room
Ladies' room with toilet behind
Refreshment room with scullery and attendant's room behind
Smoking room

A steel and wood glazed verandah 66½ ft long, matching the length of the main building, was also provided in 1905 to shelter passengers waiting on the platform. Beyond the main building and set at the back of the platform was a porters' room faced with glazed bricks (the author remembers a very large kettle on a gas stove inside which was always alight whilst the station was open) and beyond that the fish dock, as it was called. The platform and its rooms were lit by gas right up to closure, a long chain hanging either side of each glass globe, one chain for 'on' the other for 'off', a pilot light (usually) ensured automatic ignition.

Nearest the platform line was a run-round loop which, until the introduction of auto-trains, would have been used after arrival of every train to transfer the engine from one end of its train to the other. Latterly it was seldom used for that purpose and so could hold fish trucks if the yard was particularly full. Beyond that were two sidings holding 13 and 12 wagons respectively, then the goods shed road which held 11 wagons; the building contained a 2 ton crane. The part of the shed covering the track was about 56 ft long. Alongside the southern boundary wall was a short siding used to unload coal trucks which could accommodate six or seven wagons.

The GWR employed a colour coding for engine route availability, 'uncoloured' engines (the lightest) having the greatest availability, through 'yellow', and 'blue' to 'red' and 'double red', the heaviest. The Brixham branch, in 1945, was allowed all 'uncoloured' types, 'yellow' *tank* engines and '57XX'-'97XX' tank engines in the 'blue' category, these latter being limited to 20 mph. By 1954 '57XX' tanks had been re-classified 'yellow' except for Nos. 9700-9710 which remained 'blue' but were cleared at 20 mph. Rather surprisingly, considering the track required imposition of speed restrictions and resleepering just before closure, in 1960 the branch was cleared for all types, excluding 'Kings' which were 'double red'. After this the only restrictions were that '41XX', '51XX', '61XX', '81XX' locomotives could not use the bay at Churston and were restricted to 20 mph. 'D63XX' diesels were restricted to 20 mph. Permitted engine loads for passenger, parcels and fish trains were, in 1945, as shown below:

			Class of Engine			
	3206-3455				
	4400-4410		2-4-0T		
	4500-4599		'Metro'	0-4-2T	
	5500-5574	0-6-0 and	0-4-2T	'517' class	
	'36XX', '37XX',	0-6-0T	'48XX', '58XX'	1334	
	'57XX', '77XX',	0-6-2T	898	1335	
	'87XX', '97XX'	'A' group	900	1336	
	Tons	*Tons*	*Tons*	*Tons*	
Churston-Brixham	220	190	180	160	
Brixham-Churston	196	168	144	120	

These were 'standard' loads; auto-trains worked by '48XX' (later renumbered '14XX'), between Churston and Brixham were restricted to 168 tons, but in the opposite direction it was the same as for a 'standard' passenger, etc. train, 144 tons. By 1954 the first column had been extended to include BR Standard class '3' 2-6-2T, '96XX' and '94XX' locomotives.

Freight train loads were more complicated and loads depended on whether the hauling locomotive was in group A, B or C ('A' included '48XX') and whether traffic conveyed was class 1, 2 or 3 or empties (class 1 was the heaviest traffic). In any case the maximum freight load in either direction over the Brixham branch was 30 vehicles.

The maximum speed over the branch was 45 mph except between Churston station and 225 m. 30 ch. and 226 m. 60 ch. to Brixham station where the limit was 35 mph. (Nowadays, 45 mph is the maximum speed over the erstwhile main line between Newton Abbot and Paignton - what a come down!) For at least the last eight month's of the branch's life there was a 15 mph restriction at the Churston end, 225 m. 15 ch. to 225 m. 69 ch. (nearly ¾ mile) because of the condition of the track.

David Fish, whose wonderful photographs of the South Devon railway scene bring back so well the age of steam in the West Country, now some 35 years after it finished, farmed for many years at Churston Court farm, whose fields were bisected by the Brixham branch. He recalls an incident where a tractor and harrows crossed the line immediately in front of an auto from Brixham to Churston. The train cut the harrows off which lodged underneath the auto-coach and caused considerable damage before the train stopped. It turned out that the train driver did not see the tractor, and the tractor driver did not hear the train because the wind was against him.

On another occasion a heifer jumped over a low wall and went up the bank from the farm lane to the line. David heard the auto start from Churston and waved his arms to stop the train. The train shut off steam and Fish thought that the driver had seen him, but when about 150 yds away the driver opened up and ran into the heifer, killing it. The driver had not seen his warning; eventually the railway paid compensation.

David thinks that in the 1920s he once saw a truck over the platform line buffer stop at Brixham and down the steep bank at the end of the line. He feels sure he did not imagine it. [This could be quite easily done, if careless, when placing vehicles here because the approach was on a sharp curve; alternatively a movement could have been trying to fit into the limited space between the points and the buffers prior to running via the loop and been too long. Fortunately, because of the extreme difficulty in recovering any derailed vehicles, it does not seem to have been done often. *Author*]

Jack Eveleigh joined the GWR as a lad porter at Kingswear in June 1937. In August 1941 he transferred to Brixham as porter and enlisted in the RAF that December. He returned to Brixham (as porter) in September 1946. There had been two signalwomen working at Brixham during the war, Daisy Easterbrook and Dot Lusty; the latter was still there at the end of the war but wanted to finish. Jack, who had been appointed signalman at Moretonhampstead (class 5), applied for and got Brixham (class 4) in March 1947 without going to Moretonhampstead. He remembers learning the job within a week. Apart from eight months temporarily employed in Churston box in 1951 he remained at Brixham until March 1953, when he was promoted to Churston (class 3). Thereafter further promotions took him to Torre (1957), Kingswear (1958), eventually becoming a district relief signalman for Paignton (1967) and Newton Abbot (1973); he retired in 1987.

When Jack first went to Brixham station master C.V. (Cecil) Williams was there, and also in charge of Churston and had been for some time [GW establishment records show this dual arrangement started sometime between March 1931 and March 1932.] Williams retired in September 1949 and L. Nickels took his place early in 1950. In 1941 the early porter at Brixham had a busy time; coming on duty at 5.15 am he was booked off for two (one hour) meal breaks and went off duty at 3.15 pm, but as it was wartime he was expected to work overtime, often finishing at 8 pm or later! His duties included lighting the fires, booking the first few trains, shunting, cleaning the station and carriages, sorting the parcels for the van driver, loading fish and attending to any signal lamps not dealt with by the signalman. At night he returned to the station for fire watching or went on Home Guard duty!

For many years, he recalls, the early morning Brixham goods, which left Hackney at 3.45 am or thereabouts, was hauled to Churston by a tender engine which then ran 'light' to Kingswear to work the 7 am thence to Bristol. The Brixham engine followed it down 'light', attached to the goods and worked it to Brixham at 5.20 am. After shunting the yard it worked the passenger service for the rest of the day, returning 'light' to Newton Abbot about 11.15 pm. The yard hand point near the signal box was detected through the down home to loop signal and if this signal was 'off' the hand points could not be turned. This precaution was employed to safeguard the practice of gravitating wagons from the home signal to the yard. The guard on the 3.45 am freight was employed as a passenger guard until about 9 am when he returned to Newton Abbot. This was in the period from 1941 to the curtailment of the service in 1951, to Jack's knowledge. After the guard left, the signalman kept and filled in the 'Passenger Train Journal' and sorted the tickets for the Railway Clearing House.

The former engine shed siding was used every day during this same period to stable one of the auto coaches. The first few trips were worked with two coaches, then after the school children had gone to Churston (*en route* to Dartmouth or Torquay) one of the coaches was detached until the afternoon. The coaches were swapped around to allow for cleaning. Of course in the peak summer both coaches might be used nearly all day.

The February 1951 coal shortage, and subsequent curtailment of the branch service, caused the box hours to be shortened and a reduction in staff to signalman and porter-signalman only, hence Jack's temporary transfer to Churston. But in October he was displaced at Churston by a man moving there under compassionate grounds and returned to Brixham. Also in 1951 the oil depot sidings were used extensively, this was their last time used; movements lasted for some months. Tank trains from Micheldever were split into two manageable loads at Churston.

During Jack's time as signalman at Brixham, there were sometimes 'Q' fish specials from there on Sundays, with the signalman called out as required at short notice, or maybe told he was not required if on 'standby'. A porter was brought out under the same arrangements for loading.

Clifford Pearce, who had previously worked in the PW department in Cornwall and Devon, on marrying a Torquay girl managed to transfer to the traffic department and started at Brixham as a porter on 5th November, 1945. After 12 months he moved closer to home as a porter at Torre, then went to Moretonhampstead as a class 5 signalman in October 1947. In 1949 he was promoted to class 4 signalman at Kingskerswell, and in 1957 became a class 3 signalman at Torquay. He stayed there until the box closed (except for summer Saturdays) in October 1968, becoming signalman at Torre shortly afterwards, from where he retired in December 1978.

On the early turn at Brixham (5.15 am-1.15 pm) Clifford would travel down on the branch engine; he lit the station gaslights and booked the first train (around 6.58 am). The late turn started at 1.30 pm and, at the finish, the two trailers were stabled in the fish dock. He would then return to Torre on the light engine. The late turn was particularly busy with fish traffic and Clifford said that when walking from Torre station to his home in Carlton Road he would often sit on a seat for a rest and, on occasion, wake up two hours later!

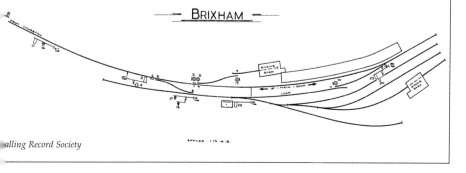

THE STANDARD REGULATIONS FOR BLOCK WORKING ARE SHEWN IN THE BOOK OF REGULATIONS FOR TRAIN SIGNALLING ON DOUBLE AND SINGLE LINES.

Additional Instructions for the Brixham Station Signal Box.

Regulation 4.

The "Is Line Clear?" Signal must be sent for Up Trains just before the Train is ready to leave.

Regulation 5.

Whenever vehicles standing at the Fish Platform are on the Churston side of the points leading to the Loop Line, Down Passenger Trains must be accepted under the Warning Signal (Regulation 5), the train stopped at the Signal Box by the exhibition of a red hand signal and the Driver advised of the position of the vehicles. A green hand signal, held steadily, must then be exhibited to the Driver.

Regulation 8 A.

A Freight Train working between Brixham or Churston Station and Northfield Sidings must be dealt with in accordance with Regulation 8 A.

Down Passenger Trains must be brought to a stand at the Home Signal before being admitted to the Platform.

Down Freight Trains must be accepted with the points set for the Loop Line and the points must remain in that position until the Goods Train has come to stand at the Home Signal.

Before lowering the Down Main to Loop or Yard Home Signal the Signalman must satisfy himself that the hand points are set for the line on which the train has to run.

_1948_   _Personal Signature of Divisional Superintendent_

(9)-6.48-P.O.

Alan Babbage joined the GWR in 1944 at Teignmouth S&T Depot and was at first a member of the telegraph gang and moved into the signal gang three months later. The telegraph gang had to climb poles using climbing irons, ladders were banned because, if being carried, they could be turned and foul the line. Alan did not like the irons - if one slipped you could end up with an armful of splinters! From 1948-1959 he worked on the Kingswear line, at first as assistant to Charlie Rawlings the S&T lineman. Charlie was a strong Labour supporter and Alan can remember Charlie standing on top of the box steps at Torquay cheering and applauding Clem Attlee who was walking from the Grand Hotel to Torquay station - he was the sole supporter; if it had been a Tory minister the station approach would have been full! Clem came over and had a word with him. In 1954 the S&T area was divided and he became lineman, responsible for Paignton North to Aller Jn and Aller Jn to Totnes (exclusive). Alan went into the newly formed Work Study department in 1959, first at Plymouth then Reading and Old Oak Common areas, eventually leaving BR in 1970 (he says Work Study worked themselves out of a job!) and went to work for Thames Water. He kindly supplied some memories of Churston and Brixham:

Churston signal box was rather unusual in that it had three E.T. Token instruments (when Brixham was still open). All of these had different configurations on their respective tokens (there being only four types normally made). We had occasionally to carry out a transfer of tokens when too many would accumulate at one end of the section.

One of the regular signalmen here was George Snell [pictured in the author's book *The Newton Abbot to Kingswear Railway* published by Oakwood Press] who had a very strong Devonshire accent and referred to the kettle as the 'Tay Ketto', usually kept permanently on top of the Valour oil stove, except when he was having one of his massive fry-ups!

Jim Cook, the regular branch fireman for a number of years, used to take the occasional dip in the water tank on the bay platform during the hot summers we used to have - but he did it very discreetly.

One of the relief signalmen at Churston was a keen motor cyclist and was driving an H.R.D., a very potent machine. On one occasion he offered to take one of our assistants back to Paignton to collect some battery jars needing replacement. Our chap came back looking very pale, but with the jars remarkably intact!

We were scheduled to visit Brixham every two weeks. It wasn't a very big signal box and did not have a particularly large number of train movements. I don't think the smell of fish at the station end of the yard will ever be forgotten, or the noise of schoolchildren at play (unseen) over the wall opposite the box.

I can only remember one of the signalmen, 'Ginger' Brown, whom I recall made a complete stair carpet or rug from 'Readicut' wool or similar to occupy some of his time there. Most of the batteries required to work the Token instrument and telephones, etc. were of the Leclanche type of cell, but those found here were particularly old and still working! Most of these cells on the Kingswear line were of the sac pot or fabric covered type, whereas those at Brixham were of the earlier porous pot type. Some had the date that they were put into service scratched into the pitch seal at the top of the pot; a date around the 1890s!

The box must have been 'blacked out' during the war years as I found several blackout screens stored under the box. They were made from a type of roofing felt fitted to wooden screens. (I later dismantled one of these and used the wood to make a clothes-horse, timber being almost unobtainable in those days.)

Once a porter here was accused by a railway policeman of stealing sprats from a barrel being loaded into a van on the fish dock. When the charge was made at the local

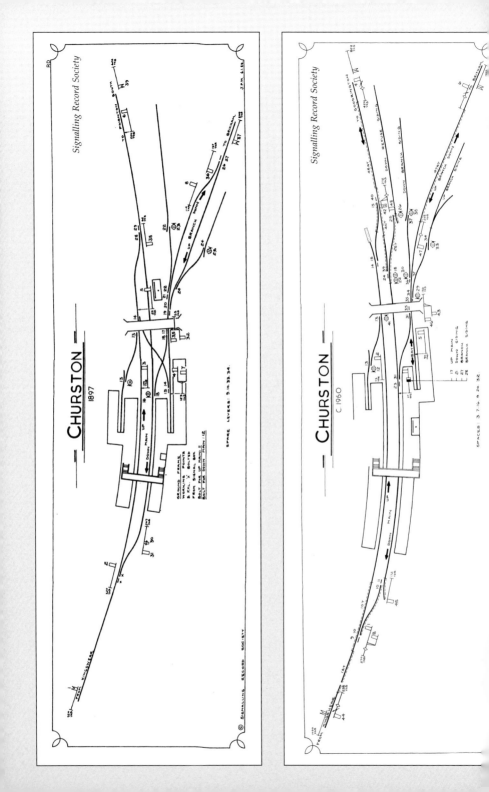

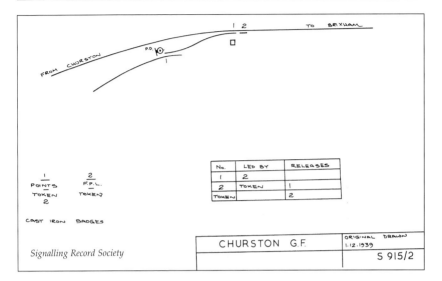

CHURSTON G.F.

No.	LED BY	RELEASES
1	2	
2	TOKEN	1
TOKEN		2

POINTS
TOKEN

F.P.L.
TOKEN

CAST IRON BADGES

Signalling Record Society

ORIGINAL DRAWN
1.12.1939

S 915/2

magistrates court, the question of whether the porter was actually seen taking the fish was brought into some doubt. As the magistrate was a former station master here and knew that the gas lighting was particularly poor, making it almost impossible for someone inside a van to be seen, the case was dismissed. [In the author's experience, so many sprats were 'wasted' because they fell out of the boxes or barrels, which in the case of sprats only were not covered, this must have been a case of a policeman particularly desperate for a prosecution.]

Jim Cook was the branch fireman at Brixham from 1945 to 1959. Having been based at Newton Abbot what attracted him to the job was the turns of duty - 8 am to 4 pm and no Sundays. He had been working double home turns to Shrewsbury and Paddington and quickly decided that waiting an hour and a half for a Cardiff man to vacate a bed in the lodgings provided by the railway, after working a long turn through the night, was not his cup of tea.

Before Jim went to Brixham he fired to Bob Wise (who appears in the picture on p. 128) for a couple of years. Bob was a past master on rules and regulations and the engines. They would leave Hackney yard, and after exchanging hand signals with the guard, he would ask a question and expect the answer by Teignmouth! Sometimes this would continue for most of the turn of duty. Jim found this very instructive, and at the end of the two years was as good as, or better than, many of his mates.

When Jim came to Brixham, Reg Westaway was the Brixham driver. Reg had already been there some years, having transferred in 1940 in the grade from Cardiff back to Brixham where he had originally been a cleaner and fireman. He had swopped with the former Brixham driver, Bob Stamp, who was a Cardiff man! Reg lived in Brixham and liked his 'scrumpy'. The fact that there was a pub opposite the station at both ends of the line probably compensated for the low earnings he made.

When Jim Cook first started on the 8 am-4 pm turn, three sets of enginemen were involved in working the line. A Newton Abbot set brought a goods down from Newton Abbot, shunting at intermediate stations and then started the branch passenger service. They were relieved just after 8 am by the Brixham men (Jim travelled down from Torquay where he lived, whilst Reg walked across from the other side of Brixham). Finally another set of men travelled down from Newton Abbot to relieve Reg and Jim at 4 pm and then worked the remainder of the service, which in those days continued until 9.30 pm, returning the branch engine to Newton Abbot.

This sociable turn of duty did not last long, however, and the Brixham men's hours were changed to 10 am to 6 pm about 1947. This turn was worked until about 1951 and then changed to a very unsociable 1.30 pm-9.30 pm which Jim and Reg worked continuously until 1959 when Jim was promoted to driver at Newton Abbot. This involved booking on, relieving a Newton Abbot set of men (who worked the early turn as part of their 'link', perhaps only coming to Brixham one week in 30), running the branch afternoon service and then returning the engine to Newton Abbot. After that the pair returned 'as passenger' to Brixham, although Jim finished his journey at Torquay where he lived.

Except on summer Saturdays when the branch service continued until about 8.40 pm or so, the last service from Brixham was at about 6 pm. This invariably conveyed fish trucks to Churston for attaching to the 6.05 pm ex-Kingswear for dispatch to Bristol, Paddington, etc. After these trucks had been attached and the 6.05 pm ex-Kingswear cleared the section, the branch engine proceeded light to Newton, usually arriving there about 7 pm.

In an effort to reduce the unproductive time at the end of the Brixham men's turn, there were two fairly short-lived attempts to find them work. The first of these involved the '14XX' 0-4-2T engine shunting Gas House Sidings between Paignton and Torquay. These sidings are located on a short level stretch of line, with quite sharp gradients in either direction. The idea was that the branch engine would enter the sidings at the Paignton end and then segregate the loaded and empty wagons ready for the next goods to pick up the empties. This involved shunting out onto the down main line.

On the only occasion that this was tried the engine picked up about 12 loaded and 12 empties and pulled out onto the down main line, then, clear of the points, the shunter signalled Reg to stop prior to setting back into the other siding. Reg applied the brake but the coupled wheels 'picked up' and the engine slid down the steep gradient towards Paignton, propelled by its heavy load. Despite several further attempts at braking, assisted by sand and Jim Cook's efforts to apply hand brakes on the wagons using the coal pick, the shunt continued its steady progress down the bank with Reg applying the brake whistle at intervals. Eventually moving too fast for Jim to run alongside, he scrambled into a wagon, all the time thinking about the level crossing gates at Paignton North. Fortunately the signalman there had been made aware of the situation and both home signals were lowered, in fact the line had been cleared to Goodrington Yard. The runaway eventually stopped near Paignton South box, and after Jim had picked up wagon brakes, proceeded into Goodrington. Jim says that Reg never had a report to answer because the person who had arranged the shunt would have been reprimanded for not realising the '14XX' could not cope with such heavy work on a steep gradient. That arrangement was swiftly terminated.

Another short lived arrangement dictated that if the branch engine arrived at Torre before 6.30 pm the Brixham men were to relieve a Newton Abbot set shunting Torre yard on a goods from Goodrington. The Newton men would then return the Brixham engine to Newton Abbot, whilst Reg and Jim carried on shunting with the goods and ran it to Hackney. Doubtless, human nature being what it is, the engine would not have arrived at Torre before 6.30 pm too often . . .

No. 1466, now preserved at the GWS site at Didcot Railway Centre was the 'regular' Brixham engine in the 1950s although No. 1470 made quite frequent appearances. Jim Cook used to keep the front of the engine clean, also the transfers, number plates, etc. It was very seldom that '14XX' class locomotives were not available but, as Newton Abbot also had to supply these to the Ashburton and Moretonhampstead branches, occasionally the incidence of heavy repairs, etc., meant that Brixham had to have a 'pannier' or '45XX' class locomotive, and usually this lasted for a week at a time. This was a 'fag' for the fireman as he had to uncouple and re-couple after each single journey as the non auto-fitted locomotives were not allowed to propel.

Between November and January when the 'sprat season' was in full swing it was often necessary to run additional 'sprat specials' after the passenger service had finished. During much of the 1950s and early 1960s the last passenger from Brixham was either at 5.10 pm or 6.07 pm. When the last passenger was at 5.10 pm, the 6.07 pm ran as a 'Q' Fish train ('Q' = runs as required). But it was often necessary in the season to run fish specials much later than 6.07 pm and then the branch engine, after detaching the auto-coach in the bay at Churston, would return light to Brixham. It was a question of waiting for the boats to arrive with the catch and, although the fish special of three or four fish trucks and brake van would normally leave by 7 or 8 pm, the author can remember a very occasional trip as late as 9 or 10 pm. A spare goods brake van was kept at Brixham for the purpose and the special was run through to Newton Abbot, the brake van afterwards being tripped to Hackney. It was returned the next day on the early morning goods.

Incidentally, these fish trucks were pressed into service during the summer months to convey huge amounts of passengers' luggage in advance (PLA) in through truck loads to the main centres (Midlands, London, South Wales, etc.). The parcels delivery lorry trundled round the many holiday camps in Brixham collecting these trunks and they were loaded into several pre-labelled trucks waiting at the fish platform. Although the trucks were thoroughly scrubbed before use, there must have been a strong 'whiff' of fish when these trunks arrived at their owners' homes!

As the last passenger train of the day nearly always conveyed fish trucks it would be signalled into the down main at Churston. Here any passengers would detrain and the empty train, formed coach, engine, truck(s), would then proceed to the up main after arrival of the train from Kingswear. The truck(s) would be attached and the empty branch train would be signalled back, via the down main line, onto the branch line, coming to a stand at the bracket signal just beyond the road bridge. The coach was uncoupled and Jim Cook transferred to the driver's compartment therein. After the bay signal was lowered Reg Westaway smartly loose-shunted the coach into the bay platform line. However, this unofficial practice was stopped after a member of the staff at Churston did the shunt and applied the hand brake in the coach too slowly, causing a heavy collision with the stop block!

After Jim Cook was promoted to Newton Abbot in 1959, to the best of his knowledge no permanent fireman was appointed in his place, relief being supplied from Newton Abbot each week. Reg Westaway remained until the end of steam in March 1961, retiring soon afterwards.

The late Bill Glanville spent his early working life on the trawlers and in the World War II his trawler was taken over by the Navy; he spent the war ferrying stores, etc. through the hazardous mine-strewn Bristol Channel. Wartime leaves spent in Brixham often involved hitching a lift on the early morning goods from Churston to Brixham.

After the war he decided that he would like to spend more time at home and joined the GWR in 1945, becoming a lengthman in PW gang No. 113, based at Churston and covering from 'West Bridge' at Churston, a mile towards Kingswear, to just before the second (Broadsands) viaduct between Churston and Goodrington, also the Brixham branch. He said that it was exactly 2 miles 5 chains from the buffer stops in the Brixham bay at Churston to the buffer stops at Brixham. Before the auto-trains were introduced on the branch in 1929, 3- or 4-coach passenger trains were run with guards, and two regular guards employed, Jim Griffin and Bill Casely, on alternate early and late turns. In July 1924 for example the early turn was 6.20 am to 2.20 pm and the late turn 3.25 pm to 11.25 pm (WFSX) 4.15 pm to 12.40 am (WFSO). A porter-guard worked from 2.22 pm to 3.22 pm (WFSX), 4.12 pm (WFSO). (The Summer Sunday service was worked by Newton Abbot guards.) However, the introduction of the push-pull trains made these men redundant, and the trains were subsequently run without guards, until dieselisation.

Despite the make-do-and-mend condition of the track on the branch there were few derailments. Apart from the one in the engine shed road already described, Bill Glanville could only remember one other during his time on the branch. This took place in the yard at Brixham where the track was really worn out and one could see the sleepers and chairs move up and down as the engine passed over them. As far as he could recall this was in the early 1950s and the station master was in the signal box at the time. The derailment was due to 'condition of track'.

Not long before closure about ¾ mile of the branch between Churston (Bridge Road) bridge and the end of Bascombe Road cutting 225 m. 15 ch. - 225 m. 69 ch.) had to be re-sleepered because there was no alternative. Also, to Bill Glanville's amazement, a new PW Inspector managed to get Brixham yard relaid with new rails and sleepers, whereas everything had been second- or third-hand before. All this material was lifted and re-used after the line closed. The track of the branch was lifted early in 1964.

The author lived opposite Brixham station from 1957 to closure and, as a schoolboy, spent all his holidays at the station, the sea being unable to lure him away from No. 1466! Thanks to the friendliness of station master Stan Cook, fireman Jim Cook and the office and platform staff, I was allowed to work on the station. I participated in the drudgery and the delights - loading fish and parcels, sticking up posters at the station and at sites in the town (good experience for later wall-papering!), coupling fish trucks to the passenger services, selling tickets, acting as vanboy in the parcels lorry and - best of all - travelling on the footplate of 1466. Hardly any door was closed to me, what wonderful experiences for a boy!

The first engine to be preserved by the Great Western Society, No. 1466 was moved from Totnes to Didcot in 1967. Built in 1936 and withdrawn by BR in 1963 it has now been in preservation longer than it was in service. Here it stands alongside Didcot engine shed, part of Didcot Railway Centre. Currently (2000) the engine is repainted in GWR green and bears its original number, 4866.   *GWS Heavy Freight Group*

Revenue and Traffic Details 1868-1882

Revenue details 1868-1882

Period ending	Passenger	Parcels Fish	Goods	Misc.
31st December, 1868	696	n/a	n/a	n/a
31st December, 1869	768	n/a	n/a	n/a
31st December, 1870	806	n/a	n/a	n/a
31st December, 1871	904	n/a	n/a	n/a
31st December, 1872	916	n/a	n/a	n/a
31st December, 1873	985	n/a	n/a	n/a
31st December, 1874	963	n/a	n/a	n/a
30th June, 1875	450	121	163	19
31st December, 1875	522	171	158	38
30th June, 1876	464	184	237	13
31st December, 1876	598	638	208	59 *
30th June, 1877	505	241	311	120
31st December, 1877	671	389	307	80
30th June, 1878	534	232	301	27
31st December, 1878	623	360	295	83
30th June, 1879	538	228	276	58
31st December, 1879	625	393	324	70
30th June, 1880	559	286	279	96
31st December, 1880	670	343	287	30
30th June, 1881	513	262	266	71
31st December, 1881	697	410	312	96
30th June, 1882	578	354	290	48
31st December, 1882	643	412	324	117

n/a = not available
* Plus £2,135 award from Railway Commissioners.

Traffic details 1868-1882

Period ending	No. of Passengers	No. Parcels	Fish (tons)	Goods (tons)
31st December, 1868	60,729	n/a	n/a	1,248 *
31st December, 1869	68,856	n/a	800	2,133 *
31st December, 1870	73,822	n/a	1,200	3,802 *
31st December, 1871	69,154	6,833	1,144	4,412
31st December, 1872	69,190	5,700	1,174	4,952
31st December, 1873	73,160	5,658	1,407	5,341
31st December, 1874	73,583	5,813	1,454	5,211
31st December, 1875	74,606	6,170	1,661	5,751
30th June, 1876	28,670 (?)	n/a	n/a	n/a
31st December, 1876	41,213	3,034	1,192	1,629
30th June, 1877	33,345	2,967	782	2,824
31st December, 1877	45,600	3,249	1,352	2,534
30th June, 1878	36,883	3,038	734	2,572
31st December, 1878	42,995	3,565	1,220	2,375
30th June, 1879	35,684	3,242	705	2,183
31st December, 1879	41,993	3,755	1,337	2,587
30th June, 1880	38,493	3,511	921	2,242
31st December, 1880	45,065	3,958	1,116	2,234
30th June, 1881	34,619	3,491	832	2,171
31st December, 1881	46,950	3,733	1,398	2,559
30th June, 1882	39,840	3,290	1,206	2,337
31st December, 1882	45,232	4,230	1,452	2,517

n/a = not available

* These figures are for minerals (limestone) only, no figures are available for coal or general merchandise. The limestone traffic ceased in 1870, it is not known whether it resumed later.

Appendix Two

Station Masters at Brixham

March 1868	Henry Wood (7, Prospect Place) (Resigned 7th August, 1887, aged 62)
August 1887	Edward George Tripp (until October 1888)
1888	Sidney Francis Garford (Furzeham House, South Furzeham Road)
13th February, 1893	Robert Arthur Higginbottom
24th July, 1899	Thomas Mills (Died in service October 1907)
December 1907	Henry Louis Mayland
1922	Ernest Willcocks (Retired early, ill health)
1925	Henry G. Fear
(?) 1931 or 1932	John Penwarden JP (3, Victoria Place)
1935	Cecil V. Williams
1950	Leonard F. Nickels
1955	G. Stanley Cook (remained until closure in 1963)

The station master at Brixham (class 2) took charge of Churston (class 3) also, sometime between March 1931 and March 1932.

This is thought to be a complete list of Brixham station masters, Mr Tripp, who had a very brief stay, having been 'discovered' since the First Edition. All dates have been verified from staff records or the *GWR Magazine*, except for the starting date of Mr Penwarden. A complete examination of the *Magazine* failed to reveal any announcement of Mr Fear's promotion, retirement or demise, which is most unusual. However, in either 1931 or early 1932 the two stations (Churston and Brixham) were combined under one station master and this seems the most likely time for Mr Fear to have left and Mr Penwarden (who had been appointed to Churston in 1927) to have taken over. He certainly retired from Brixham in 1935.

There were three very lengthy stays. Mr Wood, the first appointment, lasted 19 years and Messrs Mayland (who came from Teignmouth) and Williams (previously SM Bovey on the Moretonhampstead branch) shared second place with nearly 15 years each. Taking Mr Penwarden's earlier Brixham service into account (*see Chapter Six*) he served at least 17 years at that station.

Inevitably, with two stations to control after 1932, the station master's time had to be split between them, but Brixham probably always had the lion's share of his time, being both busier and with more staff. Certainly in Stan Cook's time he normally spent more time at Brixham, but would start his day at Churston, and usually make another visit there later, before leaving Brixham mid to late afternoon, with one final look at Churston before returning to his home in Torquay by train. Probably a more demanding job than the earlier station masters who only had responsibility for Brixham.

Appendix Three

Correspondence

between J.C. Wall, J.W. Batten and A.P. Prowse
regarding the purchase of the Torbay & Brixham Railway

Note: J.C. Wall was Goods Agent of the Bristol & Exeter Railway, J.W. Batten a Parliamentary Agent and friend of R.W. Wolston and A.P. Prowse, Chief Accountant of the South Devon Railway.

The correspondence opens with this letter from J.C. Wall to Mr Batten:

Bristol, 11th December

Sir,

Mr Prowse, Chief Accountant of the South Devon Railway Company, stated at their Board Meeting yesterday, that you told him I was the real purchaser of the Torbay & Brixham Railway, and that all the others would have little to do with it, adding that I had made a capital thing out of the purchase.

Now as three of my own Directors were sitting at the South Devon Board, this statement was most unwelcome news to them, and as such calculated to do me much injury.

I am determined to sift this gross and false report to the very bottom and I shall feel therefore obliged by your explanation by return of post.

I am, Sir,
Your obed. Servant
(Signed) J.C. Wall

To J.W. Batten, Esq.,
35 Palace Garden Terrace,
Kensington,
London.

to which Batten replied:

3 Harcourt Buildings,
Temple E. C.
Dec. 14 1874

J.C. Wall. Esq.,

My dear Sir,

I only came up from Plymouth today, and received your letter on my arrival at Chambers. Someone must have made a mistake in the repetition of the conversation with our mutual friend Mr Prowse, for I certainly never had the faintest idea, that you were the purchaser of the Brixham Railway, and the absurdity of my saying so will be patent to you when I tell you that I have advised Mr Wolston throughout as to his rights and wrongs, and know exactly how each and every share of the Company is held. I cannot see, however, how your three Directors could receive such an intimation with disfavour, they would be certain that in your hands the trade of Brixham would be developed to its utmost, and *ex necessitate* increase traffic sent over their line and the B&E unless perchance they were afraid that your knowledge of Railway Traffic and terminals might secure a larger share for the Brixham Railway than the S.D. have been accustomed to allow. But into this I need not go at present, I simply deny ever having said that you had purchased a single share in the Brixham Railway, or had made a capital thing out of it, but I must add that if I thought you had, I should not hesitate to say so, believing as I do, that in the right hands the Brixham line is a most valuable property.

Yours very truly
(Signed) John W. Batten

He received this acknowledgement from Wall.

Bristol 15th Dec. 1874

My Dear Sir,

I have to thank you for your courteous and straightforward reply to my letter of the 11th inst., and I shall now endeavour to make Mr Prowse smart for his unwarrantable conduct.

My strong feeling in the matter arose from the fact that my Directors have for twentyfour years treated me with the utmost confidence, believing that nothing would induce me to become connected with any railway interest directly or indirectly without their knowledge and permission, and to this position I intend rigidly to adhere for the short time which I hope will be necessary for me to continue in harness.

My Dear Sir,
I am, Yours very Truly
(Signed) J.C. Wall

J.W. Batten, Esq.

Batten then wrote to Mr Prowse:

3 Harcourt Buildings
Temple E.C.
December 15th 1874

My dear Mr Prowse

Someone with more wit than wisdom has told J.C. Wall! that a South Devon Director said!! that you said!!! that I said!!!! that J.C. Wall had purchased the Brixham & Torbay Ry. and had made a good thing out of it.

I do not for a moment imagine that you invented this pleasing fiction, but I shall be obliged if you will write to Mr J.C.W. and let him know what I did say. Conversations, like engines on an incline, acquire force by transit. That Mr Wall has not purchased the Brixham Rly none knows better than myself as I prevented Mr Ellis getting hold of it in its entirety, and got one half reserved for my friends, but Mr W. will no doubt be best pleased at hearing direct from you the contradiction of a report which was too good to be true.

Yours very truly
(Signed) John W. Batten

and received the following, undated reply, written on 16th December:

My dear Mr Batten

After the Mayor of Devonport had left speaking with you at the Duke of Cornwall Hotel you addressed me . . .

'I say Prowse! Wall will wring a pretty round sum out of you for the Brixham terminals'
I replied:

'What has Mr Wall got to do with it? We do not interfere in matters affecting the Bristol & Exeter and its branches'
You said:

'I expected to have got the line for £8,000 but Wall has got half of it for £6,500'
I said:

'I thought Ellis was the purchaser' and you replied 'Mr Wall is at the bottom of it, and they are looking to have a considerable sum out of you'

This is exactly what passed, and I presume you will not question the accuracy of the meaning conveyed, or of even the words used. I send a copy of this to Mr Wall as you desire.

I remain
Yours very truly
(Signed) A.P. Prowse

Mr Prowse also wrote to J. C. Wall, enclosing a copy of his undated letter to Batten:

Plymouth
16th Dec. 1874

My Dear Sir,

You will see from the enclosed correspondence what Mr Batten said to me at the Duke of Cornwall Hotel.

I do not understand that he denies what he said then, but only that you did not buy the Brixham Railway in its *entirety*. His letter appears to convey this meaning.

Yours very truly
(Signed) Albert P. Prowse

J. C. Wall Esq.
Bristol

On 17th December, 1874 John Batten wrote the following reply to Prowse:

3 Harcourt Buildings
Temple E.C.
Dec. 17th 1874

Dear Mr Prowse,

I am obliged to you for writing to Mr Wall who evidently thought I had been making mischief between him and his Board; but I think you have drawn largely on your imagination for your facts and figures. It is always difficult to recall a conversation which has not an object, but I am quite certain that I never said anything which implied that Mr Wall was owner of the line, or would do anything more than advise Ellis as to what terminal charges were, and as to the sums mentioned in your note of the conversation they must be wrong as the sum I offered was £8,000 for the whole but Ellis got the half for £3,250.

It seems to me a great pity that you should have gone out of your way to repeat my conversation to your Directors. I often hear persons say 'Scott is backing you up' or 'the L&SW are finding you the funds' without going off and repeating to the Board remarks which can only have a foundation in the brain of the utterer. Besides what difference can it make whether Ellis is buying for himself or as trustee for the B&E or whether Mr Wall advises him or not, he can only get from your Company what is fair and surely there can be no cause of complaint in that.

I would suggest that you write Mr Wall explaining to him, that what we call the 'gossip of the Court' has been repeated as the 'gossip of the Board Room', and has been no doubt retailed to him by his Directors, in words, figures and accounts very different from the original, and quote to him the proverb of 'The Three Black Crows'. He is much too sensible a man to take offence where none was intended. I would write to him myself, but I do not wish to make a mountain out of a molehill.

Yours truly
(Signed) John W. Batten

On 18th December J.C. Wall wrote to Batten but this letter is not on the file. Batten replied on 19th, enclosing a copy of his letter of 17th December to Prowse and received the following acknowledgement from Wall.

Bristol
Dec. 21 1874

My dear Sir,

I enclose you, as you desire, the copy of Mr Prowse's letter to you dated 17th inst. [actually Batten's letter *to* Mr Prowse].

I now make it a Board question for the S.D. Directors and shall await the result of their deliberations before I move further in the matter. According to *your* shewing Prowse has been guilty of inventing a foul and contemptible lie.

Yours truly
(Signed) J.C. Wall

J.W. Batten, Esq.,
3 Harcourt Buildings,
Temple, London

On 31st December Wall wrote to the South Devon Railway in strong terms, and almost illegible handwriting, enclosing copies of all the correspondence (fortunately copied in very neat handwriting). Unfortunately only a copy of the SDR's incomplete draft reply has been preserved on the file.

Draft Reply

My Dear Sir,

Having laid before my Board your letter of the 31st ult. with correspondence between yourself, Mr Batten and our Mr Prowse relating to the purchase of the Brixham Railway, I am desired to inform you that my Directors have no doubt that Mr Prowse correctly reported the general purport of what was said to him by Mr Batten as he came straight from the Duke of Cornwall Hotel where the conversation took place to the Board Room and mentioned it incidentally on a discussion which was then going on in reference to an interview of our Chairman with Mr Ellis.

At the same time my Directors think that probably Mr Batten's remarks, whatever they really were, must have been made jestingly and as idle gossip rather than having any significance which should be seriously noticed. [this paragraph deleted]

It is of course unnecessary to add that my Directors have not the faintest idea that the remarks can in any remote degree have had any justification in fact - so far as they relate to you.

No further correspondence, or details of Wall's reaction, is available.

Appendix Four

List of Officials
Torbay & Brixham Railway 1868-1882

(Details taken from *Bradshaw's Shareholders Guide* for the year shown)

Date	Directors	Secretary	Manager	Others
1868	Arthur Hill Wolston W.T.P. Wolston Wm P. Spark	John Howard		Richard W. Wolston (Solicitor) S.G. Stewart (Engineer)
1869	A.H. Wolston W.T.P. Wolston W.P. Spark	R.W Wolston	R.W Wolston	

Note: all shares held by R.W.W. and the three Directors

Date	Directors	Secretary	Manager	Others
1870-4	all as for 1869			
1875	Henry S. Ellis (Chairman) A.H. Wolston (Deputy) W.T.P. Wolston W.M. Spark Robert T. Campion	R.W Wolston C. Ashford (Asst)		William Morgan (Auditor) Charles Ashford (Auditor)
1876	H.S. Ellis (Chairman) A.H. Wolston (Deputy) R.W. Wolston W.P. Spark R.T. Campion	C. Ashford		Arthur C. Pain (Engineer) John Daw (Solicitor) W. Morgan (Auditor)
1877	as for 1876	as for 1876	H. Cecil Newton	as for 1876 plus H. Cecil Newton
1878	as for 1876	as for 1876	as for 1877	J. Daw (Solicitor) W. Morgan (Auditor) T.F. Robinson (Auditor)
1879	A.H. Wolston (Chairman) R.T. Campion (Deputy) R.W Wolston W.M. Spark	as for 1876	as for 1877	J. Daw (Solicitor) W. Morgan (Auditor) A.C.R. Wolston (Auditor)
1880	all as for 1879			
1881	all as for 1879			
1882	J. Daw (Chairman) R.T. Campion (Deputy) A.H. Wolston R.W Wolston W.M. Spark	remainder as for 1879 except 'Solicitor' not shown		

From 1868-1874 the company's offices were New Road, Brixham. From 1875 onwards they were 8 Bedford Circus, Exeter.

Appendix Five

Heads of Agreement between the Great Western and Torbay & Brixham Companies (1876)

1. The Great Western Company to lend the Torbay & Brixham Company Broad Gauge rolling stock on the following terms:
    One Composite with break £2 per calendar month
    One Third class carriage £1 10s. per calendar month
2. The GW Company to provide trucks for the conveyance of goods and fish traffic, horse boxes and carriage trucks at the usual Clearing House rates and conditions.
3. The GW Company will, when practicable, temporarily lend the T&B Company when required in consequence of break downs, etc., an extra engine at £2 5s. per day the T&B Company finding engine driver and stoker and all fuel, stores, etc. for the use of the engine.
4. The GW Company to pay the T&B Company 1s. 3d. a trip when their engine is required to take vehicles over the down main line to the Kingswear end of the points and push them thence over the up line to the tail of the Great Western trains. The station master at Churston to decide when it is necessary or advisable to so work for the convenience of adding vehicles to the up passenger trains. In other cases no charge is to be made for attaching vehicles by means of the T&B Company's engine.
5. The T&B Company to pay into their Bankers all moneys received on account of through and local traffic, and monthly private settlements to be made with the GW Company.
6. The T&B Company to pay to the GW Company for the user of and services rendered at Churston station including interest on the capital cost of the station a sum equal to one half the cost of the working expenses of the station including maintenance and stores.
7. In the case of all through goods traffic, the T&B Company to be allowed a three mile toll and the usual Railway Clearing House (RCH) terminals on general goods and mineral traffic. In respect of fish and passenger traffic the local charges of the T&B Company to be made and allowed to that Company in division (as per Schedule A attached).
8. The T&B Company to pay the Brixham carting agent's cartage and commission out of the RCH carted terminals with which they will be credited in division of the receipts.
9. The T&B Company to have complete control of the working and management of the line and to fix the local passenger and goods rates.
10. The GW Company to insert the Brixham train service in their Time book.
11. The GW Company to arrange for through passenger fares from Brixham to the principal stations on their system.
12. The Agreement to take effect as far as practicable from the 1st February, 1876 and to be determinable by one month's notice on either side.
13. All questions and differences arising under this Agreement to be determined by arbitration.
14. The T&B Company to provide substantial security in the sum of £1,500 in respect of the GW Company's proportion of the receipts from through traffic which are to be collected by the T&B Company and other payments which may from time to time be due to the GW Company.

For the Torbay & Brixham Railway Company

H. Cecil Newton - Manager

Schedule A

The following charges to be added to the GW rates to and from Churston and credited to the Brixham Company.

Fish

Consignments up to 56 lbs	4*d*.
56-112 lbs	6*d*.
1 cwt to 1½ cwt	9*d*.
1½ to 2 cwt	1*s*.
above 2 cwt	10*s*. per ton

Parcels other than Fish

Consignments up to 14 lbs	3*d*.
14-28 lbs	4*d*.
28-56 lbs	6*d*.
56-112 lbs	1*s*.
above 112 lbs	20*s*. per ton

Carriages	1*s*. 6*d*. each
Horses, etc.	1*s*. each
Cattle	9*d*. each
Dogs, Pigs, Sheep	6*d*. each

For the Torbay & Brixham Railway Co.

H. Cecil Newton - Manager

Paddington
6th June, 1876

[Reference: GWR Miscellaneous Deed No. 2440]

Appendix Six

Engines shedded at Brixham 1902-1929

1902 Jan.-April 540; Apl-Aug. 1468; Aug-Sept. 628; Sept.-Oct. 643; Oct.-Dec. 217
1903 (whole year) 529
1904 Jan. 529; Feb. 534; Mar.-Apl 529; Apl-June 1443; July-Aug. 13; Sept.529; Oct. 535; Nov. 1466; Dec. 535
1905 Jan. 1466; Feb. 535; Mar. 1466; Apl-Dec. 13
1906 Jan.-July 13; Aug. 1457; Sept. 13; Oct. 217; Nov. 13; Dec. 217
1907 Jan. (?); Feb.-June 13; July 470; Aug.-Sept. 3593; Oct. 1449; Nov. 628; Dec. 470
1908 Jan. 863; Feb. 628; Feb.-Mar. 1443; Apl-May 1448; June 470; July 468; Aug 470; Sept-Oct. 468 ; Oct-Dec. 1431
1909 Jan. 470 and 1431; Feb. 470; Mar.-May 1431; June 470; July-Nov. 559; Dec. 1449
1910 Jan-Feb. 559; Mar. 569; Apl-May 559; June-Dec. 1440
1911 Jan.-Feb. 1440; Mar. 468; Apl 470; May 1466; June-July 863; Aug.-Nov. 845; Dec. 470 and 845
1912 Jan. 845; Feb. 1449; Mar.-Apl 845; May-June 217; July-Aug. 1467; Sept 217; Oct.-Nov. 1467; Nov 217; Dec. 845
1913 Jan. 1440; Feb.-Dec. 845
1914 Jan. 845; Feb.-Apl 217; May 845; June 205; July 1439; Aug.-Oct. 845; Oct. 217; Nov.-Dec 845
1915 Jan. 845; Feb.-Mar. 217; Apl-June 845; July 217 and 563; Aug. 563; Sept. 845; Oct. 563; Nov.-Dec. 845
1916 Jan.-Apl 1433; May-Aug. 217; Sept. 1433; Oct. 217; Nov. 1433; Dec. 217
1917 Jan.-Sept. 217; Sept. 1433; Oct.-Dec 217
1918 Jan.-Mar. 217; Apl-May 1433; June 845; July-Oct. 1433; Nov. 1308; Dec. 1433
1919 Jan.-Sept 1433; Oct.-Dec. 217
1920 No records
1921 Jan.-May 571; May-Aug. 1466; Aug.-Dec. 845
1922 Jan. 571; Feb. 1158; Mar.-July 571; Aug.-Sept. 1158; Oct.-Nov. 1466; Dec. 1158
1923 Jan. 1440; Feb.-Apl 1466; May-Aug. 1158; Sept. 1466; Oct.-Nov. 1158; Dec. 1466
1924 Jan.-Apl 1466; May-Sept. 1439; Oct. 1467; Nov.-Dec. 838
1925 Jan.-Feb. 838; Mar. 1439; Apl 838; May-Aug. 1439; Sept. 1439 & 1466; Oct. 571; Nov.-Dec. 1244
1926 Jan. 1244; Feb. 838; Mar. 2050; Apl-Sept. 838; Oct. 1466; Nov.-Dec. 845
1927 Jan.-May 838; June-July 1439; Aug. 1941; Sept.-Oct. n/a; Nov.-Dec. 1439
1928 Jan.-Aug. 845; Sept.-Dec. 838
1929 Jan. 1464; Feb.-May 831; June 530; July 1165 (shed closed 22.7.1929)

n/a = not available

Classes contained in above list
'517' 0-4-2T: 205, 217, 529, 530, 534, 535, 540, 559, 563, 569, 571, 831, 838, 845, 1158, 1165, 1431, 1433, 1439, 1440, 1443, 1466, 1467, 1468
'Metro' 2-4-0T: 468, 470, 628, 1448, 1449, 1457, 1464
'633' 0-6-0T: 643
'850' 0-6-0T: 863, 1941
'2021' 0-6-0T: 2050
'1076'0-6-0T: 1244
4-4-0T: (unclassified 'one-off' locomotive, formerly 2-4-2T) 13. Heavily used 1905-07.
2-4-0T: (ex-Liskeard & Looe Railway) 1308 *Lady Margaret*
2-4-2T: (non standard 'Metro', altered to this wheel arrangement in May 1905) 3593

Note: The census of locomotives at depots was taken 4-weekly so the allocations shown only reflect what was there on that particular *day* in the month shown. There will have been other locomotives used covering breakdowns, boiler washouts, etc., but on a short line like the Brixham branch it seems unlikely that much variation occurred to what is shown above.

The author is grateful to David Braun who copied all the above information from records at PRO Kew (RAIL 254).

Appendix Seven

Brixham Station
Inventory of Accommodation (1963)

Parcels Office	17 ft 10 in. x 11 ft 6 in.	}
Booking Office	28 ft 6 in. x 6 ft 11 in.	}
Booking Hall	10 ft 10 in. x 11 ft 3 in.	}
Ladies Waiting Room	12 ft 2 in. x 12 ft 0 in.	} Wooden construction with slate roof
Ladies Toilet	12 ft 0 in. x 5 ft 6 in	} and gas lighting in poor condition
Waiting Room	7 ft 6 in. x 19 ft 6 in.	}
(L - shaped) and	12 ft 3 in. x 11 ft 10 in.	}
SM Office	11 ft 10 in. x 13 ft 8 in.	}
Gents Toilet	15 ft 0 in. x 10 ft 0 in.	} Stone construction with slate roof
Coal Store	12 ft 8in. x 7ft 1 in.	} and gas lighting in poor condition
Stationery Store	4 ft 9 in. x 5 ft 6 in.	Wooden lean-to in poor condition
Porters' Room	13 ft 6 in. x 10 ft 6 in	Brick construction with tiled roof in fair condition
Garage (ex stable)	38 ft 0 in. x 18 ft 0 in.	Brick construction with slate roof in good condition
Fish Checker's Office	8 ft 0 in. x 8 ft 0 in.	Stone construction in fair condition
Goods Office	18 ft 0 in. x 14 ft 0 in.	Brick and corrugated iron construction in poor condition
Signal Box	24 ft 0 in. x 8 ft 0 in.	Brick construction with slate roof in fair condition
Lamp Room	10 ft 0 in. x 7 ft 0 in.	Corrugated iron in fair condition

Also:

Platform Verandah	68 ft 0 in. x 13 ft 9 in.	Constructed of glass and corrugated iron in good condition
Parcels Loading Shelter	14 ft 4 in. x 11 ft 0 in.	
Fish Loading Shelter	104 ft 0 in. x 17 ft 0 in.	

Two Station Name Boards
Goods Yard Loading Gauge
Gas fittings on platform and in goods yard
Three stoves, one fireplace, one gas cooker, one gas ring and two wash basins

The following items were listed on 4th December, 1962:

	Year	Original Cost	Gross Replacement Cost	Estimated Cost of Removal	Estimated Credit
		£	£	£	£
Water tank 12 ft x 12 ft x 6 ft with swing jib under	1890	85	595	85	25
Water elevator P5	1893	7	50	5	1
Water pump P126	1866	28	200	10	5
Water wheel (driving P126)	1866	30	210	10	5
3 in. C.I. water main disused 575 yds	1890	105	1,850	Abandon	-
2 in. water main 17 yds	1890	2	38	Abandon	-
1 in. water main 90 yds	1946	15	90	Abandon	-

[Details taken from correspondence in connection with closure. As seen from the text, some of the items listed in December 1962 'survey from the desk' had gone long before this time.]
[Hand crane FM 4154 6 tons capacity, original cost £345 (plus £90 fixing and foundations) in 1938, was sold for £20 in 1960.]

Appendix Eight

A Brief Chronology of Brixham as a Fishing Port and Shipbuilder

Late 18th century. By second half of century trawling was well established at Brixham, seven vessels of only 15 tons each in 1756 had expanded to 76 vessels of 20-30 tons (sloops) in 1786 and 90 vessels by 1791. The more expensive types of fish were sent to London, even though the cost of transport doubled or even trebled the final price. For this reason cod could not be sent. As early as the 1760s at least two firms were engaged in the transport of fish to London which took between 36 and 48 hours. In the 1780s an estimated 500 carriages of fish, worth £6,500 at Brixham, were sent to London, Bath and Bristol.

Early-mid 19th century. A total of 151 trawlers based at Brixham and Plymouth in 1830 had grown to 190 by 1860. New Brixham trawlers were constructed either in the town or at Dartmouth. In the years before the branch, 1824-1862, 226 vessels measuring 15,133 tons had been constructed at Brixham. The coming of railways had made an impact in that the less expensive fish could now be sent to more distant places. In 1854 the South Devon Railway conveyed 940 tons of fish, this had grown to 3,000 tons by 1864. After 1847 many Devon vessels transferred to Hull to exploit new grounds. Wolston's evidence (*see Chapter One*) tells us that there were 146 fishing vessels in that year. In 1863 of the 152 vessels insured by the Brixham Fishing Club only 90 were based in Brixham, 41 were permanently in Hull and 21 at other places, principally Ireland.

Later 19th century. The fishing industry remained profitable and continued to expand for much of the second half of the century. Although rail costs were high Brixham and Plymouth boats stayed at sea for a shorter time than Hull or Grimsby boats and so their catch was fresher and commanded higher prices. In 1864 Brixham was created a registry port, until then boats had been registered at Dartmouth. In 1877 2,000 tons of fish were sent to London; by 1888 this had risen to 2,600 tons, according to Ellis. Brixham became a coal bunkering port in the 1880s. From 1866-1899 no less than 538 vessels, totalling 32,700 tons were built at Brixham; much of the material for these would have come in by rail to Brixham station. Towards the end of the century Brixham began to adapt to tourism, although in 1899 one writer unkindly described it as 'a sort of Devonshire Wapping with a Billingsgate smell'!

20th Century. In the early 1900s Brixham's fleet was mainly sail powered and these continued to be launched as late as 1927. By 1901 99 per cent of fish landed at Brixham were dispatched by the GWR but high rail charges were quoted as the main reason why fishermen failed to receive a sufficient return on their outlay. World War I had a disastrous impact on the fishing fleet, some hundreds of men joining the Navy, particularly in minesweeping. Of those that survived, many never returned to fishing. Ellis says that there were 300 trawlers in the Brixham fleet in 1914, only 70-80 remaining and fishing in 1919 (50 had been sunk by enemy action). The number of trawlers fell again in the 1930s, from 60 in 1933 to less than a dozen in 1936 and only 3 by the end of 1939. Wartime fish landings were kept up by the Belgian fishing fleet which had taken refuge in Brixham - in 1941/42 95 Belgian trawlers were based at Brixham (later some of the larger ones were dispersed to other ports). They stayed until VE Day in 1945. Not until 1965 when a fishermen's co-operative was formed was the trend reversed. In 1971 43 boats were registered with the 'BM' port mark. A new fish quay and ice making plant was completed in 1971. Fish landed at Brixham in 1886 was 2,400 tons, in 1901 2,900 tons, the average for the years 1919-1928 was 3,000 tons, from 1929-1938 the average only 1,700 tons, from 1952-1961 2,300 tons and 1962-1971 1,600 tons. During the whole of this period the Devon proportion of the UK fish caught was never more than 4.1 per cent (in 1886), the great bulk of fish being caught by the East Coast fleet.

Sources: *The New Maritime History of Devon (Vol. 2)* [Conway Maritime Press];
Brixham - Its history and people by Arthur C. Ellis [Brixham Museum & History Society].

Bibliography

History of the Great Western Railway by E.T. MacDermot (Revised Clinker) (Ian Allan)

A Regional History of the Railways of Great Britain Vol. 1 by D. St John Thomas (David & Charles)

The Locomotives of the GWR Part Two, Broad Gauge (RCTS)

An Historical Survey of Selected GW Stations Vol. 2 (Brixham), Vol. 3 (Churston) (OPC)

A History of the GWR by G.A. Sekon (1895, out of print)

An Historical Survey of GW Engine Sheds 1837-1947 by E. Lyons and E. Mountford (OPC)

Track Layout Diagrams of the GWR and WR Part 14 South Devon (R.A. Cooke)

Mr Wolston's Little Line by John Dilley (published by the author)

Bradshaw, various dates

GWR and WR Working and Public timetables, various dates

The GWR Magazine

GWR 'water files' (Chapter Five)

GWR staff records (Rail 264 at the PRO) and Plymouth Division staff records formerly in the Clinker Collection and not yet at the PRO

BR (WR) files on closure

Brixham in Devonia by Charles Gregory (1896, out of print)

Torbay Story by Eric Delderfield (Raleigh Press)

Brixham, a bibliographical guide by John Pike (Borough of Torbay)

A Short History of Brixham by John E. Horsley (Brixham Museum)

Brixham Its History and People by Arthur C. Ellis (Brixham Museum & History Society)

The New Maritime History of Devon (Vol. 2) edited by Duffy *et al* (Conway Maritime Press)

A Pint of Beer or a Return to Brixham by Roger Grimley (published by the author)

The source of the traffic that kept the branch open for so long - Brixham fishmarket. This card was sent in 1910. *D.K. & M. James Collection*

Index